Between *the* Testaments

Between *the* Testaments

From Malachi *to* Matthew

S. Kent Brown & Richard Neitzel Holzapfel

Salt Lake City, Utah

Visit us at www.deseretbook.com

Library of Congress Cataloging-in-Publication Data

Brown, S. Kent.

Between the Testaments : from Malachi to Matthew / S. Kent Brown, Richard Neitzel Holzapfel.

p. cm.

Includes bibliographical references and index.

ISBN 1-57008-901-9 (alk. paper)

1. Bible. O.T. Apocrypha—History of contemporary events. 2. Judaism—History—Post-exilic period, 586 B.C.–210 A.D. I. Holzapfel, Richard Neitzel. II. Title.

BS1700 .H65 2002
220.9'5—dc21 2002013732

Printed in the United States of America 18961-7049
R. R. Donnelley and Sons, Crawfordsville, IN

10 9 8 7 6 5 4 3 2 1

For our children

Karilynne, Julianne, Heather, Shoshauna, and Scott

—S. Kent Brown

Nathan, Zac, Zanna, Marin, and Bailey

—Richard Neitzel Holzapfel

Contents

Part 4: Spiritual Light

Maps

Preface

Even the most casual reader of the Bible senses vast differences in the tone, texture, and doctrines of the Old and New Testaments. After reading Malachi and then turning to Matthew's Gospel, we sense that more than unspoiled time has passed lazily between the end of the Old Testament period and the beginning of the New Testament. The nearly five centuries that separate the two parts of the Bible represent far more than a mere chronological divide. They also represent a hefty cultural gap.

By almost any account, an entirely new group of people rises into view within the pages of the New Testament in contrast to the group portrayed in the Old. Certainly the people, one group in the Old Testament and another in the New, inhabited the same geographical area, shared a basic religious point of view, and were of the same families and clans. Yet these two chronologically separate peoples seem deeply dissimilar in significant ways.

One obvious example of differences that we encounter between the Old and New Testaments appears in common personal names. In the Old Testament, we become familiar with the names *Jacob*, *Joshua*, *Miriam*, *Hannah*, and *Elijah*. In the New Testament, we read regularly of *James*, *Jesus*, *Mary*, *Anna*, and *Elias*. In actuality, the New Testament names are the Greek equivalents of the same names found in the Hebrew Old Testament. The case is much like the names of *Paul* and *Pablo*.

They are the same name, but one is English and the other is Spanish.

However, the major differences between the Old and New Testaments do not lie simply in language. The Old Testament has come down to us in Hebrew, with a few Aramaic sections, and the New Testament comes to us in Greek. Nevertheless, the central difference between the peoples who lived at the end of the Old Testament period and those at the beginning of the New was the ever-shaping, ever-renewing passage of time. Those nearly five centuries brimmed with far-reaching changes that included periods of crippling crisis, brilliant inventiveness, cautious adaptation, and painful transition. By all odds, the major influence in that era arose from Hellenization (from *Hellas*, the term for Greece). By definition, Hellenization sought to repackage the world as Greek. Making its relentless influence felt initially with the coming of Alexander the Great into the Near East in the late fourth century B.C., Hellenization affected people in profound ways and explains many of the differences in tone and texture between the Old and New Testaments.

This book, *Between the Testaments: From Malachi to Matthew*, attempts to connect the Old and New Testaments by opening a window onto events that unfolded from the time that members of the covenant people returned from their Babylonian exile, not long before the end of the Old Testament age, to the period when Jews lived under Roman dominion at the beginning of the first century A.D., coinciding with the beginning of the New Testament era. Admittedly, one of the nettlesome challenges that faces any student of this period is the lack of sources for vast expanses of time. For these gaps, we have tried to be restrained in what we can legitimately conclude.

We introduce this period by reviewing the end of the Old Testament age before painting the story of people, places, and events between the Old and New Testaments, an era usually called the intertestamental period. We discuss the developing canon of sacred scripture and other important religious texts, such as the now-famous Dead Sea Scrolls as well as the lesser-known Apocrypha and Pseudepigrapha. We describe groups whom we meet in the New Testament—Pharisees, scribes, Sadducees, priests, Samaritans, Essenes, and Zealots—all of whom either originated during this period or made important adaptations therein.

Additionally, we review the religious practices and beliefs that framed the world of the people of God during this sometimes calm, sometimes turbulent period, including their messianic hopes that pierced the frequent dark clouds of turmoil; the religious feasts and festivals that punctuated their holy calendar, joyously reminding them of ancient covenants established with Abraham, Isaac, and Jacob and renewed at Mount Sinai; and the growing Jewish law that deeply influenced people's lives and fomented much debate and divergent practices among Jews. We end our discussion with a brief overview of the immediate setting of the birth and ministry of Jesus of Nazareth, reviewing important passages from Matthew and Luke. Finally, we provide a detailed chronology of major events.

One challenge we have faced is what to call the region in and around Jerusalem, one of the most intriguing and studied pieces of land in the world. The birthplace of two of the world's dominant religions, Judaism and Christianity, this area has often carried the name conferred by its conquerors. For the sake of variety, we have chosen to use names from differing eras as if they were contemporaneous with one another—Judah, Judea, Palestine, the Holy Land. Although each of these names brings forward cultural and historical peculiarities, as well as chronological differences, we decided not to be overly pedantic and have treated them as interchangeable.

To make this book reader-friendly, we decided that each

chapter should stand independently as much as possible, allowing readers to choose specific topics without the necessity of reading others chapters. This decision forced us to be occasionally repetitive.

We hope this book will help readers more fully appreciate this shaping, watershed period of history—the centuries between the Old and New Testaments—for its own sake. It was a colorful era of change and constancy and of despair and rising hopes for peoples of the Holy Land. Ultimately, we hope that *Between the Testaments* will also help make the Old and New Testaments into one continuous story—from Genesis to Revelation—instead of two stories separated by wide chasms of history, culture, and doctrine.

Acknowledgments

Many people helped move this project along from research through publication. We appreciate the efforts of Cory H. Maxwell, Jack M. Lyon (our editor), Tom Hewitson (our designer), and Kent R. Minson (our typographer) at Deseret Book Company. Patricia J. Ward, Ancient Studies secretary at Brigham Young University, helped transcribe early drafts of chapters. Ted D. Stoddard, professor of management communication at Brigham Young University, copyedited the entire manuscript. Our competent student research assistants, Marc Alain Bohn, Zanna L. Holzapfel, Robert D. Hunt, Karyn Hunter, Keri Lynn Karpowitz, Melanie R. Munson, Robert F. Schwartz, and Jocelyn R. Sparks, were invaluable in assisting with library work, checking sources, and producing the chronological chart included herein. Our colleagues, Eric D. Huntsman and Thomas A. Wayment, read various chapters and provided helpful suggestions, preventing some errors. Cory D. Crawford and Matthew P. Roper read the final draft. Kent P. Jackson, Dana M. Pike, Richard D. Draper, and D. Kelly Ogden kindly answered questions and made suggestions along the way. Andrew D. Livingston prepared the maps. Any mistakes of fact and interpretation are ours alone.

Sources and Further Reading

As we noted in the preface, one of the nettlesome challenges that faces any student of the intertestamental period is the lack of ancient sources for various periods of time. However, the now-famous Dead Sea Scrolls, as well as the lesser-known Apocrypha and Pseudepigrapha, do provide illuminating information for certain decades during this era and supply an important context for many subjects that we address in this book. We discuss each of these sources in separate chapters and often draw from them. There is one further important source.

Josephus

Even though Flavius Josephus wrote his books in the last quarter of the first century A.D., his literary works are without peer for the intertestamental period. Born in Jerusalem as Joseph ben Matthias in A.D. 37, he tied himself to the Roman Flavian family following the Jewish War against Rome (A.D. 66–70). Josephus was a priest of royal Hasmonean descent and Pharisaic persuasion. He took a prominent but apparently reluctant part in the Jewish revolt, leading the Jewish troops in Galilee until he surrendered to Vespasian's Roman troops sometime in July 67. From the Roman side of the war, Josephus witnessed the last stages of the revolt, including the siege of Jerusalem that ended with the destruction of the temple in August A.D. 70.

Vespasian, the general sent to Judea to put down the Jewish revolt, was eventually proclaimed emperor by his troops in Judea after the succession crisis that followed Nero's suicide in A.D. 68. Vespasian's elevation to the imperial throne in A.D. 69 established a new dynasty (Flavian), eventually producing three emperors: Vespasian (A.D. 69–79), Titus (A.D. 79–81), and Domitian (A.D. 81–96).

Josephus obtained Roman citizenship and spent the second half of his life at Rome, where he dictated to scribes—mostly in Greek—his invaluable historical works. The first of his works, *The War of the Jews*, completed about A.D. 78, covers the period of the Jewish revolt, including the final operations at Masada in A.D. 73; it is customarily cited as *Jewish War*.

Josephus' second work, *The Antiquities of the Jews*, which he finished about A.D. 94, covers the entire sweep of Jewish history through the end of the first century A.D.; students usually refer to this work as *Jewish Antiquities*. His third book was both an autobiography and a supplement to *Jewish Antiquities*, entitled *The Life of Flavius Josephus*, and was written about A.D. 95. His final work, *Against Apion*, consists of a defense of Judaism, also written about A.D. 95.

Because of its wide availability to Latter-day Saint readers, we have cited the translation of Josephus by William Whiston (*Josephus' Complete Works* [Grand Rapids, Michigan: Kregel Publications, 1963]) when quoting from Josephus.

Josephus is the sole surviving source for our knowledge of some of the events of the intertestamental period. Although his reports in *Jewish War* and *Jewish Antiquities* are sometimes inconsistent and contradictory, Josephus' histories reveal much about this period because he had access to and quoted from sources that are now lost, such as the writings of Nicholas of Damascus, a non-Jew and an associate of Augustus who authored Herod's memoirs.

Further Readings

At the conclusion of each chapter, we provide a section called "For Further Reading" that highlights some of the important works dealing with topics we discuss. Readers may on occasion notice that our discussion on a given topic diverges from the position taken by authors noted in the "For Further Reading" section. We believe that our positions, when they differ from those of others, rest on solid grounds. Nevertheless, our intention in citing these works is to provide examples of seminal and recent scholarly works that are within reach of the wider reading public.

Additionally, we highlight publications of other LDS scholars who have written on topics included in this book and whose views may or may not agree with our interpretations. Again, our purpose is to guide readers to important studies by other Latter-day Saints who are contributing to this field of study.

We include reference to a few of our own previous studies on topics discussed in this current study. New discoveries, interpretive studies by other scholars, helpful comments by friends and colleagues, and our own continued research have in some cases caused us to update or modify positions we took in earlier publications. For example, after the publication of a study on Herod's life (see Richard Neitzel Holzapfel, "King Herod" in *Masada and the World of the New Testament*, John F. Hall and John W. Welch, eds. [Provo, Utah: BYU Studies, 1997], 35–73), Dr. W. Reid Litchfield at Brigham and Women's Hospital in Boston, Massachusetts, provided an alternative medical diagnosis of the symptoms of Herod's fatal illness that has caused us to reevaluate the evidence and has shaped our discussion in chapter 7, "Herod Rules." Additionally, sometimes our previous publications provide more detail or discuss related aspects of the topic that are not addressed in this current study and therefore may prove useful for readers to consult.

Finally, we would like readers to be aware of another helpful and readily accessible source for studying events, personalities, and topics discussed in this book. Some of the relevant entries in the Bible Dictionary in the LDS Edition of the King James Version of the Bible (Salt Lake City: The Church of Jesus Christ of Latter-day Saints, 1979) are: Alexandria, Anoint, Anointed One, Antioch, Antiochus Epiphanes, Apocrypha, Aramaic, Artaxerxes, Assyria and Babylonia, Augustus, Authorized Version, Bible, Caesar, Canon, Christ, Codex, Cyrus, Daily Service, Dead Sea Scrolls, Diaspora, Essenes, Ezra, Feasts, Haggai, Hagiographa, Hasidaeans, Hellenists, Herod, High Priest, Jerusalem, Judaea, Law of Moses, Lost Books, Maccabees, Malachi, Masoretic Text, Messiah, Nehemiah, New Moon, Persia, Pharisees, Priests, Pseudepigrapha, Roman Empire, Sabbath, Sabbatical Year, Sacrifices, Sadducees, Samaritans, Scribe, Septuagint, Syria, Temple of Zerubbabel, Temple on Mount Gerizim, Zachariah, Zadok, and Zerubbabel.

Part I

History

Land of Judah in the Days of the Return

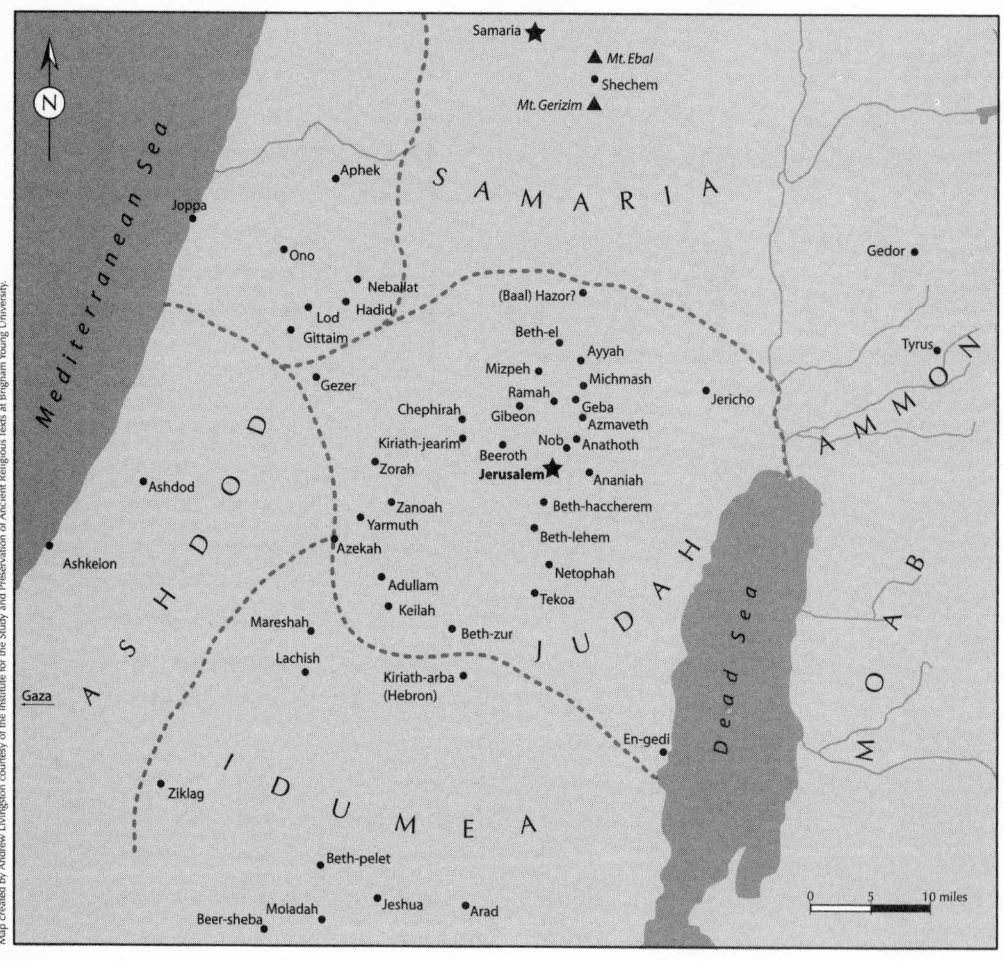

Map created by Andrew Livingston courtesy of the Institute for the Study and Preservation of Ancient Religious Texts at Brigham Young University.

CHAPTER 1

The Jewish Exiles Return

Cyrus the Persian king stood at the window of his palace. Below him he saw soldiers patrolling the streets of his new capital, Babylon. He was anxious, expecting word from his generals in the East who were trying to put down squads of Median resistance fighters. The old Babylonian military had crumbled months before when his warriors had swept into Babylon without a fight. But now that his empire was more or less secure, Cyrus knew he had to turn to the business of building unity within the realm and loyalty to himself and his successors. A hundred years ago, the Assyrian kings had moved people around to keep them from rebelling. More recently, Babylonian rulers had relied on tremendous military might to keep the peace. But each of those efforts had made subjects more restless and less loyal. For the past couple of years, Cyrus had been rolling an idea over and over in his mind. He had finally come to believe that returning people to their original homelands was a way to cement their loyalty to him. They would be grateful, he had reasoned, for reinheriting their former homes. To his advisors and confidants, he would demonstrate the wisdom of this course of action by returning the Jewish people to their homes in the land of Jerusalem. He then turned to his secretary and directed him to take dictation for a decree that would free the Jews to return to their homes in Palestine.

Hundreds still living could remember the horrible scenes that filled their memories of those dark days when the Babylonian army fought its way into the city. The people of Jerusalem had trusted their king, Zedekiah (597–587 B.C.), who had assured them for years that his pro-Egyptian stance in political matters was the right one for the realm. He was wrong. The Egyptians had made only a halfhearted attempt to engage the Babylonian forces and then retired behind the desert into their lush river valley. After their retreat, the Babylonian army tightened its grip on the city. This military force had already burned town after town near Jerusalem, plundering and raping and slaughtering. Standing on the tops of the walls, people in the capital city could see the smoke from miles away.

Fall of Jerusalem (587 B.C.)

If we hold up Josephus' account of the siege of Jerusalem in his day as a lens, we see that people in the earlier city learned of the Babylonians' terrible acts firsthand from fleeing refugees who sought safety in Jerusalem. After eighteen months, the city bulged with these blighted people. Food began to run out, and prices skyrocketed. Friends began to fight with friends for the smallest scraps of food. Family members, depressed and angry over the situation in the city, feuded among themselves over trivial matters. Some were sorely tempted to eat animals that the Mosaic law said were not kosher. Then came the Babylonians' fearsome march toward Jerusalem. Burning the stubble in fields and razing houses as they came, soldiers surrounded the city and worked to penetrate the walls. At first they failed, and the walls held. Even so, people within the city became frantic. They had a right to be frantic; it was the worst of days. (See 2 Kings 25:1–4, 8–21; 2 Chronicles 36:17–20; Jeremiah 34:1–3, 7, 17–22; 37:6–10; 39:1–2, 8–9; Lachish letters.)

Beginning with Isaiah more than a century before, prophets had raised their voices against injustices and wickedness in high places. Briefly, King Josiah (640–609 B.C.) had outlawed and pushed out the worship of foreign deities. But after his death at Megiddo in 609 B.C., people turned back to old habits, including the outlawed worship practices and other social injustices. In a desperate bid to bring people back to Himself while the Babylonian army stood before the gates of Jerusalem, God had asked through Jeremiah that people make a covenant in the temple to release their slaves whom they had held longer than the law of Moses allowed. Such an act would be a first step in placating God's anger for a host of iniquities. People in the city agreed and in the numbing crisis came together to make solemn covenant to do so. But then, astonishingly, they reneged. Among the offenders were princes and priests. In response, God withdrew His protective care not only from the rebellious city but also from the temple, the "place which the Lord" chose "to dwell there." The Babylonians swarmed through the walls. The month was July, and the year was 587 B.C. (Jeremiah 34:1–22; Deuteronomy 12:11; 2 Kings 25:2–3).

Less than eleven years before, in March of 597 B.C., King Nebuchadnezzar of Babylon (605–562 B.C.) had raised Zedekiah to the throne of Judah in place of his young nephew Jehoiachin, whom Nebuchadnezzar took with him as a hostage to Babylon. He took many others as hostages too, including princes, craftsmen, and warriors. King Nebuchadnezzar looted treasures from the temple, which Cyrus sent back fifty years later (2 Kings 25:8–18; Ezra 1:7–11).

Nebuchadnezzar wanted no trouble from this small kingdom on the southwest corner of his new empire. Among the group of several thousand hostages were Ezekiel and Daniel, who would become God's prophets in faraway Babylon. These exiles had not been settled long in their new land before Zedekiah rebelled against Nebuchadnezzar, thinking to ally himself with Egypt. But it did not work. Instead, when the Babylonians finally broke into the city, Zedekiah fled. He was quickly captured and, after Nebuchadnezzar had forced him to witness the execution of his sons (except one who escaped to the New World), Zedekiah was blinded and taken by force to Babylon, where we hear of him no more (2 Kings 25:4–7; Helaman 6:10; 8:21).

The second wave of exiles arrived in Babylon barely ten years after the first. We can safely assume that, with the aid of the first exiles, the second group eased its way into life in a different land. According to Ezekiel, some of his people had settled along "the river of Chebar," a major canal that ran through the rich soil of southern Mesopotamia and passed a locale called Tel-Abib (Ezekiel 1:1, 3; 3:15). We also assume that the Babylonians forced the exiles to perform some sort of compulsory service. The fact that Ezekiel and Daniel seem to have moved about rather freely indicates that the exiles were not thought of as prisoners, and they probably lived in their own villages. They apparently owned their own homes and planted gardens, were allowed to practice their marriage customs, and gathered together freely (Jeremiah 29:4–8; Ezekiel 33:30–33). But one thing was missing—their beloved temple. They thought of themselves as dwelling in a strange land, in a defiled land (Psalm 137:1–6; Ezekiel 4:13). In that place, they felt it was impossible to worship God as they had done in Jerusalem. They pined to go back. Their chance came in 538 B.C., fifty years after Jerusalem had burned.

CYRUS (550–530 B.C.)

The new ruler was Cyrus, the Persian who toppled the Babylonian empire. Cyrus was an extraordinarily gifted man who had drawn the interest of heaven long before his time (see Isaiah 44:28–45:4). Someone captured his attention on behalf of his exiled Jewish subjects, and in a major turnabout from the policies of previous Babylonian kings, Cyrus set policies that were at once humane and respectful and would continue long beyond his own reign. He decided against the Babylonians' forced removal of people from their homelands, thus allowing displaced people to return to their lands, and outlawed the disrespectful practice of looting temples. From all appearances, the Jewish exiles were the first beneficiaries of his changes.

This reversal of fortune came as a blessing to the exiles, some of whom could remember their home city and its temple. But much had happened in fifty years. The Babylonians' destruction of Jerusalem had brought changes that would not disappear with the return of the exiles to their homeland. First, Babylonian actions had created a Jewish dispersion, a diaspora. To be sure, earlier, in 722 B.C., the Assyrian kings Shalmaneser (727–722 B.C.) and Sargon II (722–705 B.C.) had sacked the capital city of the northern kingdom of Israel after a three-year siege and dragged off thousands of exiles—27,290 by Sargon's count—to destinations within the northern sector of the Assyrian empire (2 Kings 17:1–6). But these Israelites disappeared from ancient historical records. It was only the exiles from the southern kingdom of Judah who formed a genuine diaspora. Most of them stayed on in Babylonia, creating a significant Jewish population who lived away from their homeland. Moreover, a second group moved to Asia Minor, modern Turkey, as an inscription dated to the sixth century B.C. shows. In addition, a third major Jewish population forged a home in Egypt. Its roots evidently go back to the flight of a group that feared Babylonian reprisals after the governor appointed by Nebuchadnezzar was assassinated. This group even forced the aging Jeremiah to go with them (Jeremiah 40–46).

We do not know how long those who took Jeremiah remained in Egypt. According to a warning from the prophet, they would not survive long (Jeremiah 42:19–22). Perhaps significantly, almost contemporaneously we find a group of Jewish people hundreds of miles to the south on the Elephantine Island of the Nile in Upper Egypt. They were there to guard the southern frontier of Egypt. Although we do not know whether a connection ties the Elephantine Jews to those who earlier fled to Egypt with Jeremiah in tow, we surmise that one exists. From papyri that came to light throughout the nineteenth century and into the twentieth, it is clear that the Jews in Upper Egypt moved there during the reign of Nebuchadnezzar or one of his successors. Moreover, they kept aspects of the law of Moses—not all of it—and worshiped at a temple they had erected on the island where they lived. What is crucial to recognize is that the forced exile of people from Jerusalem to Babylon had broken the sense among Jews that they had to live in their homeland to worship and carry on their lives. This fundamental change in outlook was an important watershed for how they viewed themselves, just as the destruction of the city and the temple had been. In a word, life would never be the same.

Other adjustments forced themselves on the former citizens of the kingdom of Judah. In the absence of their temple, sacred actions that could be performed away from the temple took on added significance. We think immediately of the Sabbath day as an expression of the covenant link between God and His people. Profaning the Sabbath, in God's words, is the same as profaning Him (Ezekiel 20:12, 19–20; 22:8, 26). A second aspect of religious life, which evidently received increased emphasis, was that of circumcision, which God said was to "be a token of the covenant betwixt me [God] and you [Abraham and his people]" (Genesis 17:11). Such performances, of course, did not and could not replace temple worship. But they were something that the devoted could grasp and embrace as an indicator of their devotion to God.

Also, the imposed absence from Jerusalem must have led some to wrestle mentally with the matter of how to worship away from the spot where the temple had stood. Although there is no indicator that synagogue worship arose immediately after the loss of the temple and though there is no hint that such worship came because of a command from God, it seems certain that synagogues and their associated worship services initially came into being because of people's deeply felt need to pay devotion to God in a sacred place away from the temple. Indeed, Ezekiel met with other Jewish exiles in Babylon and instructed them. There is even a hint that music, a feature of temple devotions, may have been a part of such occasions. However, we do not know whether these meetings took place on the Sabbath day as a worship service (see Ezekiel 33:31–32).

When the exiles returned from Babylon, especially those who could remember Jerusalem from their youth, they wept (Ezra 3:12). The sight of the city must have been horrible. The extent of the damage to the city is underscored by the fact that Nebuchadnezzar's appointee as governor over the area was stationed at Mizpah, a town that lies a few miles north of the capital city and was part of Benjamin's tribal territory (Joshua 18:26). This spot, also called Mizpeh, had served as an important and sacred gathering place in Israel's ancient past (Judges 20:1; 21:1). Presumably, Mizpah had not suffered as other towns during the Babylonian incursion. Because the governor, Gedaliah, set up his operation in Mizpah, we conclude that it was not possible to take up residence in the burned-out fragments of Jerusalem (Jeremiah 40:5–6).

The exiles returned with a charge from King Cyrus to rebuild the temple. However, it seems plain that other Israelites who had survived the Babylonian destruction had continued to worship at the place of the altar, at least in the months and years immediately following. Such worshipers included people "from Shechem, from Shiloh, and from Samaria," all cities north of the capital city (Jeremiah 41:5). From what we can learn, it also seems plain that these people did not attempt in any serious way to rebuild the altar or the sanctuary. This is a compelling point when we seek to understand what happened when the exiles arrived. Perhaps the natives felt that to repair the altar they needed a divine mandate—or perhaps not. The fact that they had not attempted any reconstruction led to a

The Return to Zion

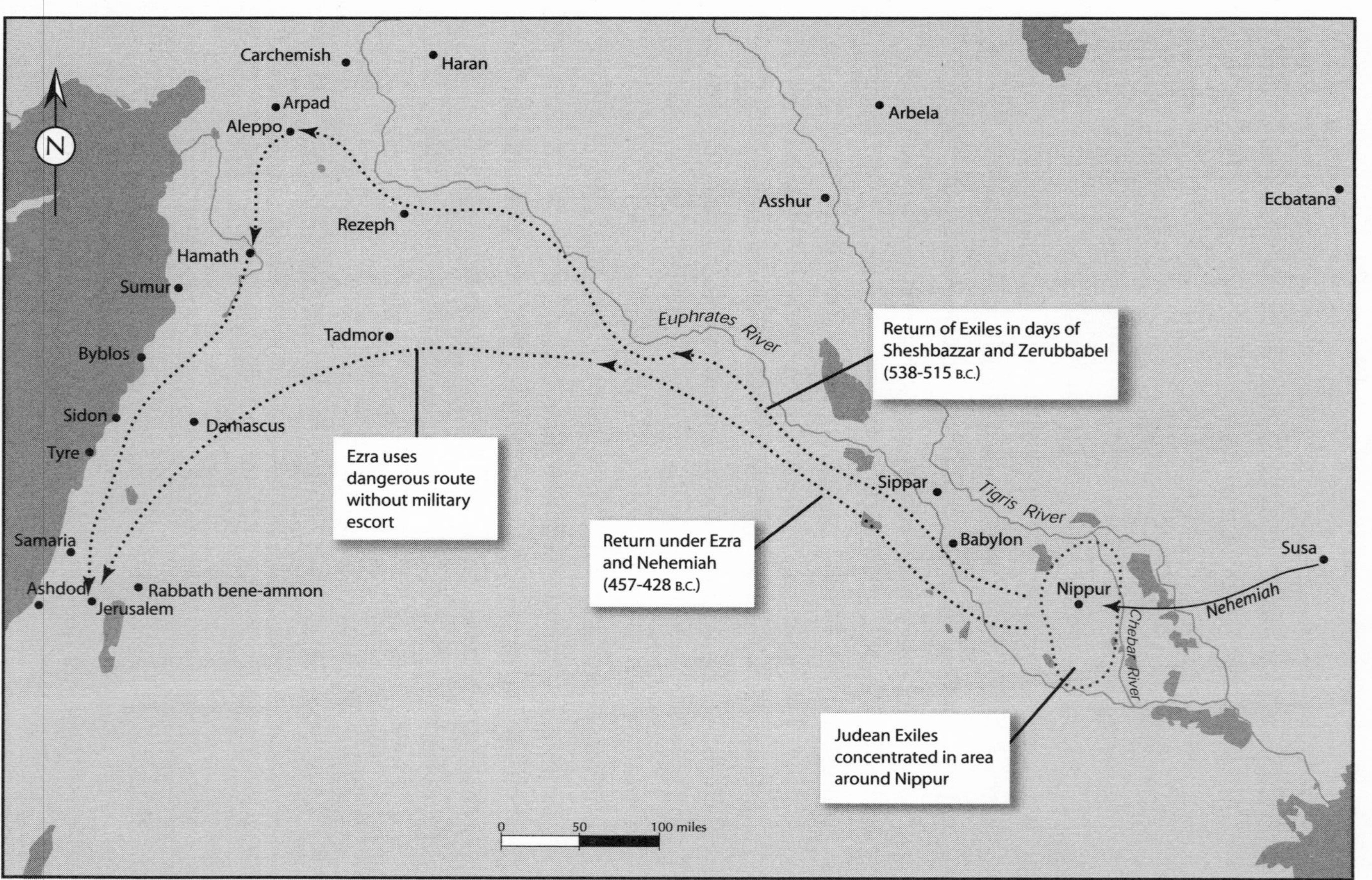

Map created by Andrew Livingston courtesy of the Institute for the Study and Preservation of Ancient Religious Texts at Brigham Young University.

serious rift between the returning exiles and those who had continuously resided in the environs of Jerusalem.

Those who returned from Babylon saw themselves as the true Israelites and viewed the other inhabitants, who were also Israelites, as hardly better than gentiles. Within months of returning, because they had come with a charge from King Cyrus, the former exiles staged an elaborate ceremony to lay the foundation for the altar on its former site. They pointedly excluded the others; and, when representatives of the indigenous people pled to be allowed to join in rebuilding the temple itself, the returnees rebuffed them (Ezra 3:1–4:3). The lines were drawn.

Haggai (520–515 B.C.)

The drawing of the lines seems to have been one of the objectives of the former exiles, at least after they arrived. Their grand, announced plans to rebuild the temple would actually come to nothing for another sixteen or seventeen years until the prophet Haggai came at God's behest to push the work forward. In an act of surprising generosity, Cyrus had opened the treasury and allowed the materials looted from the temple to go back (Ezra 1:7–11). Hence, the builders enjoyed access to funds from the Persian royal treasury and had even hired artisans and purchased materials (Ezra 3:7). Still, the work did not move forward. Evidently, people's efforts to carve out a life for themselves and their families amid the rubble simply drained them of energy and focus. Besides, most returnees lived away from Jerusalem (see Ezra 3:1). Moreover, it appears that the numbers of returning exiles were not large. Most Jews remained in Babylon, at least for the time being. Hence, the potential numbers of people who could help may have been small. In time, of course, they rose above their challenging circumstances and began to live quite well. At this point, Haggai appeared and brought God's harsh reminder to them.

It is evident that each year the former exiles had found reasons to put off rebuilding the temple. The common refrain, as quoted by Haggai, was, "The time is not come, the time that the Lord's house should be built." But God had lost patience. Through His prophet, He reminded the returnees that they lived in "cieled houses" while "this house [the temple] lie[s] waste" (Haggai 1:2, 4). It is apparent that, from God's viewpoint, there was an urgency to build the temple. To be sure, as we have seen, people had apparently continued to offer sacrifices at the site of the altar even after the destruction of the city and temple. But the full range of temple rites and blessings was not available without the temple itself, a notion underlined when God said, "In this place will I give peace" (Haggai 2:9). But that is not all.

The former exiles were paying another price. By their lack of action, they were denying themselves and their families temporal blessings that God wanted to bestow on them. We listen to His words uttered through His prophet: "Consider your ways. Ye have sown much, and bring in little; ye eat, but ye have not enough; ye drink, but ye are not filled with drink; ye clothe you, but there is none warm; and he that earneth wages earneth wages to put it into a bag with holes. . . . Therefore the heaven over you is stayed from dew, and the earth is stayed from her fruit" (Haggai 1:5–6, 10). In a word, people were missing the full range of blessings that God was willing and eager to bestow on them and their families, blinding themselves from seeing the real reasons for drought and bad harvests.

ZECHARIAH (519 B.C.)

The very next year, 519 B.C., the prophet Zechariah joined his voice as witness to that of Haggai. In a series of visions, Zechariah saw dimensions of the future of Jerusalem and the people of Judah. To aid Zechariah's understanding of the meaning of the visions, God said specifically about the city and the temple, "I am returned to Jerusalem with mercies: my house shall be built in it." Further, He said, "I will dwell in the midst of thee, and . . . the Lord shall . . . choose Jerusalem again" (Zechariah 1:16; 2:11–12). Through His prophet Zechariah, God designated that Joshua the high priest and Zerubbabel the governor were to lead out in this effort. He would not sidestep proper channels (Zechariah 3–4).

God's words through His two prophets did not fall on deaf ears. The former exiles stirred themselves to action. But almost immediately, the governor in Samaria objected to the work. We imagine that the old rebuff against assistance offered by the people of Samaria in rebuilding the temple played a role in his action. He wrote to the Persian king and demanded that the work stop (see Ezra 4:11–22). In a short time, the dispute came to involve the satrap or provincial governor of this part of the world, the "governor on this side [of] the river [Euphrates]" (5:6). We are fortunate to have at least partial copies of the letters this man exchanged with the Persian royal house in Ezra 5:6–6:12. From this correspondence, we learn that a copy of King Cyrus' earlier commission to build the temple still lay in the archives of the Persian palace and that it was still valid. As a result, the Persian king allowed the people of Jerusalem to rebuild the temple. A bit of background helps us see the picture more clearly.

Cyrus ruled the Persian Empire until 530 B.C. and was succeeded by his son Cambyses (530–522 B.C.). Because Cambyses' son had preceded him in death, there was no heir to the kingship of this huge empire that now reached from India and southern Russia to southern Egypt and halfway across North Africa. Of the pretenders to the throne, Darius I (522–486 B.C.), who was a relative of King Cambyses, was successful in bringing order out of the ensuing chaos and in engendering loyalty to himself. In total time, Darius' unifying efforts took about two years. About the time that Haggai began to prophesy in

Jerusalem, Darius had consolidated his power. In fact, because of the coincidence of Darius' rise and the appearance of Haggai and Zechariah as prophets in Jerusalem, we presume that God may have timed His message through His prophets to coincide with the new day in the empire and the new opportunities that would come with it.

But why would King Darius pay attention to a dispute in Jerusalem, which was at the time a rather small settlement amid ruins? A couple of reasons spring to mind. First, it is evident from the books of Daniel and Nehemiah that from time to time, certain Jews rose to positions of prominence within the governments of Babylon and Persia and even enjoyed personal access to the reigning king. It is therefore highly probable that well-placed Jews in Darius' government were able to take up with him the subject of the crisis in Jerusalem over the construction of the temple. Second, important land routes between Persia and North Africa ran through or near the territory of Judah. Any turmoil that might affect, even hinder, official traffic along these routes would pose a threat to the smooth functioning of internal affairs in the empire. Hence, it was to Darius' advantage to pay attention to issues that affected people whose territories sat astride these routes.

Sheshbazzar and Zerubbabel

Of course, erecting the temple and bringing life to normal levels were not the only challenges that faced the returning exiles. There was the matter of how to reconstruct the regularity in civil life that they had enjoyed before Nebuchadnezzar had overwhelmed the city. It would not be easy. Help came first from outside their numbers. Cyrus first appointed Sheshbazzar as governor of the territory in and around Jerusalem (Ezra 5:13–14). Zerubbabel, a descendant of King David, succeeded him (Haggai 1:1, 14; 2:21). It appears that, along with the high priest, Zerubbabel was involved in the appointment of those who would serve and work in the temple (Ezra 3:8). He led out in rebuilding the altar on its site and later in constructing the temple itself (Ezra 3:2; 5:2). But neither Sheshbazzar nor Zerubbabel was an independent prince in his homeland like earlier kings of Judah before them. Instead, each was subject to the authority of the Persian satrap, the regional "governor on this side [of] the river [Euphrates]" (Ezra 5:6). In a way, both men stood in a similar position to earlier Judahite kings who had served as clients to Assyrian and Babylonian kings, beginning in the first year of the reign of Ahaz (735–715 B.C.), when he appealed to the Assyrian king for aid against his enemies (2 Kings 16:7–9). But the exile had made everything different. There was to be no descendant of David on the throne of Israel or Judah. The Persians did not want a royal rival in power. Instead, each governor's authority was minimal and probably evaporated at Zerubbabel's death, for we learn of no one succeeding to his responsibilities. Within this political vacuum, the high priest became the most powerful person in Judah's society. This situation would endure until the arrival of Nehemiah almost a century later.

High Priests

Why the high priest? After the temple was rebuilt and dedicated in the spring of 515 B.C. (Ezra 6:15–18), it became the unquestioned center of life in the wider community. Even though the city itself still lay partially in ruins and remained without a wall, the people of Judah came to the temple for festivals enjoined by the law of Moses, including the Feast of Tabernacles and Passover (Ezra 3:4; 6:19–22). The head of this institution, of course, was the high priest. But God kept check on the temple priests through His prophets.

About 450 B.C., the prophet Malachi came on the scene. Through the sixty or so years that separated Zerubbabel and Malachi, priests had become complacent about divine mandates.

The prophet's reference to "thy governor" (Malachi 1:8) is a clear indicator that the people of Jerusalem were still under a Persian official, the "governor on this side [of] the river." But more important, through Malachi, God scolded the now-powerful priests: "The priest's lips should keep knowledge, and they should seek the law at his [God's] mouth. . . . But ye are departed out of the way; ye have caused many to stumble at the law; ye have corrupted the [priesthood] covenant of Levi. . . . Therefore have I also made you contemptible and base before all the people" (Malachi 2:7–9).

As a proof of these charges, God pointed out that the priests who "despise my name . . . offer polluted bread upon mine altar" and "offer the blind [animals] for sacrifice" as well as "the lame and the sick" (Malachi 1:6–8). Other parts of social and religious life were coming apart. Easy divorce had evidently become usual, and people had stopped paying tithing (Malachi 2:14–15; 3:8–11). Whether people responded to Malachi's pleas remains unknown. But the stage was set for strong leaders such as Nehemiah and Ezra.

Conclusion

One of the most vexing issues that was never solved was the relationship of the people of Judah with the people of Samaria to the north. In the minds of the returning exiles, the people of Samaria were mixed in their lineage. Centuries before, in 722 B.C., the Assyrians had conquered the northern kingdom of Israel and, after taking tens of thousands of prisoners and transplanting them elsewhere in the empire, had moved foreigners into the Israelites' cities and villages (2 Kings 17:6, 24). Over time, descendants of these foreigners evidently intermarried with the Israelites who had remained in the land after the Assyrian conquest. Even though children of the former exiles living in Jerusalem had themselves begun to intermarry with non-Israelites (see Malachi 2:11), in their minds, the earlier intermarrying of the Israelites in the north disqualified them as true descendants of Israel. This is one reason they did not want the northerners to participate in rebuilding the temple (Ezra 4:1–3). Over time, each group found more and more reasons to despise the other. Finally, the people of Samaria built their own temple on Mount Gerizim above the place where Joshua had led the Israelite tribes in a sacred ritual of entering formally into the promised land, a ritual that had been commanded by God through Moses and had led to establishing the earliest sanctuary in the country in that region (Deuteronomy 27:1–8; Joshua 8:30–35; see also chapter 14, "Samaritans"). By that point, the separation was complete, and old animosities would not be healed until the establishment of the modern state of Israel, which has promoted the education and well-being of the tiny Samaritan community that still lives on the slopes of Mount Gerizim.

For Further Reading

Elias Bickerman, *From Ezra to the Last of the Maccabees* (New York: Schocken Books, 1962), 3–40.

John Bright, *A History of Israel*, 3d ed. (Philadelphia: Westminster Press, 1981), 343–402.

F. F. Bruce, *New Testament History* (Garden City, New York: Anchor Books, 1972), 1–13.

David B. Galbraith, D. Kelly Ogden, and Andrew C. Skinner, *Jerusalem, The Eternal City* (Salt Lake City: Deseret Book, 1996), 94–123.

Simon Hornblower and Antony Spawford, ed., *The Oxford Classical Dictionary*, 3d ed. (Oxford: Oxford University Press, 1996), s.v. "Cambyses," "Cyrus," "Darius I," "Persia."

Martin Noth, *The History of Israel*, 2d ed. (New York: Harper & Row, 1960), 300–45.

Jerusalem in the Days of Nehemiah

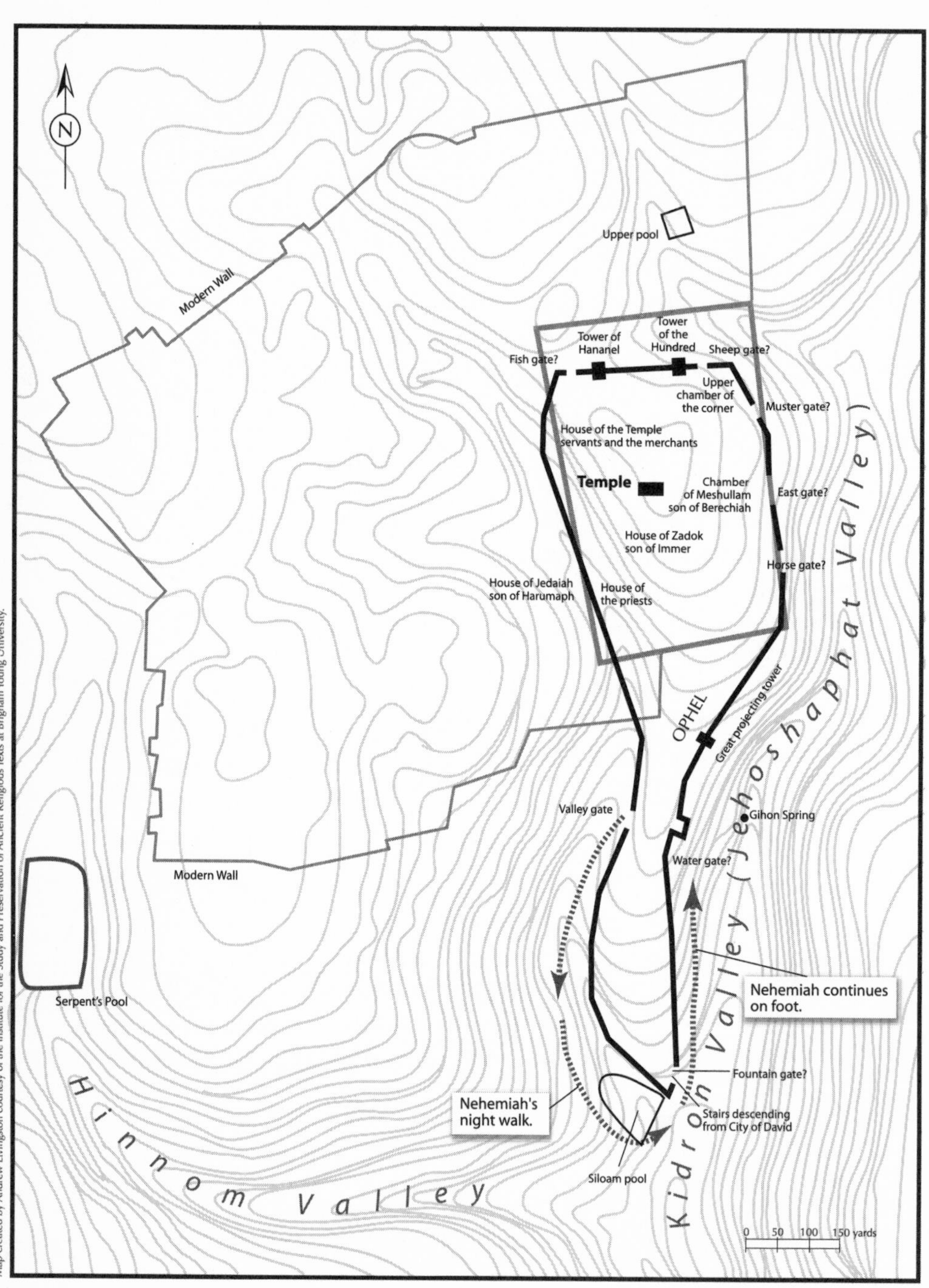

Map created by Andrew Livingston courtesy of the Institute for the Study and Preservation of Ancient Religious Texts at Brigham Young University.

CHAPTER 2

JERUSALEM ARISES FROM THE ASHES

The full moon illumined the flimsy walls of Jerusalem. Nehemiah sat on his donkey, feeling frustration that, since the people's return from Babylon almost a hundred years ago, they had not rebuilt the walls in such a way that they could resist their enemies. People in the city had responded only reluctantly to Haggai's prophetic threats that they must rebuild the temple. Even then they had not carried out the task very well. And although Nehemiah was himself a Jew and had arrived only three days ago with a commission from the Persian monarch to govern the city and its territories, some in the city had already resisted his initial suggestions to make life better for all citizens. Instead, the rich and powerful chose to protect their own interests and their personal fiefdoms. What was he to do to surmount these problems and bring unity to his people? He had a firm sense that the answer lay in the broken, unrestored city walls. If he could coax and cajole people into uniting to build these walls, that effort would leave a feeling of security and, with it, a residue of goodwill among people that would carry over into their daily interactions with one another. He tightened his right hand around the rope tied to his donkey's nose. He urged the beast forward. He needed to see the rest of the walls by moonlight. Tomorrow he would urge, no demand, that influential leaders in the city gather in a meeting and agree to rebuild the walls. The alternative, he knew, was to leave the city open to the pillaging of desert tribesmen and, worse, to an invading army.

Jerusalem became a city of safety and importance with the farsighted assistance of two Jews who neither were natives of the city nor had relatives living there. But they did not create a nation—a people united by a common purpose and a set of shared memories. That would not happen for another three centuries, beginning with the Maccabean War (167–164 B.C.). What we glimpse is a city whose spiritual life centered on its temple and whose economy literally grew out of the ground in the agriculture of the surrounding towns and villages.

Significantly, the two Jews came from the Jewish community residing in distant Babylon and bore royal commissions from the respective Persian kings who empowered them to engage in making Jerusalem a safe place where people could once again express fully their faith in God. These men were Nehemiah and Ezra. The first arrived with a mandate to bring security to the still largely ruined city. The second came with a charge to bring order and meaning into the city's religious life.

The most troublesome issue linked to the work of these two leaders concerns the dates of their arrival. A first reading of the books of Ezra and Nehemiah leads to the conclusion that Ezra preceded Nehemiah. But on that view, a host of insoluble problems arises, such as why the people of the city were still engaging in strange religious practices and marrying foreign spouses when Nehemiah arrived—features of religious and social life that Ezra's reforms had supposedly eradicated. The consensus among those who have studied this era—the latter part of the fifth century B.C.—is that Nehemiah arrived several years before Ezra did. We have adopted this view because it fits the evidence best, both inside and outside scripture (see Bright, 391–402, and the order of names in Nehemiah 12:26).

Nehemiah

According to Josephus, Nehemiah arrived in Jerusalem in 440 B.C. (*Jewish Antiquities* 9.5.7). When he reached the city, it was in abominable condition. Both the buildings and people's morale suffered terribly (Nehemiah 4:2, 10). To understand this situation, we look toward the broader world for the forces that affected the city and its citizens.

From the decree of King Cyrus in 538 B.C., permitting Jews to return to Jerusalem, until the coming of Alexander the Great in 332 B.C., the fortunes of Jerusalem and its people were tied to the Persian empire, which, as we have noted, stretched from southern Russia to a point halfway across the Mediterranean coastline of North Africa. On the one hand, this situation allowed people to move much more freely than they ever did when there were several kingdoms that covered these vast areas. As an added bonus, the enlightened Persian monarchs respected local customs of their subjects, including worship practices, which was a boon for Jews who worshiped in ways very different from their neighbors. On the other hand, incidents occurring hundreds of miles away could affect daily life in the land of Judah. For example, if people in Egypt rebelled, the Persian king would dispatch an army that would march through the Jews' territory demanding sustenance and other aid. On balance, however, the Persians' liberal policies offered opportunities that benefited their subjects' lives. So why were the lives of people in Jerusalem and the land of Judah in such difficult straits? Why did Nehemiah find a dispirited and broken people? The reasons are many.

The first was a lack of security, particularly in Jerusalem. Though our sources are meager, they indicate that after the days of Zerubbabel, the Persians had appointed no Jewish governor over the territory. Instead, the seat of the local governor was in Samaria among people who distrusted Jews and against whom some Jews held enmity. Moreover, evidence shows that the governor was himself a Samaritan and that the governorship was passed from father to son, meaning that a certain level of distrust was also passed on. Because the governor and people in Samaria did not want a strong, secure Jerusalem, citizens of the city were not allowed to undertake public works, such as building city walls, which would effectively make the city a rival to Samaria. According to correspondence preserved in the book of Ezra, this matter had arisen in 520–519 B.C. when, at the behest of the prophets Haggai and Zechariah, people began in earnest to rebuild the temple while Zerubbabel was still governor of Judah (Ezra 5:6–6:12). On that occasion, or an earlier one, the people of Samaria had made the people of Jerusalem stop construction by force of arms, an act that underscores the Jews' unrelenting worries (Ezra 4:23).

A second reason has to do with the size of the population of Jerusalem and the land of Judah. Archaeological remains and other evidence indicate that the total population was no more than twenty thousand when Haggai and Zechariah came on the scene. Not many people had taken the opportunity to return from Babylon to Judah. And they seem to have come in small groups. There was no evident, organized effort to return. By the time of Nehemiah's arrival about eighty years later, the population had grown to an estimated fifty thousand, distributed in Jerusalem and throughout villages around the city. But that number was too small to provide an effective defense against marauders and invaders from nearby states. Further, the population was not sufficiently large to provide a substantial work force to raise the walls of the capital city without a superb, charismatic organizer like Nehemiah. For when he arrived, he found the city and countryside fractured into little fiefdoms run by the wealthy, for whom poor Jews, because of bad harvests, worked as servants (Nehemiah 5:1–5).

A third reason is related to the first and second. Because Jerusalem was not secure and because the population was too small to defend itself successfully, outsiders began to encroach into the land of Judah. From the north, the people of Samaria pushed their control of land almost as far south as the hills that overlook Jerusalem. On the south of Judah, people of Edom had crossed the Jordan Valley and taken control of the fine vineyards and lands north of Hebron, almost to Beth-zur. Arab tribes had forced the Edomites out of their homeland and, under the pressure, they came into southern Judah and took Jewish lands (see Malachi 1:2–4). What is more depressing, the violating presence of the usurping Edomites on Judah's southern border would also have reminded Jewish people about the horrible acts that the Edomites' ancestors committed against the citizens of Jerusalem when the city fell to Nebuchadnezzar 150 years before (see Obadiah 1:1–12).

The fourth reason is tied to the prior reasons. Because of a lack of security, a small population, and encroachments into Judah, people chose to live away from Judah. In the prior chapter, we took note of a large Jewish group that lived on the southern frontier of Egypt as a garrison force against invasion. The fact that these people had built a temple and adopted worship patterns consistent with both their former temple and their new Egyptian environment shows that they saw themselves as living permanently away from the land of Judah. In addition, a Lydian inscription shows that Jews had moved into Asia Minor by 455 B.C., evidently not wanting to go back to Jerusalem. Further, large numbers of Jewish people remained in Babylon, apparently preferring to reside there rather than move into an unsafe and dismal situation. Of course, it was the forced exodus from Jerusalem under Nebuchadnezzar and his Babylonian warriors that had initially shattered the tie that people felt to the city and its environs. This, too, was a contributing factor to people's willingness to establish lives away from their beloved Jerusalem. Into this bleak and uninviting situation walked Nehemiah.

As we noted in the prior chapter, the stories of Daniel and Nehemiah demonstrate that Jewish men could and did rise to positions of trust within both the Babylonian and Persian empires. Nehemiah became the cupbearer for King Artaxerxes I, a Persian king who enjoyed an exceptionally long reign (465–424 B.C.). Nehemiah's lofty position meant that fellow

Jews could bring issues through him to the notice of the king. Moreover, because there was contact back and forth between Jews living in Judah and Babylon, news reached Nehemiah through his brother Hanani that things were bad in Jerusalem (Nehemiah 1:1–3). Saddened by this news, Nehemiah appeared downcast before Artaxerxes, whereupon the king asked what was wrong. The upshot of their conversation was that Nehemiah was appointed governor of the province of Judah, complete with official letters that allowed him to draw upon the royal purse for needed supplies (2:1–8). It was an impressive beginning, but trouble lay ahead.

Trouble came from inside and outside the citizenry of Jerusalem. Naturally, no one was expecting Nehemiah's arrival, even though he had taken months, perhaps even a couple of years, to reach the city. Apparently, word did not travel ahead of him. According to his own record, he received his appointment in December 445 B.C., the twentieth year of Artaxerxes' reign (Nehemiah 2:1). According to Josephus, he did not arrive in the city until 440. The discrepancy largely evaporates when we note that work began on the city wall soon after Nehemiah's coming. Evidently, he had stopped to acquire and then to see to the transport of the needed timbers to support the gates and walls (2:8). We can also assume that he had gathered other Jews to accompany him before he started his journey. If they had decided to move permanently to Jerusalem, they would have needed time to settle their affairs before departing. From their numbers may have come the "few men" who attended him on his famous nighttime inspection of the city's "broken down" walls (2:12–13). In addition, we can safely assume that Nehemiah stopped and presented his credentials to the satrap who governed the entire region. How long he may have stayed with the satrap we can only guess. In any event, it seems that more than three years passed between his fateful conversation with Artaxerxes and his arrival in Jerusalem. Now he was ready to work.

Nehemiah probably guessed rightly that the governor in Samaria, a man named Sanballat, kept spies in Jerusalem, for almost as soon as Nehemiah arrived, the governor learned the news (Nehemiah 2:10). But there was nothing he could do. Nehemiah was carrying letters from the king, which established his position. Sanballat then tried undercutting Nehemiah's confidence in his task, but the attempt did not succeed (2:19–20). Sanballat next tried raising the anger of other local peoples against the project to rebuild the walls (4:7–8), but the resulting coalition army apparently did not attack the workers in the city. Unfortunately, in the towns away from Jerusalem, according to Josephus, some died at the hands of Sanballat's army (*Jewish Antiquities* 11.5.8). But Sanballat failed to disrupt the work in Jerusalem. Nehemiah had surmounted the trouble from outside.

Trouble just as serious lurked inside the city, but it would be of a different sort. In Nehemiah's effort to rebuild the city walls, he had recruited people from all around the land of Judah. In fact, the long list of participants tells us where the land of Judah reached in that era. It was not large. For instance, we learn that the land included Mizpah and Gibeon, towns in the north that had been part of the tribal area of Benjamin (Nehemiah 3:7). In addition, the territory reached eastward to Jericho and south to Beth-zur, past Bethlehem and Tekoa, the birthplace of the prophet Amos. On the west, the land took in Beth-haccerem, where the hills fall sharply toward the maritime plain, if this town is indeed the same as Ein Kerem, which lies just to the west of modern Jerusalem (3:2, 5, 14–16, 27). It is part of Nehemiah's charismatic genius that he rallied people from these distant places, as well as those in the city, to help build the walls. All of them, of course, knew the economic and political value of a secure Jerusalem to the entire society.

To the dismay of Sanballat and his allies, the work

succeeded. People labored day and night for fifty-two days, apparently stopping only for Sabbaths. When Sanballat's coalition forces menacingly approached the walls, Nehemiah divided his people into two groups, half taking up weapons and the other half working feverishly without stopping. All the while, Nehemiah called out encouragement (Nehemiah 4:13–14). It was high drama. The work also unified the people as never before. Then trouble erupted inside the city, splintering the spirit of unity.

The labor through fifty-two days meant that people had not tended to their fields for almost two months. Besides, there had been a shortage of water, so crops were all the more fragile. To meet costs such as mortgages and taxes, some of the poorer people had borrowed money. They were now in deep debt to lenders in the city. To escape their debts, some had sold the services of their sons and daughters; others had sold their vineyards and homes. In effect, one part of the society held the other in bondage (Nehemiah 5:1–5). Perhaps significantly, this complaint, this "great cry" from the poor, brought out an aspect of Nehemiah's personality that we have not seen heretofore. In addition to his organizational skills and his evident charisma, he could become furious—"I was very angry when I heard their cry" (5:6). But Nehemiah knew that anger carried only so far in relationships with people. After all, even though he possessed authority from the king, he had been in Jerusalem only three months or less. In a revealing note, we learn that he tried to wrestle down his jagged feelings before confronting "the nobles." From his account, we read, "I consulted with myself" (5:7). Bringing his feelings under control, he took up the labor of convincing the lenders to forgive the interest—the "usury"—of the loans and to restore properties and children to those in debt. In an extraordinary turnabout, the lenders agreed. Not leaving anything to chance, Nehemiah put everyone under solemn oath to do as they had said (5:7–13). The crisis passed. The oaths would secure the future.

We learn only a little about matters that concerned Nehemiah during the rest of his first term as governor, for he would come back to serve again. His first term lasted twelve years. It is perhaps notable that throughout these years, he and his fellow officers had "not eaten the bread of the governor" (Nehemiah 5:14). That is, he and they did not demand the perquisites that normally came with their offices. Like other honorable men, he did not ask for favors that would lift him unduly above others (see 5:15). In addition, because the wall was weak in many spots owing to the speed of construction—"if a fox go up, he shall even break down their stone wall" boasted Sanballat's assistant (4:3)—one of Nehemiah's tasks was to strengthen the wall so that it would offer permanent, genuine security to the citizens within (5:16). An allied job was to convince people that it was in their interests to keep the gates shut at night and to guard the walls against intruders. To keep watch would have meant extra work for some (7:3). He also faced the challenge that the city held a rather small population: "The city was large and great: but the people were few" (7:4). To solve this apparent lack, he undertook the difficult task of convincing one person in ten to move into Jerusalem to buttress the numbers within the city. It would mean giving up life as rural people had known it (11:1–2).

All of these tasks dealt with the city's internal mechanisms. Outside the walls, enemies still sought to undo Nehemiah and his work. But he was shrewd enough that he refused invitations to meet such people outside the city, where he was vulnerable to foul play. Moreover, he resisted a false warning from outsiders that he should confine himself within the temple for safety from alleged enemies in the city, an action that would have discredited him both inside and outside Jerusalem (Nehemiah 6:1–4, 10–13). Finally, at the end of his term he departed, reaching

Babylon "in the two and thirtieth year of Artaxerxes" (13:6). It was 433 B.C. But he did not stay long in Babylon. He saw that his real service belonged to Jerusalem and its citizens.

We do not know when Nehemiah arrived back in the city, except that it appears to have been during the harvest season (see Nehemiah 13:12, 15). He writes simply, "I came to Jerusalem" (13:7). However, he was gone long enough that a host of problems faced him upon his return. Solving these problems seems to have taken up much of his second term as governor. Fortunately for the people in Judah, he was up to the test.

Immediately upon his return, he learned that the high priest himself, Eliashib, had prepared "a chamber in the courts of the house of God" for Nehemiah's most bitter adversary, a man named Tobiah, who enjoyed close ties to Sanballat, the governor of Samaria. Tobiah had even placed his "household stuff" in the chamber that was used as a storage area for "the vessels of the house of God." Offended at this desecration of the holy place, Nehemiah "cast forth all the household stuff" of Tobiah out of the temple and offered sacrifices for its cleansing (Nehemiah 13:7–9).

It soon became clear to Nehemiah that the priests, who should have been leading out in acts of devotion within the society, had slid into a state of laxness that affected the whole populace. For example, the priests had withheld "the portions" of the sacrifices and gifts that the Levites and the singers were to receive for their maintenance. As a result, these people had "fled every one to his field" to grow food for their families (Nehemiah 13:10–11). Moreover, none of the priests had taken responsibility for creating a system for storing and distributing the harvest donations that came to the temple for priesthood members and their families. So Nehemiah stepped forward and organized a system that saw these items distributed fairly and in a timely fashion (13:12–13). In addition, he observed people working on the Sabbath, "treading wine presses . . . and bringing in sheaves, and lading asses" with produce. What is worse, these people were bringing such items "into Jerusalem on the sabbath day" to sell in the market (13:15–16). Incidentally, the fact that he observed these actions in the countryside indicates that people of his era could travel farther on the Sabbath than the two thousand cubits allowed by later Jewish law.

What was Nehemiah's response to these Sabbath activities? He took up the issue with "the nobles of Judah," scolding them for their sin of allowing such enterprises and then ordered that the gates of the city be closed from before sundown on Friday afternoon until after the Sabbath had passed (Nehemiah 13:17–19). And when some of the more enterprising merchants and farmers brought their goods to a place outside the city wall to sell them on the Sabbath, Nehemiah threatened to arrest them. They left (13:20–21). Perhaps more disturbing to him were the mixed marriages with one Jewish spouse and the other of a different ethnic origin. He felt that somehow these marriages did not match God's will, so he put pressure on people not to continue the trend. Unlike Ezra after him, Nehemiah did not demand that the Jewish spouse divorce the non-Jewish spouse. But he "contended with them, and cursed them," and pulled the hairs of the beards of some men in a forceful effort to make his point. In one celebrated confrontation, he drove one of the grandsons of Eliashib the high priest out of the city because the grandson had married one of the daughters of Sanballat, the governor of Samaria (13:23–28).

In all of these cases, Nehemiah's exertions responded to varying situations that had arisen within the society. Strictly speaking, he did not attempt to introduce anything like a unified program of reforms, especially the kind that would touch the spiritual lives of people. That effort would come from Ezra. Significantly, Nehemiah's responses to these *ad hoc* situations would harmonize with Ezra's. For while the community in Jerusalem had taken the posture of reaching out to foreigners, even allowing one prominent outsider to take over a chamber on the temple grounds and permitting marriages between couples of different ethnic backgrounds, Nehemiah's position was to narrow the bases on which he and his people would involve themselves with outsiders. In that sense, he and Ezra stood on common ground.

Ezra

In contrast to Nehemiah, whose official work covered parts of three decades and was centered chiefly on temporal matters, Ezra in a very short period introduced religious reforms that would outlast him by hundreds of years. Ezra probably arrived in Jerusalem about 428 B.C. Even though we read that he came in the seventh year of Artaxerxes' reign, 448 B.C., it seems unlikely that this notice is correct, as we have noted. The reforming effort of Ezra seems to have given religious ballast to the work of Nehemiah's second term as governor instead of introducing a covenant that people quickly ignored. In addition, the walls of the city were already up by Ezra's arrival (Ezra 9:9).

One further piece of evidence points to Ezra's arrival in Jerusalem as being later than that of Nehemiah. This evidence appears in the letter signed by King Artaxerxes, which empowered Ezra as his agent and concerns the provision that allowed Ezra to spend treasury money to meet the basic needs of running the temple (Ezra 7:18–20). We have already seen that, when Nehemiah returned for his second term of office, he found that the Levites and singers had left temple service so they could produce food for their families (Nehemiah 13:10–11). Such a situation appears to precede and lie behind the king's allowance of monies to Ezra for "whatsoever more shall be needful for the house of thy God" (Ezra 7:20).

We also presume that the two men knew each other. Nehemiah may even have involved himself in the arrangements to bring Ezra to Jerusalem, but we cannot say more than this. Unfortunately, our sources allow us only a glimpse of Ezra. However, they are full enough to preserve the tremendous impact that he had on Jewish society and its religious practices.

As in the case of Nehemiah, Ezra's mission apparently resulted from the influence of fellow Jews in the Persian court of Artaxerxes. Certainly, the letter setting out Ezra's commission reads as if a knowledgeable Jewish person drafted it (Ezra 7:11–26). And the letter's provisions are extraordinary in their sweep, giving Ezra authority from the crown to undertake religious reforms within his own community. Such should not surprise us, given the policy of the Persian kings to encourage subjects to exercise their religious faith and practices. In effect, Ezra went as the royal commissioner for religious affairs for his people. That is the basic meaning of the title that the king conferred on him at the beginning of his letter: "a scribe of the law of the God of heaven" (7:12), for the term *scribe* carried a broader meaning than simply a person who copies texts. In addition, that Ezra went as an official of the realm becomes visible in such expressions as "thou art sent of the king" and his charge "to carry the silver and gold, which the king and his counsellors have freely offered" (7:14, 15). On a different front, Ezra was a priest and thus carried authority to administer in temple matters (7:11). Hence, he stood in the worlds of both his Persian sovereign and his divine master.

Ezra left Babylon in April with an entourage and gifts for the temple and arrived four months later, in August (Ezra 7:8–9). Though he came with a royal commission, he did not come as the governor. Hence, if Nehemiah was still serving in this office, Ezra would have posed no threat. Instead, he would have brought a welcome program for regularizing religious life among their people. If Nehemiah chapter 8 follows chronologically the arrival of Ezra, he did not wait long. After all, Ezra carried the solemn charge to "teach" to his people "the laws of . . . God" (Ezra 7:25). According to the note in Nehemiah

8:1–2, people of the city, perhaps more curious than serious about what Ezra might do, invited him "to bring [out] the book of the law of Moses." It was October and the Feast of Tabernacles. Standing with friends and officials "upon a pulpit of wood, which they had made for the purpose," Ezra read until time for the midday meal. These friends and officials translated the Hebrew of Ezra's copy of the law into Aramaic so that the audience could understand clearly the meaning, an indicator that people had begun to lose their abilities with Hebrew, the language of the country before the destruction of Jerusalem by Nebuchadnezzar (8:4–8). This is the first occasion we know of when an interpretation of scripture was made in another language. This practice would eventually grow into a written tradition that became known as the targums, an aspect of scripture that we discuss in chapter 8, "What Is Scripture?" The response to Ezra's reading was touching: "All the people wept, when they heard the words of the law" (8:9).

Matters did not stop there. During each day of the feast, Ezra continued to read out of the Law (Nehemiah 8:13, 18), with an immediate impact. For example, when people learned they were to celebrate the Feast of Tabernacles by dwelling "in booths" and by carrying "olive branches and pine branches" and the like, they gladly conformed (8:14–17). Clearly, it was a learning experience for them. Moreover, at the end of the month, separating themselves from others in their midst, the Jews "assembled with fasting" and entered "into an oath, to walk in God's law, which was given by Moses" (9:1; 10:29). Significantly, they pledged to live in accord with the stipulations of the Law, including keeping the Sabbath properly, making the required donations to the temple, and not intermarrying with outsiders (10:30–39). Everything was now in place. Or so it seemed.

The points at which threads of life began to unravel again had to do with people who continued to marry outside their ethnic group and pugnaciously retained their economic and other relationships with outsiders (Ezra 9:1–2). Ezra's first response was to pray fervently for God's forgiveness for his people (9:5–15). In light of Nebuchadnezzar's devastating blow 150 years before, he knew the enormity of turning against God, for God was their real protection. In December, he took action (10:9).

Ezra had brought the Law with him, carrying it in his hands (Ezra 7:14, 25). Most investigators conclude that this corpus of law consisted of the Pentateuch basically as we know it, the materials from the beginning of Genesis to the end of Deuteronomy. It was this law that he had read throughout the eight-day Feast of Tabernacles two months before. Although many had been thrilled to learn of God's requirements for their lives, even weeping as they listened, somehow they had not internalized what they heard. For the people to seriously come to grips with what Ezra had brought to them, he would have to drive a very large stake in the ground. But what would it be? The answer to his prayers came on the lips of one of the ranking officials in the city, a man named Shechaniah. Turning to Ezra, he said, "We have trespassed against our God, and have taken strange [foreign] wives of the people of the land. . . . Now therefore let us make a covenant with our God to put away all the wives, . . . and let it be done according to the law" (10:2–3). Though such an action would be harsh and would raise opposition against him, Ezra courageously pushed the issue forward, asking through "the princes and the elders" that every Jewish male within the territory of Judah gather to the city three days hence or pay the penalty of forfeiting "all his substance." They came, in a heavy rainstorm (10:7–9).

In one of the most important scenes in Israelite history, within the temple grounds Ezra put these men under covenant to "separate [themselves] from the people of the land, and from the strange wives." In solemn response, those in the congregation "said with a loud voice, As thou hast said, so must we do" (Ezra 10:11–12). Within ten days, a great many had taken the fateful step. The offending priests led out, even offering sacrifices "for their trespass" (10:16–19). There was no turning back. The profound point about conforming to the law of God had finally burrowed its way into every soul. Life would never be as it was.

The same can be said about those on the receiving end of the radical action demanded by Ezra. We imagine that they were furious, as were doubtless many on the Jewish side. It was a day of severe tests for all. On his part, Ezra showed himself equal to the huge challenge. Perhaps oddly, we do not hear of him again. He had performed his work in just a few months. Even so, by turning the hearts of his people to the Law, he laid the foundation for religious life that has persisted to modern times. In addition, from that time forward, people associated themselves with God's purposes not so much by their lineage but by their conformity to the Law. The Law, rather than God's ancient covenant established with Abraham, became the measure of a person's relationship to Him.

Furthermore, the fact that, through Ezra, the Persian king had exempted temple workers from taxation established a precedent that would persist for the next hundred years in the Persian empire and then continue under the Greeks and Romans. By such action, the governments of these empires recognized the legitimacy of the priesthood and its functions both in and out of the temple. Moreover, this recognition meant noninterference generally in religious matters. Perhaps negatively, it also meant that substantial wealth could and would accrue to the leading priests.

There was a further negative dimension to this situation. Non-priests had to pay taxes to foreigners. This became an important political issue, especially in the era just before and during the ministries of Jesus and John the Baptist. Those who violently opposed paying taxes to foreigners, even assassinating leaders who profited thereby, were the Zealots. The question posed to Jesus about whether to pay taxes to Caesar grew out of such opposition (see Matthew 22:15–22). In addition, it led to the generally low opinion about tax collectors—"publicans"—that we see in the New Testament.

Conclusion

When all was said and done, Nehemiah and Ezra had assisted their people immensely in and around Jerusalem. Perhaps significantly, they were both outsiders from Babylon. Through the forceful and charismatic efforts of Nehemiah, the wall of Jerusalem was erected, bringing security and strength to a crestfallen people. During his second term as governor, he began the process of regulating religious and social matters, such as the Sabbath day and marriages with non-Jewish spouses. But his regulations did not really influence the inner life of the people because, as we have seen, over a short time people grew lax about such matters. It was left to Ezra to seize and reform the deepest recesses of the souls of his people. Through his relentless toughness, within a few months he succeeded in demanding that certain people give up their most prized of human relationships—wives and, in some cases, children. The impact was both devastating and enlivening. The day could never be forgotten.

For Further Reading

Elias Bickerman, *From Ezra to the Last of the Maccabees* (New York: Schocken Books, 1962), 3–40.

John Bright, *A History of Israel*, 3d ed. (Philadelphia: Westminster Press, 1981), 373–412.

David B. Galbraith, D. Kelly Ogden, and Andrew C. Skinner, *Jerusalem, The Eternal City* (Salt Lake City: Deseret Book, 1996), 117–33.

Martin Noth, *The History of Israel*, 2d ed. (New York: Harper & Row, 1960), 316–45.

The Holy Land under the Ptolemies and the Seleucids

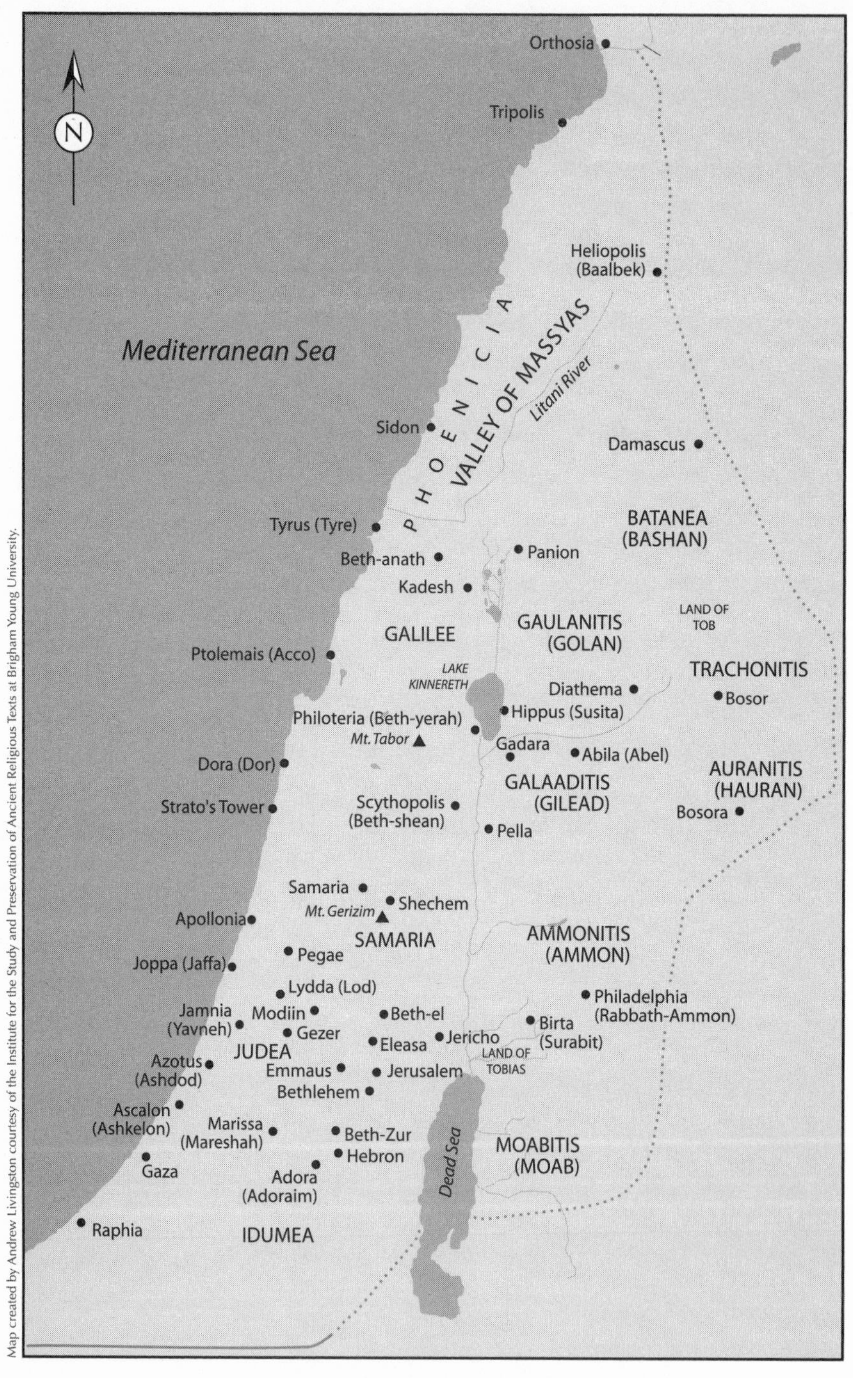

Map created by Andrew Livingston courtesy of the Institute for the Study and Preservation of Ancient Religious Texts at Brigham Young University.

.... Frontier of the Ptolemaic domain before 198 B.C.

——— Frontier between the Ptolemaic and Seleucid states after 198 B.C.

CHAPTER 3

ALEXANDER CHANGES THE WORLD

Alexander lay helpless on his bed. He was thirty-two years old. He had already conquered all the territories between his Macedonian home in northern Greece and the Punjab of India, including Egypt to the south. Tribes and nations and peoples were now his subjects, kneeling in awe and respect for this Greek warrior whose military efforts had effectively erased borders and created a grand Hellenistic body of people who, because of his conquests, would now share a common Greek language and a common Greek culture. But at this moment, a bedeviling high fever tormented his body. His physicians worked frantically to reduce his body temperature, knowing the severe consequences whether they succeeded or failed. If they succeeded in bringing down his temperature, he still might suffer damage to his brain. If they failed, he would die.

At the top of Alexander's military agenda was revenge against the Persians. After all, they had ravaged his homeland not once but twice. He was young and, at age twenty, had just succeeded his father, Philip, king of Macedon (382–336 B.C.), who had died at the hands of an assassin. No one could have guessed that by his military prowess this young man would literally change the world, from his Macedonian homeland to North Africa, from the eastern shores of the Mediterranean Sea to the Indus River beyond modern Afghanistan. By all odds, Alexander's thirteen-year reign from 336 to 323 B.C. would be the most momentous between the age of the Athenian Pericles (ca. 495–429 B.C.) and that of the Roman Augustus (63 B.C.–A.D. 14).

While Alexander's impressive military conquests carried him one-fifth of the distance across the earth, one of the most important long-term effects of his actions was the creation of a vast region whose citizens spoke and read a common language, Greek. This fact alone meant that he left a legacy of access to classical literature, art, philosophy, architecture, and social and governmental institutions that would come to influence people's lives in unexpected ways. Even people in the eastern Mediterranean region who were descendants of ancient Israel would not escape the allurements of the Greek world. The successors of Alexander carried on his dream of bringing people under the influence of Greek ideals. The lives of their subjects would be forever changed.

ALEXANDER (356–323 B.C.)

Alexander was born in 356 B.C. to King Philip II of Macedon and Olympias of Epirus. His father was massively ambitious and held influence over all of Greece, which he had gained by either military conquest or diplomacy. Moreover, he was a champion of Greek culture and spread it wherever he could. One of Philip's most cherished hopes was to invade and punish the Persian Empire, which stretched from the western shores of Asia Minor (modern Turkey) southward to Egypt and eastward to modern Pakistan. Philip was about to embark on this task when he was assassinated. Alexander adopted his father's dreams, both for military conquest and for spreading Greek culture. From his mother he inherited an unbridled, passionate spirit. But his parents were not the only major influences in his life. When Alexander was thirteen, Philip hired the famous philosopher Aristotle (384–322 B.C.) to tutor him. For three years, the philosopher instructed the young prince in Homer and the Greek dramatists as well as in politics. From Aristotle, Alexander learned the art of careful and patient thinking. This education evidently came to an end in 340 when

Philip named Alexander as his regent. The youth was all of seventeen.

When his father died in 336 B.C., Alexander knew that the individual Greek city-states would consider their old relationships with his father to be null and void. In a series of moves that began to disclose his genius, Alexander regained the support of the Greeks that his father had enjoyed by pursuing diplomacy, threats, and, when needed, force of arms. Then, with the backing of the Corinthian League, he crossed the Hellespont (known today as the Dardanelles, the narrow strait that separates Europe and Asia) into Asia Minor, never to return to his beloved Macedonia.

The events of Alexander's campaign through Asia Minor are complex to follow. But there are two features of his warfare that stand out. He first sought to free the Greek cities that lay along the west coast and that teemed with Greek colonists. By doing so, he would create a reservoir of goodwill that would both entice citizens of these cities to join his army and reduce the possibility that the Persians could attack his rear. Second, he judged that the Persian fleet would follow him and try to undo his efforts by attacking and recapturing the coastal cities he had liberated. So he hit upon a strategy that would deprive the Persian fleet of its Mediterranean bases. Early on, after dismissing his own fleet as unessential to his campaign, he besieged and captured Halicarnassus, on the southwest coast, which served as one of the Persians' naval bases. In time, he also captured the Persian bases at Tyre just north of Galilee and in Egypt, thus eventually rendering the Persian fleet of no account.

From southwest Asia Minor, Alexander turned east to face the mighty Persian emperor and his fabled army. Alexander pushed his forces across the southern regions, finally facing the Persian "grand army" and King Darius III (336–331 B.C.) in 333 at Issus, which lies at the very northeastern corner of the Mediterranean Sea where the south coast of Turkey meets the west coast of Syria. Alexander's brilliance as a leader brought victory to his army, which was severely outnumbered. King Darius fled the battlefield, leaving behind his wife and children, whom Alexander's soldiers captured. As he and his officers entered the tents of the defeated king, they were astonished at the Persian opulence, even on the battlefield. Perhaps surprisingly, Alexander refused terms of peace that were favorable to himself and his army. By his refusal, he made it clear that he intended to go beyond simply punishing the Persians, which had been the goal of his Corinthian League allies. All of Asia lay before him, and he decided to grab it.

Though the road east to Persia was wide open to Alexander, he wheeled his forces south toward Phoenicia and Egypt. He knew that the Phoenician city of Tyre, built on a small, well-fortified island just off the coast, offered a safe haven to the Persian fleet. His siege of this city in 332 B.C. lasted seven months. At times, the fighting was fierce. But Alexander's forces finally prevailed and razed the fortress city. The Persians had lost an important anchorage. Moreover, the other Phoenician cities capitulated to his army.

Alexander led his forces farther south, passing along the maritime plain that lies west of Samaria and Jerusalem. Apparently, officials of both cities sought assurances from Alexander that his army would not attack if they would surrender. Josephus tells us that the Samaritans supplied a contingent of soldiers to Alexander's army and that Alexander visited both cities (*Jewish Antiquities* 11.8.1–6). He then moved on southward toward Egypt. People of both cities must have been relieved because they knew that, based on his successful siege of Tyre, Alexander could attack Samaria or Jerusalem and reduce either city to ashes. Little did they know that it was the Greek ideals he represented that would burrow deep into the hearts of their citizens and bring about crises of faith and devotion.

Alexander went off to Egypt, where he received divine

honors, being dubbed "the son of the God Amun" during a visit to Amun's temple at the Siwah Oasis in the western desert. Further, he walked along the beach of the Mediterranean Sea and laid out the city that would be called after his name, Alexandria, which in time would become the chief cultural and intellectual center of the ancient world. Satisfied that all of Egypt was his, he began to retrace his steps northward. At some point he learned that, inexplicably, the Samaritans had rebelled. During the melee, Alexander's prefect, a man named Andromachus, was burned to death. Alexander exacted revenge on the people of Samaria, destroying their city. His forces pursued hundreds into a cave in the Wadi Daliyeh where they were suffocated by smoke from fires built at the cave's entrance. Picking up the pieces of their lives, Samaritans reestablished themselves a few miles eastward in Shechem. They had felt the indelible print of the horribly heavy hand of the Macedonian king. For his part, Alexander went on toward the heart of Persia. He would not deny his lust for conquest.

In short, Alexander's army invaded the Persian heartland. King Darius, who tried to make a stand with another numerically superior army near Arbela, was driven from the battlefield again by Alexander's disciplined troops. But Alexander never caught the rival king, for Darius was soon assassinated by a satrap, one of his own governors. Alexander then seized Babylon and Susa in succession, finally reaching territories beyond the Indus River. Because his soldiers refused to go farther, he turned back to Babylon, where he fell ill and died in 323 B.C. at the age of thirty-three. His conquests had eclipsed those of any other ruler in the known world.

Alexander's Successors

Almost immediately, Alexander's generals—known as the Successors—began to quarrel among themselves about what territories belonged to whom. For our purposes, the most important figures in this struggle are Ptolemy I, the founder of the Ptolemaic dynasty in Egypt (323–285 B.C.), and Seleucus I, founder of the Seleucid empire in Syria (312/11–280 B.C.). In the year of Alexander's death, Ptolemy snatched the reins of government in Egypt, finally declaring himself king in 304 B.C. (The last Ptolemaic ruler was Cleopatra VII [69–30 B.C.]. After her suicide, Egypt became a Roman province.) Soon thereafter, Ptolemy conquered Palestine and the island of Cyprus. Seleucus, on the other hand, tried to take control of the former satrapy of Babylonia, finally succeeding in 321. But he had to flee for his life to Egypt in 316, returning to power only in 312. Both men coveted Palestine. Even though Ptolemy gained decisive control of Palestine at the battle of Ipsos in 301, those who succeeded these two sovereigns would later struggle over this territory. Through it ran important trade routes that connected their respective territories. And control meant revenues and power.

Before Ptolemy's death in 283/282 B.C., he came to rule over a large population of Jews who lived in Egypt. More than two hundred years before his arrival, Jews had arrived in the country as mercenary soldiers on the southern border, residing on the island of Elephantine, which sits in the middle of the Nile River at modern Aswan. These Jews helped guard the frontier of Egypt and settled in well enough that they built a temple and even carried on correspondence with Samaritans and fellow Jews, as evidenced by the Elephantine papyri. In the decades following Ptolemy's ascent to power, Jews moved into Egypt in large numbers, particularly into the capital city of Alexandria, where they became a major segment of the population, reaching an estimated one million in the first century A.D. Within a couple of generations, they lost their ability to read and speak Hebrew, one of the major reasons for translating the books of the Hebrew Bible into Greek, producing the Septuagint. According to the *Letter of Aristeas*, this translating effort occurred in Egypt under the sponsorship of Ptolemy II Philadelphus (285–246 B.C.).

Although the details of Aristeas' story are probably legendary, it does seem certain that Egypt was the site for translating the Old Testament into the Greek language.

After Ptolemy took control of Palestine in 301 B.C., he became sovereign to a large Jewish population that inhabited Jerusalem and its environs. Because of the lack of sources, it is not completely clear what his relationship was with his Jewish subjects. Nor do we know much about how his successors got along with such people. Perhaps this hiatus in our knowledge means that Jews flourished during his reign and thereafter, paying their taxes and living normal lives. This certainly seems to be the case for the neighboring Samaritans, as disclosed by the Zeno papyri. These papyri consist of letters to and from a certain Zeno who was a financial agent in the government of Ptolemy II. Two of the letters came to Zeno from a Samaritan official named Tobiah. Since the ancestors of this man had served as governors of territory along the Jordan River under the Persians, it seems that the same family was serving the Egyptian government, seeing to domestic tranquility and the payment of taxes. We assume that there was a similar arrangement with officials in Jerusalem and elsewhere in the country. This kind of arrangement, which evidently respected the religious and cultural values of Samaritans and Jews, lasted for just over a century. Then, in 198 B.C., one of the descendants of Seleucus, a man named Antiochus III (223–187 B.C.), took control of Palestine from the Ptolemies of Egypt in a battle near Panias (later known as Caesarea Philippi), and things began to change.

According to Josephus, when Antiochus wrested sovereignty of Palestine from the Egyptian king, Ptolemy V (203–181 B.C.), he received a hero's welcome in Jerusalem (*Jewish Antiquities* 12.3.3–4). Further, he signed a decree ensuring to Jews that they would be allowed to continue worshiping at their temple as they had in past ages and would be able to keep out of their city even animal carcasses that were unlawful under the law of Moses. There was reason for Jews to rejoice. But Antiochus would soon overreach his own military strength, introducing a new kind of day.

Antiochus had received the Carthaginian general Hannibal into his court after the Romans had defeated Hannibal in 202 B.C. With Hannibal encouraging him, Antiochus invaded Greece in 192. The Romans drove Antiochus and his army back to Asia Minor and, following him, forced him into a humiliating surrender at Apamea in eastern Syria in 188 B.C. Antiochus lost his navy and most of his territories that produced revenue in the form of taxes. From that moment, rulers of the Seleucid Empire were to pay a huge monthly tribute to Rome and thereafter became desperate for cash. The fact that Antiochus was killed in 187 while trying to loot a Mesopotamian temple to meet the tribute that he owed to Rome makes the point.

The Romans' appearance in the eastern Mediterranean began to affect political and military affairs. But the Romans had little impact on religious matters. Rome was in the process of making the Mediterranean basin its own. That is why Romans reacted so sharply to Antiochus' invasion of Greece. As they took control of larger and larger territories, the Romans appointed representatives who managed governmental aspects of life. Otherwise, the Romans took little interest in local worship practices and the like. To this point, Rome had not bothered with Palestine. And even after Pompey conquered Jerusalem in 63 B.C., both Jews and Samaritans followed their own worship traditions largely without interference. But one of the Seleucid successors of Antiochus, also named Antiochus, made life miserable for Jews and, presumably, for Samaritans as well.

He was called Antiochus IV Epiphanes, and he ruled from 175 to 163 B.C. He was the third son of Antiochus III. His name *Epiphanes* meant "God manifest." And he acted as if he were in fact deity in the flesh. Most of all, he was a devoted follower of the Greek gods and of Greek culture in general. This part of his character rubbed Jews and Samaritans like sandpaper.

Eventually, Antiochus sent an edict that overturned all the concessions his father had made to the Jewish people. This meant that sacrifices at the temple were suspended and that people had to eat pork under penalty of death. Things had changed quickly; a mere thirty years before, people of the city had hailed Antiochus' father. Now they watched helplessly as their temple became the house of the Greek god Zeus and pigs were offered on the altar that had been dedicated to Jehovah. Although no records exist for the relationship between Antiochus and the Samaritans, we have to assume that he carried on a campaign to make their society into a host for Greek culture as well.

CONCLUSION

It now appeared that Greek ways had won. All that Alexander had stood for had seemingly triumphed, in the worst possible manner. The time had come for action of some sort. Fortunately for Jews and Samaritans, a family of five sons was equal to the task. Their leader would be the middle son, Judas Maccabee (166–160 B.C.).

FOR FURTHER READING

H. Idris Bell, *Egypt from Alexander the Great to the Arab Conquest* (Oxford: Oxford University Press, 1948), 28–64.

John Bright, *A History of Israel*, 3d ed. (Philadelphia: Westminster Press, 1981), 405–22.

F. F. Bruce, *New Testament History* (Garden City, New York: Anchor Books, 1972), 1–13.

Michael Grant, *From Alexander to Cleopatra* (New York: Charles Scribner's Sons, 1982), 1–18, 37–64.

Simon Hornblower and Antony Spawforth, eds., *The Oxford Classical Dictionary*, 3d ed. (Oxford: Oxford University Press, 1996), s.v. "Alexander," "Aristotle," "Philip II."

Martin Noth, *The History of Israel*, 2d ed. (New York: Harper & Row, 1960), 346–67.

Cecelia M Peek, "Alexander the Great Comes to Jerusalem: The Jewish Response to Hellenism," in John F. Hall and John W. Welch, eds., *Masada and the World of the New Testament* (Provo, Utah: BYU Studies, 1997), 99–112.

W. W. Tarn, *Alexander the Great* (Cambridge: Cambridge University Press, 1948).

———, *Hellenistic Civilisation*, 3d ed. (Cleveland, Ohio: Meridian Books, 1952), 126–238.

Victor Tcherikover, *Hellenistic Civilization and the Jews* (Philadelphia: Jewish Publication Society, 1959), 1–203.

CHAPTER 4

The Maccabean War Breaks Out

Mattathias sat in the dark cave trying to shift his weight to find a comfortable position among the rocks that littered the floor. He and his sons faced a problem. Ever since he had assassinated the Greek soldiers who tried to force fellow villagers to sacrifice to the hated god Zeus, he, his sons, and their sympathizers had been in hiding. But they had also managed to raise a ragtag army to fight the hated, arrogant Greeks. For Mattathias and the rest, it was beyond belief to think that their beloved temple and their time-honored way of life had changed. He was fiercely determined to change everything back, even at the cost of blood and life. But the Sabbath posed a dilemma. For centuries, his ancestors had honored God's Sabbath day, even in war. At times, God had blessed them and brought them victory over oppressive enemies. At other times, Jews had suffered because they would not take up arms on the Sabbath. What were he and his fellow partisans to do?

Mattathias' armed struggle against efforts to Hellenize the Jews began as a single act of defiance in a small village north-west of Jerusalem. It soon became a full-fledged revolt for religious freedom and ultimately ended in national liberation.

Antiochus IV (175–163 B.C.) became the king of the Seleucid Empire following the murder of his brother, Seleucus IV (187–175 B.C.), in 175 B.C. At the time, his kingdom was threatened from all sides—Rome from the west, Parthia from the east, and Egypt from the south. Also, he faced the unrelenting financial crisis that grew out of the monthly tribute

Seleucid Empire at Its Greatest

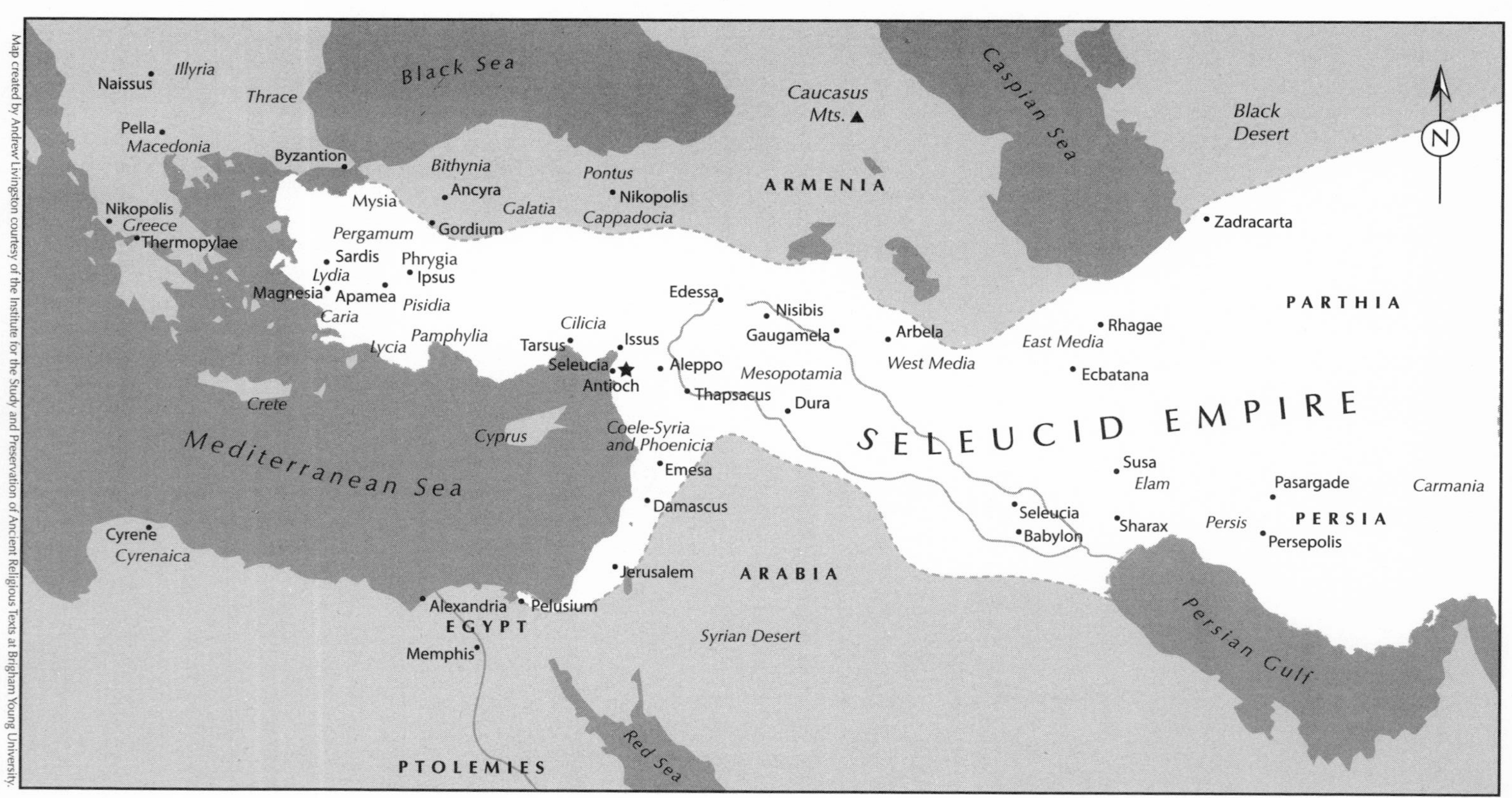

Map created by Andrew Livingston courtesy of the Institute for the Study and Preservation of Ancient Religious Texts at Brigham Young University.

imposed by the Romans on his father thirteen years before. In the ancient world, the places where people brought precious possessions for safekeeping and where kings lavished wealth were temples. Moreover, nonroyal people who sought influence within a kingdom, such as serving as a chief priest of a temple, would approach the sovereign and offer money to be appointed to such an office. In the days of Antiochus IV, the Jerusalem temple and its priesthood offered such a combination of wealth and people vying for high office.

In the face of external pressures, Antiochus attempted to unify his religiously and ethnically diverse empire, believing that complete Hellenization of the regions he ruled would give stability and strength to his kingdom. However, this decision brought him into direct conflict with devout Jews in and around Jerusalem.

By the time Antiochus IV took up the reins of power, Greek ideas and institutions had come to Jerusalem. Influential people in the city were at odds over how to respond, debating whether to adopt Greek ideas and other trappings of life, such as stylish clothing and theaters. The Jewish high priest at the time, Onias III, had gone to meet with Antiochus' brother, then the king, when the king was assassinated. While the high priest was still away, his brother Joshua, who was known as Jason, the Greek pronunciation of his name, approached the new king Antiochus and offered a large sum of money to be appointed as high priest. Desperate for cash and not guided by high principles, Antiochus agreed that Jason would serve in the top job at the temple, deposing Onias in the process. Not until this moment in Jewish history was the high priest appointed by an occupying power. Heretofore, those chosen, whether devout or not, were at least biologically descended from the proper family line, in this case the family of Zadok, the priest at the time of David who anointed Solomon to be king (see 2 Samuel 8:17; 1 Kings 1:32–45).

To understand the revolt, we must take into account the divisions within Jewish society itself. There were certainly pro-Seleucid and pro-Ptolemaic (Egyptian) factions, just as there were pro-Tobiad and pro-Oniad factions (families who held the office of high priest). And then there were those Jews who were openly attracted to Greek ideas and social institutions—in fact, most Jews were partially Hellenized by this period. There were even those who voluntarily abandoned their faith for a new way of life, particularly among the urban elite in the Holy City of Jerusalem. And within these groups, various factions were found, as there were pro-Seleucid Tobiad and pro-Ptolemaic Tobiad factions. Nevertheless, the impact of Hellenization upon faith and sacred tradition remained the major issue among Jews of the period.

Besides adopting Greek dress, young men in the city began to participate in sporting events sponsored by the new Greek gymnasium. Because they did so without clothing, their appearance created an uproar. Some of them even went so far as to undergo the painful operation that reversed their circumcision so that they would look like Greek youths when they participated in sports. Consequently, feelings against Greek culture continued at a high pitch.

But a mere three years after Jason came to the office of high priest, a man named Menelaus, who was not a member of the high priestly family, offered more money to King Antiochus and received the job. The family origin of Menelaus remains unknown. Certainly, he was not from one of the priestly families of the country. At least Jason was from a family of high priests. Like Jason, Menelaus continued the intense interest in Greek life in the city. To add insult to injury, Menelaus began to take items from the temple to pay the bribe he had promised to the king. Moreover, it was whispered that Menelaus had Onias assassinated when he protested his behavior. Further, in 169 B.C., when Antiochus was returning from a successful military expedition to

Egypt, Menelaus helped the king steal articles from the temple, including gold leafing. People of Jerusalem were beside themselves. Still, there were those who supported Menelaus because they believed in holding on to Greek ways. In the next year, 168 B.C., matters came to a sharper focus.

Antiochus attempted another expedition against Egypt. This time, a Roman officer named Popilius Laenas, on the authority of the Roman Senate, ordered Antiochus out of that country. Antiochus knew better than to resist. When his father had been forced to accept the Roman terms at Apamea, the younger Antiochus was taken to Rome as a hostage. There he saw firsthand the might and grandeur of this new power in the Mediterranean. Thus, when Popilius Laenas gave him an ultimatum, he complied and withdrew. But, we can imagine, that action did not make him feel better. In fact, feeling humiliated and then hearing that Jason had recaptured Jerusalem and the temple from Menelaus, he decided to humiliate the city and its citizens. The next year was fateful; in 167 B.C., Antiochus sent one of his military commanders, Apollonius by name, to Jerusalem. At first feigning goodwill, he ultimately turned his army on the populace and pulled down the city walls.

At the same time, a foreign colony was established within the Acra, a fortress overlooking the temple. (Scholars are divided on the exact location; the majority view is that it was located at the southern edge of the Holy Mount. A minority view, however, is that it was located at the northwestern edge of the Holy Mount where the Antonia Fortress, mentioned in the New Testament as "castle" [see Acts 21:34; 22:24], was later built.) The population of the Acra was augmented by staunch Jewish Hellenists loyal to Menelaus. The gentiles brought their false gods and their rites of worship into the very heart of the Jewish world.

In the end, the character of the city began to change. Some of the faithful, now dispirited, left the city and established themselves in villages and towns away from Jerusalem. Mattathias and his family were among those who left Jerusalem during this period.

Then Antiochus announced a drastic policy change in Jerusalem and Judea—he made obedience to Jehovah's commandments a crime. Ironically, in so doing, Antiochus actually abandoned the traditional Greek idea of religious toleration.

In his nasty effort to eradicate Jewish religious practices, Antiochus prohibited Sabbath observance, reading or teaching the Mosaic Law (he even had copies of the Torah confiscated, torn up, and burned), performance of circumcision, and observance of the Mosaic dietary laws, which included a prohibition against eating pork.

As if these steps were not bad enough, Antiochus took the ultimate drastic step of converting the holy temple into a pagan shrine. The process involved several steps. First, the altar dedicated to Jehovah was desecrated through the sacrifice of unclean animals, in this case pigs. Second, an altar of idols—three meteorites representing the three principal deities of the pagan cult (accounts differ on what was actually erected)—was placed on or over the one dedicated to the Lord. Third, sacred prostitution was established within the walls of the temple. The day was an intolerably dark one for most Jews.

At first, persecution was sporadic because few resisted in a public way. Eventually, royal officials, including apostate Jews, began enforcing the new policies in a relentless, systematic manner. Some Jews assimilated rather than allow their loved ones to suffer torture and death. Others secretly continued obeying the Lord's commandments, choosing martyrdom instead of apostasy if discovered. It may well have been the first time in human history that such mass martyrdom occurred among a people as it did during this bleak period.

Thousands were killed when they disobeyed the new edict. In one case, officers tied the dead bodies of the two young infants whom they had killed to their mother's neck before she was also executed. Her crime was that she had had them circumcised according to God's commandment. In effect, the edict condemned not only the young infants and their mother but also the father and the man who performed the circumcisions.

Antiochus' persecution was a first, for Jews died not in battle defending their country against invaders but for simply practicing their faith. It is not unthinkable that people believed their way of life was in mortal jeopardy. Antiochus' two-pronged policy of attacking the institutions that bound the people together and simultaneously forcing conversion of the Jewish people could have easily made it impossible for Jews and Judaism to survive as they were.

First and Second Maccabees

Our principal sources for the ensuing war against the Greeks are the first and second books of Maccabees, found in the Apocrypha (see chapter 10, "Apocrypha and Pseudepigrapha"). The First Book of Maccabees is an important historical account of the Maccabean War, covering the period preceding the persecution under Antiochus, from about 175 B.C. to the death of Simon, the last of the sons of Mattathias, about 135 B.C. It was written in Hebrew or Aramaic by an anonymous author who not only had access to important primary sources at the end of the second century B.C. but also followed the biblical model of historical writing in his composition.

The Hebrew text eventually disappeared, and First Maccabees survived only in a Greek translation. The author was decidedly pro-Hasmonean, glorifying the family of Mattathias and his descendants. He therefore often omitted anything that would be considered embarrassing or that might undercut the legitimacy of their rule, which was established after the defeat of the Greeks.

The Second Book of Maccabees was written by another

anonymous author during the middle of the second century B.C. and claims to be a truncated account based on the work of Jason of Cyrene. Unlike the First Book of Maccabees, the Second Book was originally composed in Greek and decidedly follows a Greek model of historical writing. Another difference between the two works is the tight focus on Judas, the son of Mattathias, while basically covering the period between 167 and 161 B.C. In this book, the author provides detailed stories of the torture, mutilation, and death of those who would not violate the covenant. The author of the Second Book of Maccabees does not support Hasmonean dynastic claims—at least not the regime as it was at the time he wrote the book. Second Maccabees also unabashedly supports the adoption of Hanukkah, the festival that grew out of the rededication of the temple in December 164 B.C., as a national celebration. In sum, both books, First and Second Maccabees, cover some of the same historical period, but from different perspectives.

Mattathias and His Sons

The story of Mattathias and his five sons begins in the small Jewish village of Modein in late 167 or early 166 B.C.: "During that time, Mattathias, son of John son of Simeon, a priest of the clan of Joarib, left Jerusalem and settled at Modein. Mattathias had five sons: John, nicknamed Gaddi; Simon, called Thassi; Judas, called Maccabaeus; Eleazar, called Auaran; and Jonathan, called Apphus" (1 Maccabees 2:1–5).

In Modein, possibly Mattathias' ancestral home, royal officials attempted to force a public pagan sacrifice. Even though he was promised special favors if he complied, Mattathias refused; and when a villager came forward to offer the sacrifice in his place, Mattathias "was filled with zeal and trembled with rage and let his anger rise, as was fitting; he ran and slew him upon the altar. At the same time he also killed the kings' official in charge of enforcing sacrifices, and he destroyed the altar.

He acted zealously for the sake of the Torah, as Phineas acted against Zimri the son of Salom" (1 Maccabees 2:26; compare Numbers 25:6–15).

The First Book of Maccabees continues, "Mattathias cried out throughout the town in a loud voice, 'All who are zealous for the sake of the Torah, who uphold the covenant, march out after me!' Thereupon he and his sons fled to the mountains, leaving behind all their possessions in the town" (1 Maccabees 2:27–28). That day began a process that would bring Mattathias' family into prominence for the next 130 years.

As noted earlier, history is often more complex than we would like it to be. The Maccabean war is no exception. It is too simplistic to imagine only two sides in conflict—a group of devout Jews coming together to fight for religious freedom under the leadership of Mattathias and his family and another group of royal officials trying to enforce Antiochus' edicts with the support of apostate Jews.

In actuality, reactions against Hellenization were complex and diverse, and the Jews were not the only ones to fight against this movement. Among devout Jews, some believed that God forbade violent rebellion against earthly powers that He had placed on earth, and still others believed it was their religious duty to rebel against an evil government bent on destroying them. Even among those who believed that it was not a violation of the Mosaic covenant to rebel, some refused to defend themselves on the Sabbath, trusting that God would protect them.

One group, numbering a thousand, fled into the desert. Greek soldiers pursued them and offered to spare their lives if they would accept the new way of life demanded by Antiochus. When they rejected this offer of amnesty, the soldiers waited until the Sabbath to attack because they knew that devout Jews would not violate the Sabbath. As predicted, the Jews offered no resistance, so every man, woman, and child was killed (1 Maccabees 2:29–38).

For Mattathias and his sons, the Sabbath posed a true dilemma. If they refused to defend themselves on the Sabbath, they would certainly die as had those who fled into the desert. If they chose to fight on the Sabbath, God might punish them for violating His law. "On that day they came to a decision: 'If any man comes against us in battle on the Sabbath day, we shall fight against him and not all die as our brothers died in their hiding places'" (1 Maccabees 2:41). This proved to be the most important decision that they made in their ultimately successful revolt.

Significantly for Mattathias' army, many Hasideans ("Pious Ones"; see chapter 13, "Hasideans, Pharisees, and Sadducees"), some of whose numbers were among those slaughtered in the desert on the Sabbath, accepted Mattathias' decision about self-defense on the Sabbath and joined his movement (see 1 Maccabees 2:42).

A second decision, next in importance, was that the resistance fighters would confine themselves to guerrilla operations, attacking when and where they wanted before disappearing back into the hills to regroup. These two decisions—Sabbath defense and quick-strike forays—allowed them not only to survive against overwhelming odds but also to win battle after battle.

Mattathias and his partisan supporters made two other decisions that buttressed the successful effort that ultimately undermined the power of Antiochus' army. First, Mattathias decided to confine the organization of guerrillas only to the towns and villages of Judea. Second, he and his soldiers decided to kill all collaborators, those who rebelled against the sacred covenant. All in all, these momentous rulings gradually reduced Greek control in the countryside, leaving Jerusalem virtually isolated as a place of concentrated Greek power.

JUDAS MACCABEE (168–60 B.C.)

Before his death sometime between April 166 and April 165 B.C., Mattathias blessed his sons much as the ancient patriarch Jacob had done before his own death (see Genesis 49). In Mattathias' final blessing, he counseled, "My children, be valorous and resolute for the Torah, because through the Torah will you win glory. Your brother [Simon], I know, is a man of counsel; always listen to him; he shall serve as your father. Judas Maccabaeus has been a mighty warrior from his youth. He shall be commander of your army and shall fight the war against the nations" (1 Maccabees 2:64–66). The story continues: "Judas, called Maccabaeus, his son, succeeded him. To his aid rallied all his brothers and all the steadfast followers of his father, and they gladly fought Israel's war" (1 Maccabees 3:1–2). Judas was known by the nickname Maccabeus or *Maccabee*, "[God's] hammer," the name that would characterize the war.

At first, Judas' successes did not worry the central Seleucid government; in contrast, the local administration was deeply concerned about the stunning successes in battle, as Judas continued to gather support among Jews: "Judas and his brothers began to be feared, and the terror of them fell upon the neighboring gentiles" (1 Maccabees 3:25).

A turning point came when Ptolemy, son of Dorymenes, the Seleucid military commander of Syria and Phoenicia, appointed Nicanor and Gorgias to lead a very large force against Judas' small army (see 2 Maccabees 8:8–9). At Emmaus (not the New Testament site but Emmaus Nicopolis, west of Jerusalem toward the coast), Judas inflicted a decisive defeat on an advance unit of the Greek army, which included slave traders laden with gold and silver who were anticipating the purchase of a large quantity of Jewish slaves after their defeat. Judas' brilliant military victory not only demoralized the Greeks but also provided an enormous boost to Jewish morale and the fighting reputation of his soldiers. Judas also captured considerable funds, weapons, and other goods necessary to sustain the revolt.

In the following year, the Greeks suffered another defeat, forcing the army under Lysias, a coregent of the realm, to retreat to Antioch, capital of the Greek kings of Syria. Taking advantage of the situation, Judas was encouraged to march on to Jerusalem, retaking the city without any apparent resistance in December 164 B.C. Only the Greeks and their Jewish sympathizers in the Acra remained menacingly entrenched behind walls.

Within days, the temple was restored. Following biblical precedents, Judas through the priests prolonged the Feast of Tabernacles (see chapter 17, "Feasts and Festivals") for a celebration of the dedication of the new sacrificial altar along with the temple furnishings, which included the lamp stand, altar of incense, and table of showbread. They rededicated the temple on the third anniversary of its desecration by Antiochus.

This memorable event gave birth to the Feast of Hanukkah ("Dedication"), later called the "Festival of Lights." The dedication lasted through eight days of celebration, and later tradition explains why it lasted eight days: Judas found only one cruse of pure olive oil that still bore the seal of the high priest. He needed the oil to light the Menorah in the Holy Place, but the one cruse was sufficient for one day only. Miraculously, it burned for eight days, until new supplies could be found.

In November or early December 164 B.C., Antiochus died during a military campaign in Iran, and a succession crisis ensued, allowing the Jews to take advantage of the resulting instability. In a series of seesaw advances and retreats, one faction in the empire eventually renounced Antiochus' religious policy and deposed and executed Menelaus, replacing him as high priest with a moderate Hellenist, Alcimus.

The Jewish revolt was successful, ending religious persecution and, for the time being, stopping a foreign government from forcing a wicked high priest upon the Jews. Some decided to support the new government. Judas, however, acknowledged the progress but ultimately, at least in political and military terms, believed that the current compromise with the Seleucids was nothing more than a cease-fire agreement.

It is most likely that during this period, the revolt against religious persecution became a war of total independence for Judas and his followers. Soon, Judas and the Greeks were again waging battle. Sometime in May 160 B.C., Greek forces under the command of Bacchides defeated Judas' forces at Eleasa (some miles north and slightly west of Jerusalem) and also killed Judas. The death of Judas was a stunning blow.

Defeated, humiliated, and demoralized, the Jews retreated to the hills again: "Then all the friends of Judas assembled and said to Jonathan, 'Since the death of your brother Judas there has been no man like him to go forth against our enemies and Bacchides and against the [internal] foes of our people. Accordingly, we hereby choose you today to replace him as our commander and chief to carry on our war.' On that occasion Jonathan accepted the leadership and took the place of his brother Judas" (1 Maccabees 9:28–31).

Independence at Last

When Alcimus died of a stroke in May 159 B.C., Jonathan (160–143 B.C.) retook Jerusalem. Alexander Balas, a claimant to the Seleucid throne, secured additional support by appointing this same Jonathan as the new high priest in Jerusalem. Now the family that began the revolt was recognized as the legitimate leaders of the Jewish people by one faction of the Greeks. For their part, the Greek leadership now enjoyed wide and deep support among Jews who, in their turn, proved to be loyal subjects and supporters. In 152 B.C., during the Feast of Tabernacles (Sukkot), Jonathan officiated as the high priest for the first time, beginning a 115-year role for his family.

Continued conflict among the claimants in the Seleucid kingdom also destabilized the Maccabees' control of Judea and Jerusalem as one party gained power over the other. The ebb and flow of one claimant's influence and power directly impacted Judea. Against his will, Jonathan was forced to fight more battles. Eventually, through trickery, Jonathan was lured into a trap and killed. Simon was now the last of the Maccabean brothers. Simon decided to continue the struggle and became the third son of Mattathias to lead the Hasmonean movement. By now, the majority of the Jews seem to have accepted the Maccabees as leaders of their people.

Demetrius II (129–125 B.C.), another contestant for the Seleucid throne, decided to make a variety of far-reaching concessions to the Jews in 142 B.C. This was certainly a significant date and event: "In that year [142 B.C.], the yoke of the gentiles was lifted from Israel, and the people began to write as the dating formula in bills and contracts, 'In the first year, under Simon, high priest, commander and chief of the Jews'" (1 Maccabees 13:41–42). Independence had been won, but not assured.

During the following year, Simon finally dislodged the foreigners and Jewish Hellenists from the Acra fortress, thereby removing the last formal symbol of Greek rule over the country. The First Book of Maccabees informs us that, while Judas was a hero in every sense of the word, it was nevertheless Jonathan and Simon who finally established an independent Jewish state for the first time in over 440 years.

Conclusion

Despite countless differences, the Jewish community throughout the ancient world was bound together by its collective allegiance to Jehovah, the Law, and the temple in Jerusalem. Struggling to maintain their distinctive religious identity amid the rising tide of Hellenism, the Jewish people successfully resisted attempts by Antiochus IV to eradicate their faith and practice. Led by Mattathias and later by his sons, the initial revolt led to a long guerrilla war that, despite tremendous odds, ended in victory. Together with various Jewish groups, including Hasideans and other guerrilla fighters, the Maccabees drove out occupying Greek forces and established an independent nation in 142 B.C., one of the few successful revolutions of that era.

For Further Reading

Elias Bickerman, *From Ezra to the Last of the Maccabees* (New York: Schocken Books, 1962), 112–47.

John Bright, *A History of Israel*, 3d ed. (Philadelphia: Westminster Press, 1981), 415–27.

Shaye J. D. Cohen, *From the Maccabees to the Mishnah* (Philadelphia: Westminster Press, 1987), 27–31, 34–35.

David B. Galbraith, D. Kelly Ogden, and Andrew C. Skinner, *Jerusalem: The Eternal City* (Salt Lake City: Deseret Book, 1996), 134–52.

Jonathan A. Goldstein, trans., *I Maccabees, Anchor Bible* (Garden City, New York: Doubleday, 1976).

Jonathan A. Goldstein, trans., *II Maccabees, Anchor Bible* (Garden City, New York: Doubleday, 1983).

Ben Witherington III, *New Testament History* (Grand Rapids, Michigan: Baker Academic, 2001), 38–41.

Jerusalem of the Hasmoneans

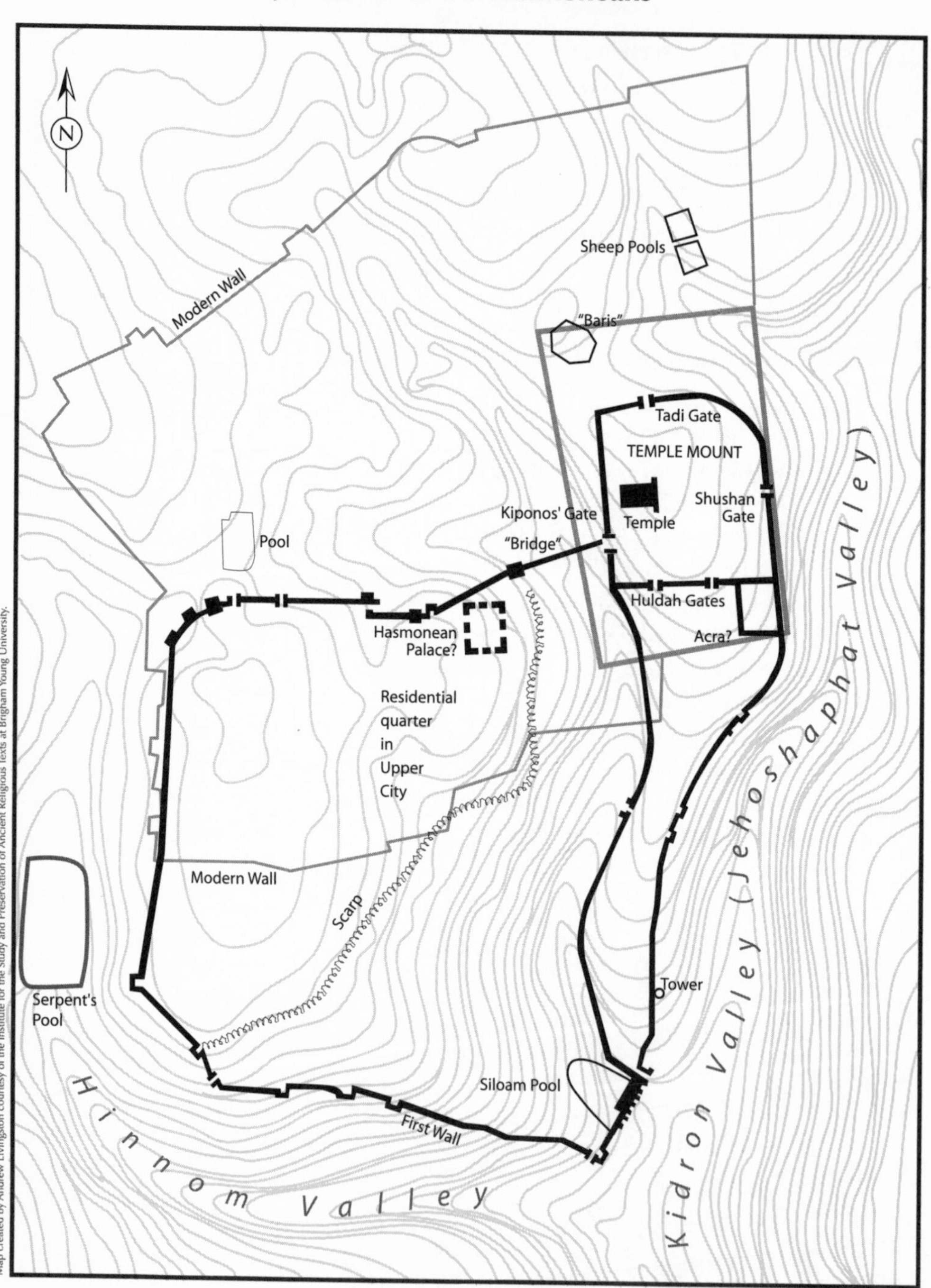

Map created by Andrew Livingston courtesy of the Institute for the Study and Preservation of Ancient Religious Texts at Brigham Young University.

CHAPTER 5

THE HASMONEANS TAKE OVER

John Hyrcanus sat intensely discussing various options with his advisors—it was the chance of a lifetime. The Greeks were again in Judea and had besieged the Holy City; but, amazingly, they had accepted a truce in honor of the Jewish Feast of Tabernacles. Antiochus VII had even sent a magnificent sacrifice, consisting of bulls with gilded horns and cups of gold and silver filled with all kinds of spices to be offered in his behalf in the temple. Unlike Antiochus IV, who had sacrificed swine upon the altars after capturing the city, this Greek seemed to be someone with whom John Hyrcanus could deal, and, to everyone's surprise, negotiations between the two rulers had proven successful—the Greeks would withdraw if Hyrcanus would pay a tribute for the cities on Judea's border now controlled by the Hasmoneans, including the port city of Joppa, which had once been under Greek control. Their discussion centered around the question, "How can we pay the tribute?" The royal treasury was depleted by construction projects and by a growing royal bureaucracy hungry for more and more funding. What were they to do? One option seemed most promising: They could open David's tomb, where there was certainly a king's treasure. With the enormous amount of silver to be found there, Hyrcanus could easily pay the tribute and rid his kingdom of the Greeks for the foreseeable future. There might be enough treasure left over to hire a mercenary army, something no Jewish leader had ever done before but something that seemed absolutely necessary now to secure the Hasmonean kingdom and even expand it by conquest.

Simon (143–135 B.C.), John Hyrcanus' father, had negotiated well with the Greeks years before when "the yoke of the gentiles was lifted from Israel," granting the Jews joyous independence after a protracted struggle against their oppressors (see 1 Maccabees 13:41). Further, according to the First Book of Maccabees:

> The land had peace as long as Simon lived. He sought the good of his people. They welcomed his rule and his glory as long as he lived. By means of all his glory he captured [Joppa] to be a port and secured access to the islands of the sea. He proceeded to extend the territory of his nation after conquering the land. . . . He eliminated the unclean things from the Akra [Acra] and there was none to oppose him. The people farmed their land in peace, and the land gave forth its produce and the trees of the fields their fruit. The old people sat in the town squares, all chatting about their blessings. . . . Simon supplied the towns with food and equipped them with weapons for defense. . . . He established peace in the land, and Israel rejoiced exceedingly. Everyone sat under his own vine and fig tree, with none to make him afraid. . . . Simon supported all the poor of his people. He sought to fulfill the Torah and wiped out all the impious and wicked. He glorified the temple and added to its furnishings. (1 Maccabees 14:4–15.)

According to the records, it was a wonderful, heady time for the Jews. But the peace was more apparent than real. In 135 B.C., at the end of eight years of rule, Simon traveled through his Hasmonean kingdom, stopping in Jericho with his wife and sons. While there, Simon was murdered by his son-in-law, Ptolemy. The sources are contradictory at this point, but most likely Simon's family was imprisoned by Ptolemy, who was attempting to wrest control over the country.

Ptolemy had made a fatal error, however. John Hyrcanus, one of the sons, escaped the assassination plot. Gathering forces sympathetic to his father, Hyrcanus attacked Ptolemy, attempting to rescue his mother and two brothers. He failed. He was unable to prevent Ptolemy from killing his family. When Ptolemy realized he was unable to resist Hyrcanus, he fled to Philadelphia, leaving Hyrcanus to succeed his father Simon. But Hyrcanus had little time to enjoy his new dignity.

John Hyrcanus (135–104 B.C.)

Antiochus VII, the Seleucid Empire ruler, besieged the city of Jerusalem shortly after Hyrcanus became the high priest and ruler. He demanded the return of the cities captured by Simon from Seleucid control. Eventually, negotiations brought about the Greeks' promise to withdraw if Hyrcanus paid a tribute for Joppa and the other cities on Judea's border. By this agreement, Hyrcanus thwarted an attempt to place a garrison of Greek soldiers in the city, presumably within the Acra, an impregnable fortress. All in all, it was an absolutely successful conclusion to a long and bitter siege.

By good fortune, the tomb of King David provided the necessary amount to pay the agreed tribute, some three thousand talents of silver. It was more than enough. In a spirit of peace and a newfound political relationship, Hyrcanus opened the city gates and allowed Antiochus and his army to enter, supplying them with whatever they needed before they returned to their homes in Syria.

For the rest of Hyrcanus' reign, partly because of his own military prowess and partly because of the continued preoccupation of the Seleucid rulers with securing their own thrones against rivals, he continued to expand the nation's territory. In the process of this territorial expansion, thousands of gentiles who lived in these regions under new Jewish control were converted. In light of Antiochus IV's efforts to force Jews to adopt paganism, it is somewhat ironic that some of these gentiles may likewise have been converted by force of arms.

Among those conquered were the Idumeans, descendants of the Edomites of Transjordan, who, under pressure from Arab tribes, had migrated west into southern Judah when the land was relatively empty following the Babylonian deportations. These people too were converted to Judaism. Incidentally, Herod the Great was a descendant of one of these Idumean converts.

During this period, one event that carried a long-lasting impact was the capture of Shechem, the Samaritan stronghold, about 128 B.C. According to tradition, Hyrcanus destroyed the Samaritan temple on Mount Gerizim during the same campaign. Hyrcanus' military successes pulverized any remaining goodwill between Jews and Samaritans (see chapter 14, "The Samaritans").

Other cities fell to Hyrcanus' forces. Even with these military successes, internal struggles tore at society's fabric, including a rebellion by the Pharisees (see chapter 13, "Hasideans, Pharisees, and Sadducees"). Hyrcanus had once been a Pharisee but later became a Sadducee. In any event, Hyrcanus repressed the opposition and spent the rest of his thirty-one-year reign peacefully, dying a natural death in 104 B.C., the first of the Hasmoneans to do so.

Aristobulus I (104–103 B.C.)

John Hyrcanus' son, Aristobulus I, ruled for only one year. Sources provide different and often contradictory views of his reign and personality. Although his rule lasted only a short time, it included several important developments. First, Aristobulus was the first Hasmonean to actually adopt the title "king." Previous leaders had avoided the term, even though they effectively ruled as kings. Second, he continued his father's policy of territorial expansion by taking Iturea in southern

Lebanon and Galilee by military force. Again, there is evidence that he may have forced the inhabitants to convert to Judaism. Bureaucratic functionaries whom he sent to Galilee to manage affairs there may have been among the progenitors of Mary and Joseph.

Alexander Janneus (103–76 B.C.)

Josephus preserves more information about Alexander Janneus, the second son of John Hyrcanus, than he does about any other Hasmonean ruler. Two major themes appear in Josephus' works *Jewish War* and *Jewish Antiquities* about Janneus' reign: relentless territorial expansion of the Hasmonean kingdom and severe internal conflicts between the king and his opponents.

Like his father and brother before him, Janneus continued the expansion of the country by capturing Gaza, Gadara, Amathus, Raphia, and Anthedon. By the end of his reign, the country resembled the biblical concept of Israelite territory expressed in the phrase "From Dan even to Beersheba" (see 1 Samuel 3:20). He also encouraged maritime trade through two ports that he acquired, Dora and Strato's Tower (the future Caesarea Maritima), and he gained control of overland routes to Egypt.

While Janneus continued to expand territorial frontiers, things at home were simmering darkly and finally boiled over at the Feast of Tabernacles. Sources are not clear about the reasons, but a riot broke out on this solemn occasion. In fact, Josephus' stated reasons seem somewhat trivial (see *Jewish Antiquities* 13.13.5). Whatever the real reason, pilgrims carried citrons as part of the celebration and began to throw them at Janneus while he officiated in the office of high priest. The king's forces swiftly and brutally gained control, slaughtering some six thousand rioters.

Janneus' wars of conquest continued, overrunning Moab

and Galaditis (Gilead); but when he was soundly defeated and almost killed by the Arab king Obodas I, his opponents took courage and for the next six years waged a bitter civil war against him, ending in 88 B.C.

As various factions had done before when they attempted to gain the advantage, these opponents asked for outside help. This time, Janneus' opponents called upon the Greek Demetrius III, one of the rivals for the Seleucid throne, who came to their aid hoping to increase his power over territories that once had been part of the Seleucid Empire. In a seesaw battle, both Demetrius and Janneus seemed to gain the upper hand. In the end, however, Demetrius retired from the battleground when it became obvious that he could not prevail.

In the aftermath, Janneus pursued and captured nearly eight hundred of his opponents. During a victory feast, he tortured and killed his opponents' family members before their eyes and then crucified these detractors. It was a horrifying action that sent a witheringly powerful message to those who continued to oppose him, some eight thousand of whom fled the country and remained outside the Hasmonean kingdom while Janneus ruled.

When he died in 76 B.C., Janneus was forty-nine years of age and had ruled the Hasmonean kingdom twenty-seven years. During his reign, he had extended the boundaries of his kingdom to rival those of King Solomon.

SALOME ALEXANDRA (76–67 B.C.)

For later Pharisees, the eight-year reign of Salome Alexandra, the wife of Alexander Janneus, was considered a "golden age" (see chapter 13, "Hasideans, Pharisees, and Sadducees"). Josephus, our most important source, confirms that the Pharisees enjoyed tremendous influence during this period, including the power to eliminate a number of their enemies. When she died in 67 B.C. at the age of seventy-three, the strife between her two sons, Hyrcanus II and Aristobulus II, finally planted the blighted seed that would end the Hasmonean kingdom.

HYRCANUS II (67, 63–43 B.C.) AND ARISTOBULUS II (67–63 B.C.)

When Hyrcanus II became the ruler of the Hasmonean kingdom upon the death of his mother, his kingship did not last long. He and his brother, Aristobulus II, plunged themselves into a protracted struggle to gain ascendancy over each other. No sooner had Hyrcanus begun to rule than Aristobulus seized the throne from his brother (67 B.C.). Hyrcanus II survived his brother's takeover by finding refuge in the temple and holding Aristobulus' wife and children as bargaining chips. Eventually, he fled to Petra to find protection under the Arab sovereign Aretas II.

Hyrcanus II's chief minister, Antipater (Herod the Great's father), convinced him that his life and the lives of his family members would always be in jeopardy unless he took back the throne. With the support of the Nabatean king, Aretas III, Hyrcanus attacked Jerusalem. But before the outcome was realized, both brothers asked for the intervention of Rome, which was then expanding its influence in the eastern Mediterranean.

The Roman general Pompey sent his lieutenant Scaurus to Syria to end the Jewish civil war. Scaurus forced the Nabateans to retire, allowing Aristobulus to defeat his brother. When Pompey arrived in Syria, he heard the arguments from the two factions himself but delayed making his decision. Aristobulus decided not to wait and headed for Jerusalem. This provocative action, which Pompey considered an affront, changed the balance of power in favor of Hyrcanus.

Pompey quickly followed Aristobulus, who now realized the utter futility of continued resistance, and met Pompey in negotiations between Jericho and Jerusalem. The city was in an uproar with various factions vying for control. Eventually,

Aristobulus' supporters decided they would defend the city instead of accepting the agreement reached between Pompey and Aristobulus on the road. They fled to the temple while Hyrcanus' supporters opened the city gates and welcomed the Romans. After a siege of the temple area lasting some three months, the Romans finally entered the holy enclosure. Hyrcanus' supporters followed and slaughtered their opponents.

Aristobulus and his sons were, in Roman fashion, taken captive to Rome. His brother Hyrcanus was restored to the office of high priest but not as king. Thus, the independent Hasmonean kingdom skidded to an end.

Conclusion

It is ironic that the Hasmonean dynasty came to power fighting against forced Hellenization. Within a short time, the dynasty itself became increasingly Hellenized, reflecting in many aspects other Hellenized societies of the period. Many Jews criticized the Hasmoneans for the very same vices they found repugnant in the political dynasties of the gentile nations: greed, ambition, and ruthlessness.

Although the process of Hellenizing of the Hasmonean dynasty was continuous, it accelerated significantly during the reign of Alexander Janneus. He called himself a king while holding the position of high priest, quite uncommon in Jewish tradition. He also feasted in public with his concubines. Such behavior was not uncommon for earlier kings such as David and Solomon, but it was traditionally unacceptable for the high priest. Janneus also provided for his wife, Salome Alexandra, to succeed him, following Hellenistic tradition. Finally, some coins issued during his reign carried Greek inscriptions along with Hebrew, a clear departure from Jewish custom.

The emergence of a military monarchy that rapidly came to reflect aspects of other Hellenized dynasties of the period was unsettling to a significant portion of the populace. It caused disillusionment, anger, and resentment. It may not be a coincidence that the birth of the three sects or "philosophies" mentioned by Josephus came about during this same period (see chapter 13, "Hasideans, Pharisees, and Sadducees," and chapter 15, "Essenes and Zealots"). Each of these "philosophies" filled needs in the larger society. One of these sects, the Essenes, was particularly critical of the Hasmoneans, ultimately rejecting their priesthood and their authority at the temple; they also withdrew from society to the shores of the Dead Sea. In contrast, the Pharisees became more popular among the people by casting themselves as the champions of the poor and the devout.

The Hasmoneans' military accomplishments were great, yet they missed the opportunity to bring long-lasting peace, unity, and stability to their people. Principally because of internal intrigues, unchecked ambitions, and even treachery, the feuding brothers Hyrcanus and Aristobulus independently made a critical decision that would curtail Jewish national autonomy: they each invited Rome into their affairs.

For Further Reading

Shaye J. D. Cohen, *From the Maccabees to the Mishnah* (Philadelphia: Westminster Press, 1987).

David Noel Freedman et al., eds., *The Anchor Bible Dictionary* (New York: Doubleday, 1992), s.v. "Hasmonean Dynasty."

Lester L. Grabbe, *Judaism from Cyrus to Hadrian*, 2 vols. (Minneapolis: Fortress Press, 1992), 1:297–307.

Ben Witherington III, *New Testament History* (Grand Rapids, Michigan: Baker Academic, 2001), 40–51.

Pompey's Territorial Arrangements

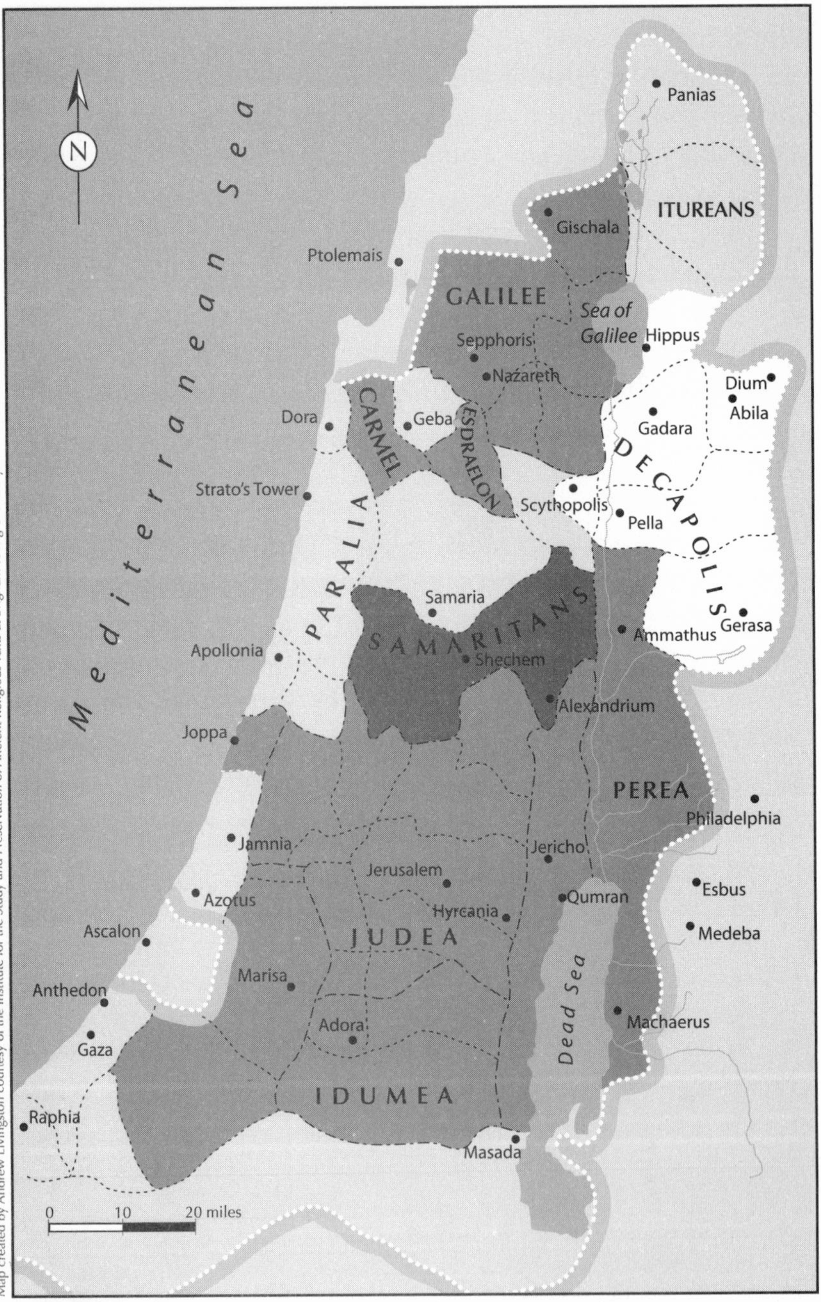

Mediterranean Sea
Panias
ITUREANS
Gischala
Ptolemais
GALILEE
Sea of Galilee
Hippus
Sepphoris
Nazareth
Dium
Abila
Gadara
Dora
CARMEL
Geba
ESDRAELON
DECAPOLIS
Strato's Tower
Scythopolis
Pella
PARALIA
Samaria
SAMARITANS
Ammathus
Gerasa
Apollonia
Shechem
Alexandrium
Joppa
PEREA
Philadelphia
Jamnia
Jericho
Jerusalem
Esbus
Azotus
Qumran
Hyrcania
Medeba
Ascalon
JUDEA
Marisa
Dead Sea
Anthedon
Machaerus
Adora
Gaza
IDUMEA
Raphia
Masada
0 10 20 miles

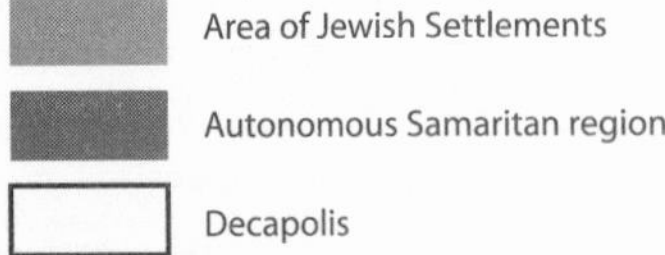

Map created by Andrew Livingston courtesy of the Institute for the Study and Preservation of Ancient Religious Texts at Brigham Young University.

CHAPTER 6

The Romans Are Coming

Judas Maccabee had heard about the Romans. Even his hated opponent, the Seleucid king Antiochus IV, had personally watched the invincible Roman military machine crush the mightiest powers of the Greek-speaking world, including his own father's army. Judas' informants told him how the Romans had subdued Iberia, Carthage, and Greece. It was a bold move, but Judas felt it was time to make an alliance that might help his people achieve independence. So he sent two trusted friends, Eupolemus and Jason, to Rome. When they arrived, the Roman Senate received them kindly, heard their pleas, and agreed to their request, issuing the following: "A decree of the Senate concerning a treaty of alliance and goodwill with the Jewish nation. No one of those who are subject to the Romans shall make war on the Jewish nation, or furnish to those who make war on them any grain, ships or money. And if any attack the Jews, the Romans shall assist them so far as they are able, and on the other hand if any attack the Romans, the Jews shall help them as allies." The Jewish envoys returned to Jerusalem with a copy, while the Senate deposited the bronze tablets containing the original in the capital.

Whoever coined the phrase "Rome was not built in a day" created a permanent reminder that Roman civilization was twelve hundred years in developing, flourishing, and ultimately disintegrating. Although Roman civilization owed much to ancient Greece, whose golden age is generally regarded as having lasted from about 490 B.C. to the death of Alexander the

Great in 323 B.C., understanding Rome's unique cultural and political development helps explain its unique approach to Hellenistic politics in the eastern Mediterranean. This is particularly important in understanding how and why the Romans became involved in Judean affairs.

According to tradition, Rome was founded on April 21, 753 B.C. The founding legends vary, but most associate Rome's beginnings with Romulus and Remus, who were the twin sons of the god Mars and a vestal virgin named Rhea Silvia. According to one version of the story, Rhea Silvia was forbidden to marry and was imprisoned by her uncle, who wanted to secure his right as king by ensuring that his brother, the rightful king, would not have any male descendants. When Rhea Silvia nevertheless miraculously conceived while in prison, Amulius, the uncle, placed Rhea Silvia's twins in a reed basket and sent them down the river. The basket was caught in a fig tree, and the twins survived. A she-wolf nursed them until a royal shepherd found them and took them under his care. Legends aside, historians believe that the Romans were a tribe of the Latini, who spoke one of the Italic dialects and settled in the immediate neighborhood of other Latini tribes in central Italy. Rome itself began as a small agricultural settlement next to a ford of the Tiber River.

The Age of Kings

During the Age of Kings (753–509 B.C.), some of Rome's basic economic, political, and social structures were established. Although ruled by kings, the independent city-state had a balanced system of government in which a council or "Senate" comprised of the heads of leading families helped select the ruler and supervised his actions. Thus, from the earliest times, Rome nurtured a tradition that supported aristocratic or oligarchic rule.

About 600 B.C. the Etruscans, a culturally advanced people

to the northwest, crossed the Tiber in force, occupied the settlement, and imposed their rule on the people living in the hilltop villages that had united under the earlier Latin kings to form Rome. The Etruscans transformed the pastoral community into a walled city, enlarged it by draining the marshlands between the hills, and further developed it with paved streets, brick, masonry, and stone. Rome was now the leading city-state in central Italy.

The Roman aristocrats eventually threw off their Etruscan overlords and founded a new form of oligarchic government called a republic in 509 B.C. The Etruscans retreated to their lands in central Italy, where some of their small cities continued to enjoy autonomy and where their language and culture flourished. Eventually, however, they came under Roman control and by about 31 B.C. were completely assimilated.

THE REPUBLIC (509–31 B.C.)

Unlike the Greeks, whose political order consisted of short-lived leagues of city-states, the Romans established a republic whose territory eventually reached the eastern Mediterranean and lasted almost five hundred years. The primary motivation for expansion during the fifth and fourth centuries B.C. was the protection of their independence.

During the Early Republic (509–264 B.C.), Roman society had divided into two separate and distinct classes, one a politically and socially privileged group (patricians), numbering about one hundred families, and the other not (plebeians). The heads of the patrician families dominated the Senate, the powerful successor to the old monarchical council, which now included and supervised all the elected officials and priests of the Roman state. This state was governed by two consuls, technically chosen by the people but always drawn from the great senatorial families, who held their office for one year at a time.

Soon after the establishment of the republic, the patricians came to dominate the Senate and the state, apparently citing their historical social and religious prerogatives as a reason to monopolize the consulship, the other state offices, and the priesthoods. This caused persistent and often violent struggles among its classes. Eventually, by 287 B.C., through continued struggles, the plebeians gained all the rights of citizenship enjoyed by the ruling patricians, and leading plebeian families began to hold offices and priesthoods in Rome and function more fully in the Senate. It was a major step forward for this class of Roman society, a step that would reverberate down through time, affecting even the Apostle Paul. For by Paul's time, nonpatricians and even non-Italians enjoyed the privileges of Roman citizenship.

During the Early Republic period, Roman military conquests of various peoples inhabiting the Italian peninsula increased Rome's power and influence. Leaders also implemented an ingenious policy that introduced stability among those whom they conquered: they began to incorporate many of the conquered communities into the Roman body politic by allowing them dual citizenship. Such privileged communities retained their own citizenship and government within the Roman state as *municipia* but also received Roman citizenship, allowing them to participate in elections and affairs at Rome. This policy allowed conquered people to retain their religious practices, to provide men for the Roman legions instead of paying taxes, and to retain much self-governing power. Those communities that were not given Roman citizenship became *socii* or allies that were bound to Rome by treaty and were obligated to provide troops for her wars. By the end of this period, Roman armies conquered all of Italy and began to establish Roman towns in an effort to Romanize the entire peninsula so that the Latin language and Roman law were universal.

During the Middle Republic period (264–133 B.C.), Rome gained her first overseas territory when she became involved in the affairs of the island of Sicily just southwest of Italy. Rome's expansion was blocked by Carthage, a Phoenician state in North Africa. During the Punic Wars (264–146 B.C.), Rome overwhelmed and finally destroyed Carthage, adding Sicily, Corsica, Sardinia, and North Africa to its territories. The acquisition of these non-Italian territories resulted in new ways of governing and relating to conquered communities. With only isolated exceptions, Rome ceased to extend her citizenship to whole communities, and only some of the conquered cities were bound to Rome by treaty. Instead, Rome organized these territories into the first provinces. Each of these provinces had a current or former Roman magistrate as its governor, whose responsibilities included maintaining the peace, defending the borders of the province, and collecting taxes. Nevertheless, each province was a patchwork quilt of cities and communities, each maintaining its own local government and retaining different degrees of local rights and obligations toward Rome.

Having made themselves masters in the west, the Romans gradually conquered the Hellenistic kingdoms to the east. Unlike the west, where the Romans took advantage of their military victories against Carthage to annex territory and establish provinces, Roman expansion in the east was characterized by a hesitancy to commit forces long-term. Instead, Roman intervention in the Hellenistic world was driven by two factors. One consisted of entangling alliances with different Greek states that brought the Romans into conflict with one after another of the great Hellenistic kingdoms. The second was the ambition of individual Roman generals, who saw these wars as opportunities to win glory and riches for themselves. As Rome was drawn deeper into eastern affairs, she initially tried to establish a balance of power there, whereby the great Hellenistic kingdoms were weakened, Roman allies were strengthened, and Roman interests—diplomatic and economic—were preserved. This attempt failed, however, and Rome found itself establishing provinces first in Macedonia and then in portions of Asia Minor. Wherever possible, however, Rome tried to maintain a system of client states in the east that would keep her from needing to exercise direct control over large swaths of territory. Nevertheless, by 146 B.C., the Romans could justly call the Mediterranean *Mare Nostrum* ("Our Sea").

The results of creating an empire in the Middle Republic led to considerable economic, social, and political upheaval in Rome. The rich grew richer and the poor poorer as leading senatorial and business families exploited the empire while the citizen farmer, who had formed the backbone of the Roman legions, was ruined by long terms of service overseas. Ambitious nobles, such as the Gracchi, took advantage of this discontent by appealing to the Roman lower classes under the guise of reform, either genuine or self-interested. It was also during this period that the equestrians, a third class located between the senatorial class and the lower classes, were established as an additional class with their own rights. Although the equestrians, originally named for their role in the Roman cavalry, had been a wealthy but nonpolitical class, because of their involvement in business throughout the empire and their exploitation of the provinces (particularly as tax collectors), they became more involved in politics at Rome.

During the Late Republic (133–31 B.C.), Rome was ruled by an oligarchy of leading patrician and plebeian noble clans whose families had held the consulship and continued to dominate the Senate and cling stubbornly to their rights and privileges. Although Roman power continued to spread throughout the Mediterranean basin, economic and social problems multiplied. Despite attempts at reform, the issues proved intractable. A particular problem lay in the ruin of the peasant farmer who had traditionally provided most of Rome's soldiers. A leading general of the period, Marius, succeeded in ending the manpower problem by forming a professional army and allowing the non-landowning poor to enroll, but this caused further problems since this new army was more loyal to its general than it was to the state. Ambitious generals used their loyal armies as political weapons, and by 31 B.C. the republic lay in ruins.

The republic's last hope for substantive reform was Julius Caesar, a major figure in Roman politics from 60 to 44 B.C. After being elected consul, Caesar spent nine years conquering Gaul (modern France). His campaigns in Gaul, Germany, and Britain marked the first expansion of Rome outside the Mediterranean region. As his popularity grew, the Senate became worried and eventually ordered that Caesar disband his army. He changed the course of history by crossing the Rubicon, the river in northern Italy that formed the boundary of his province in 49 B.C. By crossing the Rubicon—a phrase employed today for any step that commits a person to a given course of action—Caesar, in effect, declared war on the Senate and other generals who opposed him. He marched on Rome and eventually defeated his enemies to become Rome's sole ruler in 48 B.C. After one battle, Caesar sent an ally a three-word letter: *Veni, vidi, vinci*—"I came, I saw, I conquered."

His authority appears in the many titles and powers that he held, including consul, dictator (eventually for life), and head of the armies. Caesar, though acting in the name of equestrian and popular interests, held a lofty vision for Rome's future. He initiated building projects that gave work to the urban poor, and he gave the Italians outside of Rome more self-rule. He also founded Rome's first public library. But Caesar's enemies in the Senate believed that the dictator wanted to be king—a dreaded fear most likely dating back to the Etruscan era of Rome. On the Ides of March (March 15) in 44 B.C., Brutus and Cassius murdered Caesar: "Liberty! Freedom! Tyranny is dead!" Yet they miscalculated the mood of the people of Rome, who were willing to accept a successor to Caesar whose power and position stopped just short of a royal title.

The eighteen-year-old grandnephew of Julius Caesar, Octavian (the future Augustus), joined with Mark Anthony, Caesar's loyal lieutenant, to defeat Caesar's assassins at the Battle of Philippi in 42 B.C. With Lepidus, another of Caesar's supporters, Octavian and Mark Anthony formed the Second Triumvirate and shared the governing of Rome. The first had been an unofficial alliance among Julius Caesar, Pompey, and Crassus. In the Second Triumvirate, the real power was divided between Mark Anthony, who took control of the East, and Octavian, who administered Italy and the western dominions.

Octavian and Mark Anthony, who had been allies, found themselves drawn into a vortex of mistrust and conflict, culminating at the Battle of Actium in 31 B.C., a naval engagement in which Octavian's forces defeated those of Anthony and his wife, Cleopatra VII, a descendant of Alexander's General Ptolemy, who then ruled Egypt. Anthony's death and Cleopatra's suicide in 30 B.C. brought Egypt under direct Roman control and left Octavian the sole ruler of the Roman state.

After a century of civil violence, Rome was finally at peace. This was the beginning of an era known as *Pax Romana*, a two-century period of peace. A grateful Senate voted Octavian the name "Augustus" and the title of "princeps" in 27 B.C., recognizing him as the undisputed head of state. Octavian triumphantly marked the end of the ancient Roman Republic, a concept in name only as Caesar himself noted. And while his advancement cost the citizens of Rome many of their traditional political rights, they seemed willing to exchange civil freedom for the restoration of public order, political stability, and economic prosperity that Augustus' reign brought (27 B.C.–A.D. 14).

At Jesus' birth, the emperor Augustus ruled over an empire even larger and more diverse than Alexander's. Rome controlled not only most of Europe and all of North Africa but also much of the Near East.

Judea as a Roman Protectorate

Judas Maccabee had sent an embassy to Rome to arrange an alliance in 164 B.C. while engaged in a protracted war with the Greeks. An informal alliance was renewed in 143 B.C., when Jonathan sent an embassy to Rome just before the Jews gained their independence. Simon, the last surviving son of Mattathias, also sent a delegation as early as 139 B.C. to renew the alliance with Rome.

Simon's renewal was different from the previous declarations because the Jews had by now become friends and allies of Rome. The first declaration (164 B.C.) had been made between Rome and a rebel faction within the Seleucid Empire. The second (143 B.C.) had been made between Rome and an official of the Seleucid Empire. The third (139 B.C.) was made between Rome and an independent nation. Additionally, this time the Romans sent letters to at least five neighboring powers in the east, warning them not to attack Judea or to help anyone who planned to do so.

This was not the last time Jewish officials sought Roman friendship and intervention. During the Hasmonean period, several members of the dynasty asked for and obtained help from Rome.

Rome's direct intervention in Judea occurred when Aristobulus II (67–63 B.C.) and Hyrcanus II (67, 63–43 B.C.) struggled against one another to become the legitimate successor of the Hasmonean dynasty, their selfish ambitions dragging their people into another civil war. The inability of the Hasmonean royal family to solve its civil, dynastic, and religious affairs led the Roman general Pompey (one of the generals who later opposed Julius Caesar and who was eventually killed in Egypt when he sought refuge there) to take advantage of the situation when both claimants requested his personal intervention (see chapter 5, "The Hasmoneans Take Over"). Pompey had just dissolved the Hellenistic kingdom of Syria, ending the centuries-old Seleucid dynasty and reducing Syria to a province. Much of the territory in the east, however, including Judea, was organized into a system of client states meant to ensure a balance of power in the east and the preservation of Roman interests without direct Roman occupation. Pompey adjusted borders of states and provinces, installed new dynasts guaranteed to be faithful to Roman interests, and thereby expanded Roman hegemony into the region with few direct annexations.

Some Jews were relieved to see Rome intervene in what had become a seemingly endless, chaotic situation. But there was some early resistance against the occupation government, particularly in Galilee, where many gentiles had become enthusiastic converts to Judaism. Pompey eventually sided with Hyrcanus in the dispute and pursued Aristobulus to Jerusalem, where he had gone to prepare for an attack. The city was divided; Hyrcanus' supporters opened the gates of the city to the Romans, while Aristobulus' supporters fled to the fortified temple enclosure.

Following a three-month blockade, Roman soldiers brought forward a large siege engine that accomplished its designed purpose. One of the tall towers guarding the temple enclosure fell. Roman soldiers and Jewish supporters of Hyrcanus poured into the temple courtyard through the breach. The Romans and the conquering Jews killed many of Aristobulus' supporters, while other supporters committed suicide. Apparently, priests who had diligently fulfilled their duties even during the siege also perished in the bloodbath.

When the carnage ended, an estimated twelve thousand had died. Surrounded by lieutenants, Pompey walked into the courtyard and passed into the area of the temple proper. He entered where it was unlawful for gentiles to walk. Without pomp or ceremony, he continued into the Holy Place, strode across the room, and stood before the veil of the temple, which separated this room from the Holy of Holies, one of the most sacred spaces in the world for the Jews. He paused briefly, parted the curtain with his hand, and walked into the room, a place reserved for the high priest on the Day of Atonement. The room was empty. After a brief pause, Pompey turned around and left the sanctuary as quickly as he had entered it. Evidently, he did not take any of the furnishings or rob the treasury. On the following day, he commanded the priests to cleanse the temple and offer the customary sacrifices to God.

In the fall of 63 B.C., after eighty years of independence, the Jews were again subject to a foreign power, Rome, although they maintained a measure of autonomy under Hyrcanus, who was confirmed as high priest and given the title "ethnarch" instead of king. With Pompey's capture of the city that year, the Hasmonean dynasty lost most of its life. The Roman general reduced the Hasmonean kingdom, stripping virtually all the territorial gains made during the prior Hasmonean expansion. Greek and other Hellenized cities in the old Hasmonean realm were given independence and placed under the protection of the governor of Syria. Samaria and other non-Jewish regions were separated from the territory of the ethnarch, who as a Roman client was expected to maintain the Pompeian settlement and support Roman interests in the region. The real authority in the region now rested with the Roman proconsul of Syria, whose seat was at Antioch, the old Seleucid capital.

This arrangement lasted until the death of Pompey in 48 B.C. At that point, Hyrcanus and his trusted advisor Antipater, who was the father of Herod the Great, sought the support of Julius Caesar, who in turn made Antipater governor of Judea and reconfirmed Hyrcanus as high priest, also granting him a limited amount of political power. Jewish territory formerly seized by Pompey was restored to Hyrcanus, and the few Roman soldiers in the area were withdrawn.

However, in 44 B.C., Julius Caesar was assassinated, leading to more instability in the Mediterranean. This situation provided Aristobulus' last surviving son, Antigonus, a brief opportunity to establish an independent kingdom under his authority. Supported by the Parthians, who were Rome's chief rivals in the East and the successors to the Persian Empire in present-day Iran, Antigonus sought to depose his uncle Hyrcanus and to oust the Romans. In 40 B.C., he attacked Judea, captured Jerusalem, killed Antipater, imprisoned Hyrcanus, and proclaimed himself king of Judea. But Antigonus' rule did not last long. The young Herod would see to that.

CONCLUSION

When Pompey entered Jerusalem in 63 B.C., Judea came under Roman influence. At first the control was indirect, with Hyrcanus and Antipater operating as Roman clients but technically functioning as independent rulers. Although 63 B.C. represented a watershed year for Jewish and Roman relations, contact between the Jews and Rome had begun almost exactly a century before during the Maccabean War. During this entire period, Rome's influence in the region grew as its boundaries expanded eastward toward Jerusalem. Although Rome's preference for indirect control of most eastern territory made her rule of Judea in this period less of an occupation than is usually imagined, Roman control of and influence in the region would set the stage for events recorded in the New Testament Gospels.

FOR FURTHER READING

Shaye J. D. Cohen, *From the Maccabees to the Mishnah* (Philadelphia: Westminster Press, 1987).

David Noel Freedman et al., eds., *The Anchor Bible Dictionary* (New York: Doubleday, 1992), s.v. "Rome."

John F. Hall, "The Roman Province of Judea: A Historical Overview," in

John F. Hall and John W. Welch, eds., *Masada and the World of the New Testament* (Provo, Utah: BYU Studies, 1997), 319–36.

Antony Kamm, *The Romans: An Introduction* (New York: Routledge, 1995).

E. Mary Smallwood, *The Jews under Roman Rule* (Leiden: E. J. Brill, 1976).

Ben Witherington III, *New Testament History* (Grand Rapids, Michigan: Baker Academic, 2001), 49–61.

Herod the Great's Kingdom

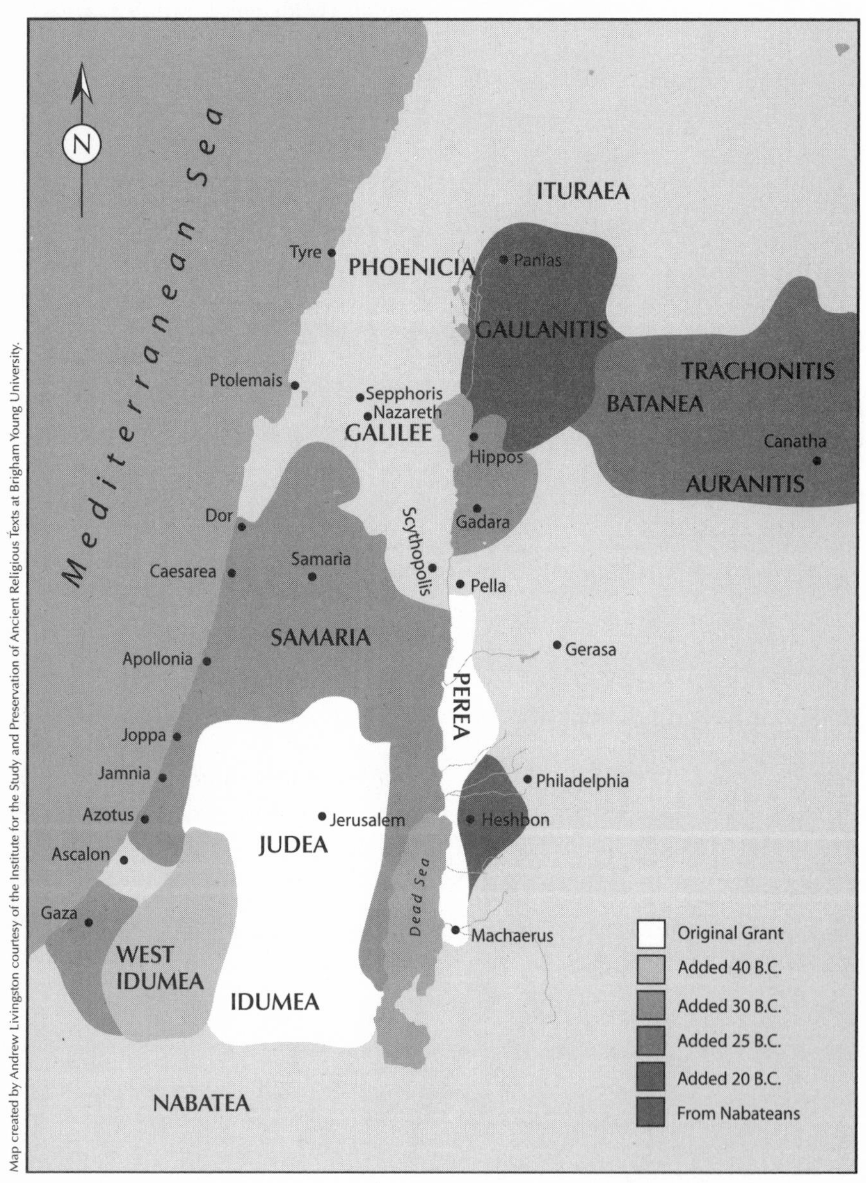

Map created by Andrew Livingston courtesy of the Institute for the Study and Preservation of Ancient Religious Texts at Brigham Young University.

CHAPTER 7

HEROD RULES

It was an occasion of both overwhelming joy and deep concern for the thirty-three-year-old man from Jerusalem. He was on his first visit to the magnificent Roman imperial capital—the very center of the Mediterranean world—but at the same time, he worried about his family, friends, and supporters back home. He had left his betrothed Hasmonean princess, Mariamne; his future mother-in-law, Alexandra; his mother, Cypros; his sister, Salome; his youngest brother, Pheroras; and some servants, supporters, and soldiers holed up on Masada while he made his way to Rome to gain additional support to oust the Parthians and their appointed king, Antigonus (Mariamne's uncle). On this day, however, his world changed unexpectedly and forever when the Roman Senate named him king of Judea, Galilee, Perea, and Idumea. At the conclusion of this momentous meeting in the august senate-house, there were cheers for Herod. Anthony and Octavian, his chief sponsors, quickly stepped forward and grabbed one of his arms to ceremonially escort him out of the building to offer sacrifice and to lay up the decree in the capital. There was to be a banquet in the evening to honor the new king, but Herod was already making plans to return home to save his family and secure his kingdom. Thus, the reign of Herod the Great began far away from the land of his birth.

Herod (37–4 B.C.), best known to modern Christians for his slaughter of children after the birth of Jesus, was the son of Antipater of Idumea (called Edom in the Old Testament), a land touching the southern part of the Jewish kingdom. It was a relatively small area stretching approximately from the southern portion of the Judean hill country to the northern part of the Negev. To the east, Idumea bordered the Judean Desert and the Dead Sea, and its territory reached west into the provinces of the port cities Gaza and Ashkelon.

Apparently, Idumea was annexed though not conquered by the Hasmoneans about 120 B.C. Much of the conversion of the inhabitants to Judaism was voluntary—not forced as has been traditionally argued. Idumea shared the Jewish allegiance to the Jewish nation, religion, and culture, as demonstrated in their unity with Jews against the Romans in the war of A.D. 66–70.

Herod's father and grandfather were men of experience and prominence who rose to importance during the reign of the Hasmonean queen Salome Alexandra (76–67 B.C.). Herod's grandfather, Antipas, was appointed praetor or general over Idumea by Salome and Alexander Janneus, her husband. Salome and Janneus had two sons, the older, Hyrcanus II, and the younger, Aristobulus II. Following Janneus' death, Salome retained the throne. Because she could not serve in a priesthood office, Hyrcanus was appointed high priest. Following Salome's sudden death in 67 B.C., Hyrcanus was also crowned king.

Herod's father, Antipater, was a wealthy man who eventually made his home in Jerusalem, where he advised the Hasmonean court of Hyrcanus. It is certainly possible that Herod was born in Jerusalem while his father served in Hyrcanus' court, making him an Idumean only in his ethnic background. In this connection, the integration of the Idumean nobility with the Hasmoneans is underscored by Hyrcanus' marriage to an Idumean woman and by Herod's later marriage to a Hasmonean princess. Most important, Josephus affirms that Antipater the Idumean possessed many positive qualities and clearly blames the Jewish Hasmonean family for frittering away its authority and power.

Cypros, Herod's mother, apparently came from a distinguished Nabatean family, possibly from the royal family of Aretas III or Obodas II. Whether Cypros was a converted Jew is unknown, and how much Jewish education Herod received is lost to us. However, during this era, identification of a child with Judaism came through the father, not the mother. Herod was, therefore, a third-generation Jew born into this aristocratic family in the late 70s B.C. (usually dated at 73 B.C.). He had three brothers, Phasael, Joseph, and Pheroras, and one sister, Salome. Two of his siblings, Joseph and Salome, had Jewish names—another indication of the family's close association with Judaism. Apparently, like Sadducees and Samaritans, Herod did not accept the prophetic section of the developing Hebrew scripture (see JST Matthew 3:4). Josephus suggests that, as a young man, Herod was athletic, agile, tall, and strong. As a member of the upper class, he played soldier, hunted, and learned to ride horses. Apparently while Herod was still a boy, the Essene Menahem prophesied that the child would eventually become king. Training, education, and family connections prepared Herod to serve his nation, but events beyond his control eventually gave him the throne.

A decade after Herod's birth, Hyrcanus and Aristobulus struggled against one another to establish themselves as the legitimate successor to their mother, Salome, and, in the process, pulled civil war onto the land. Pompey eventually sided with Hyrcanus and captured Jerusalem in the autumn of 63 B.C. The Roman general then appointed Hyrcanus as high priest and ethnarch (serving basically from 63 to 40 B.C. with several periods of interruption). Aristobulus was captured twice and taken to Rome on both occasions. Upon his second release in 49 B.C., Aristobulus headed toward Judea, intending to depose his brother. However, he was apparently poisoned under orders of Quintus Metelus Scipio, governor of Syria, preventing him from interfering in Judean affairs.

Herod's father, Antipater, had supported not only Hyrcanus but also the Roman alliance. He demonstrated his firm loyalty to Rome by providing troops and supplies (paid for by himself, not Hyrcanus), particularly for a Roman campaign in Egypt. Rome gradually drew power away from the Hasmoneans and, although Hyrcanus retained his position as high priest, increasingly Antipater came to dominate political life in Judea. Herod's own rise to prominence was rapidly propelled forward when his father was made a Roman citizen (an honor transmitted to Herod and his children) and appointed procurator or governor by Julius Caesar in 47 B.C., three years before Caesar's assassination.

To establish order, Antipater asked his two sons for help in what was a difficult task. Herod and his brother Phasael were soon appointed governors, Herod in Galilee and his brother in Jerusalem. The northern region presented a daunting assignment because the borders were infested with brigands. Herod, twenty-five years of age, soon gained a reputation for military and administrative abilities when he imposed order on Galilee by crushing a revolt led by a man named Hezekiah. He came to be admired by Galilean Jews and Roman officials in Syria for his loyal service.

During this period, Herod married Doris, one of his ten wives. This was a time when Jewish families, unlike their Roman and Greek counterparts, formed endogamous community families that were characterized by equality of brothers, cohabitation of married sons with parents, frequent marriage between children of brothers, and sometimes polygamous relationships.

One of many setbacks in Herod's career occurred in 43 B.C. when his father was poisoned by an arch rival, Malichus. It was a devastating blow because throughout his life Herod had demonstrated intense loyalty to his parents, brothers, and sister. Eventually, with permission from his Roman patrons, Herod had Malichus killed. Even Hyrcanus the Hasmonean ethnarch was apparently relieved, fearing that Malichus wanted to depose him as well. Herod made himself indispensable to Hyrcanus, cementing his position as the successor to his father Antipater in Judean affairs.

Herod's loyalty to Rome and to his father's memory, as well as his own clever abilities, kept the Romans from deserting him when members of the Jerusalem aristocracy tried to remove him from his position of power following his father's murder. In 42 B.C., Cassius reappointed Herod governor of Coele-Syria (the area around Damascus). He had been appointed to the same position in 46 B.C. by Sextus Caesar.

During the same year, Herod divorced Doris while also divorcing both a niece and a cousin whom he had apparently married before Doris. Following his divorces, he prepared to marry Mariamne I, a Hasmonean princess and granddaughter of both Hasmonean rivals, Hyrcanus II and Aristobulus II. Although this marriage certainly represented an effort to connect himself to the Hasmonean family, Herod apparently truly loved Mariamne. Her grandfather Hyrcanus approved the marriage, but it was not sanctioned by Mariamne's mother, Alexandra.

Though this marriage was Herod's first attempt to connect himself to the royal family, he would later marry the daughter of a Jewish temple priest, thus tying himself to the leading priestly families of his kingdom. Herod's efforts to make advantageous connections with other families through marriage were not limited to himself. Members of the Herodian family intermarried in complex and multiple ways, spinning a web of threads to royal and aristocratic families in an attempt to cinch down political and economic stability in the region.

Aristobulus' son, Antigonus, joined forces with the Parthians, the power in the East, in an effort to supplant both his uncle Hyrcanus, and therefore Herod, as well as to squash

Roman influence in the region. Hyrcanus was captured and disfigured, preventing him from serving as high priest. Warned of the impending attempt to capture him, Herod fled Jerusalem. Eventually, he made his way to Rome in spite of the dangers of winter sea travel, evidently fearless of the chaotic atmosphere in Rome at the time. Apparently, when Herod arrived in Rome in 40 B.C., his nomination to become king of Judea by Mark Anthony was a complete surprise (*Jewish Antiquities* 14.15.5).

Like others during this period, Herod chose dependency on Rome as the best strategy for assuring the welfare of the nation and for sustaining Judaism. This may have been his most important and success-laden decision. As future events seem to prove, Herod's prudence in accepting the political realities of Rome's dominance in the first century was a better alternative to the irresponsibility and impulsiveness of the political and religious zealots who eventually brought Judea into direct and open conflict with Rome in A.D. 66. After all, it was an era wherein people were not only ambitious but also brutal and devoid of compassion. It was a time of fratricide, savagery, murder, conspiracy, civil disturbances, and international plots and counterplots. Most important, it was a period when security was often nonexistent. A connection with Rome was the only sure thing.

After two and a half decades of strife in the region, Herod sought to unify the people and establish tranquillity. For Rome's part, the region was important because it served as a buffer state between Rome and its nemesis, the Parthians. The Parthian Empire was the only remaining formidable threat to the growing, hardening dominance of Rome in the Eastern Mediterranean world.

Under the Roman umbrella, Herod advanced his nation from being a small, landlocked state to one that rivaled the ancient Israelite kingdoms of David and Solomon, covering present-day Israel, the West Bank, Jordan to the east of the river, and southern Lebanon and Syria. Renewed in his determination to establish law and order in his kingdom, as Rome required and as he believed was in the best interest of Judea, Herod moved to forcibly eliminate all domestic opposition to his kingship and to control any institution that might threaten his ability to rule effectively.

Herod carried out proscriptions of the leading Hasmonean courtiers. Forty-five notables of Antigonus' party were executed, and all others disappeared from the historical record. He made the Sanhedrin (whatever their function had been before) more like the privy councils of other Hellenistic kings—convened at his request and made up largely of family, friends, and close associates.

Herod began appointing high priests, ending for good the Hasmonean practice of uniting the political and religious authority in one person (the high priest was formerly the king). While certainly this move helped consolidate power into his hand, it may also suggest a respect for Jewish law and tradition. He was not a descendent of Aaron and, therefore, could not assume a priestly role.

Herod did not fail to respond forcefully against any attempt to overthrow him, even if it meant executing family members, including his wife's grandfather, Hyrcanus; his mother-in-law, Alexandra; his brother-in-law, Costobar; and eventually his wife, Mariamne. Evidence suggests that Alexandra, Costobar, and Mariamne had plotted against Herod.

Instead of legitimizing his regime, Herod's marriage to Mariamne both revealed and intensified strains within the turbulent political, cultural, and societal confines of his kingdom. Intended to transcend and relieve the stresses between religion and ethnicity, priesthood and kingship, insiders and outsiders, and different generations, his marriage into the Hasmonean family became a source of nationalist intrigue and enmity.

His execution of his beloved Mariamne, however, was the

beginning of a long, downward spiral of trouble within his own family, which was paralyzed with rivalries and strains. He was vexed with her death until his own death in 4 B.C., demonstrating a persistent love-hate relationship with his young wife. In light of Mariamne's capital offense against the state, Herod apparently felt he had no other choice but to execute her.

Later, Alexander and Aristobulus, his sons by Mariamne, were executed when accused by other family members of planning to assassinate their father. Tragically, another son, Antipas, was convicted of plotting against his father and was executed just days before Herod's own death in 4 B.C. Far from being capricious acts based on anger or resentment—certainly deep emotions were involved—his ruthless actions were calculated to preserve the stability of the region. Among family matters, his actions were also based on a kinship system deeply rooted in customs of honor and shame. Betrayal by family members—real or imagined—brought shame on the king and undermined his authority. Additionally, Jewish tradition empowered him to condemn rebellious sons.

However, these incidents, as noted in Josephus, reveal the problematic nature of Herod's methods of maintaining security, particularly the most widely used means of extracting truth—physical torture. Confessions made under such conditions and the information extracted thereby were highly questionable, creating a vicious cycle that made it nearly impossible for Herod to clearly define the extent and exact nature of subversion not only within his realm but even within his own family. Like the Roman Octavian and the Hellenistic rulers of the period, particularly the Ptolemies in Egypt, Herod's family seethed with infighting as competing individuals and factions within the family sought to advance their causes for succession. Of Herod's fifteen known children, ten were sons.

Herod may have altered his will on six occasions, mirroring indirectly the struggles among family members who were vying for power and position. Certainly these circumstances betray a regime plagued by chronic suspicion, as potential claimants to the line of succession accused each other of disloyalty to Herod and the state. Even so, outside of his family struggles, there were many notable successes.

Through Herod's influence, Rome demonstrated a restrained respect for Judaism and its institutions on numerous occasions. Sosius, governor of Syria who captured Jerusalem for Herod in 37 B.C., gave gold to the temple before he left; in 15 B.C., Augustus' friend Marcus Agrippa sacrificed a hecatomb (one hundred oxen) there to the delight of the populace; and apparently all the Roman emperors welcomed and perhaps paid for the sacrifices offered on their behalf in Jerusalem. Moreover, in 22–21 B.C., in an effort to relieve economic strains among his subjects, Herod remitted one-third of the taxes following the sabbatical year. In response, Octavian, now known as Caesar Augustus, rewarded Herod generously by adding the Galilee regions of Gaulanitis, Hulata, and Panias to his territory.

During his reign, Herod distinguished himself in Roman eyes and therefore received many honors, including such titles as "friend and ally" as well as "friend of the Romans, and friend of Caesar." In addition, Herod was given the rare privilege of naming his own successor, requiring only the confirmation of Caesar. With new titles, honors, and territory, Herod moved forward in expanding Judea's influence in the region.

Creating the first Judean navy, Herod joined Marcus Agrippa, who was now coregent with Augustus, in an expedition to the Black Sea and Pontus. In 14 B.C., in a bid to renew the gratitude and loyalty of his people, Herod again remitted taxes after the sabbatical year of 16/15 B.C. Two years later, Augustus rewarded Herod by giving him half of the income of the Cyprus copper mines as well as the management of the other half—thus facilitating Herod's building programs. With his increased economic power, Herod apparently saved the

Olympic games by providing badly needed funding during the same year. The trustees of the Olympic games appointed him president of the games, a post without precedent. During the same year, the great architectural and engineering wonder, Caesarea, was opened—a stunningly beautiful seaport on the Mediterranean.

Caesarea, named in honor of Caesar Augustus (the harbor itself was named Sebastos, the Greek for Augustus), was the realization of one of Herod's many architectural dreams. It was one of the amazing construction feats of Near Eastern antiquity. Originally settled in the third century B.C., the city was conquered by the Maccabeans in 96 B.C. Eventually, Augustus gave it to Herod. Between 22 and 10 B.C., Herod reconstructed the city and built the harbor out of fine cement and colossal blocks of stone, making it a successful competitor to Alexandria. Caesarea demonstrates the geographical reach of Herod's commercial activities, for there archaeologists have found marble imported from Italy, pink granite from Aswan in Upper Egypt, and Chinese porcelain.

Furthermore, Herod did much to protect Jews outside Judea—relatively much more numerous in the Greco-Roman world than at present, representing as much as ten percent of the population (seven million out of seventy million). With Herod's help and influence, Jews of the Diaspora were guaranteed freedom to worship, to follow their dietary and sabbatical laws, to send the temple tax to Jerusalem as prescribed in the Mosaic law, and to avoid military service in the Roman army. Herod may have even helped finance a synagogue in the imperial capital itself, as the Jews there named a synagogue in his honor. It seems obvious why Diaspora Jews were favorable to Herod. They, of course, were engaged in the same balancing act of trying to live their Judaism while living within the Roman world. Because Herod was a friend of Rome, the Jews of the Diaspora experienced an unprecedented era of prosperity and security in the empire. Aside from his efforts outside the country, Herod made efforts to discourage sectarian strife and division by emphasizing Jewish worship at the temple in Jerusalem, thus contributing to the prosperity and security of the nation.

However, Herod's greatest achievement for his nation and for his Judaism was the construction of the temple in the capital city, begun in the winter of 20/19 B.C. Apparently, he paid the complete cost to train and support the priests doing the work of rebuilding and to gather the building materials from various parts of the region. The temple, known as Herod's Temple, was a magnificent structure. Innovative in its design, it included areas for women and gentiles within its grounds. A massive structure, the temple and its grounds covered some forty acres.

While Herod certainly hoped this monumental enterprise would ingratiate himself to his Jewish subjects, he also hoped it would stimulate the economy and stand as a concrete manifestation of his commitment to his Jewish faith. Likewise, Herod's memorials to the patriarchs and matriarchs in Hebron, to Abraham at Mamre, and to King David in Jerusalem may reflect such devotion. In fact, the walls surrounding the ancient oak tree at Mamre and the Herodian buildings reared over the burial caves of Machpelah in Hebron, then located in Idumea, may also demonstrate Herod's belief that no fundamental opposition existed between his Idumean heritage and his Judaism.

Another manifestation of Herod's commitment to his Jewish heritage was his careful avoidance of reproducing any animal or human images on his coins or buildings. In particular, the design of one coin minted during the third year of his kingship and the first year of his effective reign in Judea exhibits motifs from the temple, symbolizing his deep-seated attachment to his heritage. Other symbols found on Herodian coins differ little from Hasmonean iconography, which was also respectful of constraints within the Mosaic law.

His relations with the Essenes further demonstrate his sympathy with Jewish law and tradition and show off his basic piety. Some evidence suggests that the Essenes reentered Jewish life during Herod's reign. These were priests and others who opposed the Hasmonean attempt to usurp the high priest's office and thereafter to establish their own institutions, living in separate communes in towns and cities and withdrawing from the temple. Their reentry may be explained by the favor that Herod showed them as a result of the prophetic blessing he received as a young schoolboy from a member of their group, as noted earlier. Finally, Herod required non-Jewish males who wanted to marry members of his family to be circumcised.

Even so, the issue of Herod's Jewishness hung around him like a cloud. Like his father, he would have resented being identified as "half-Jewish." He demonstrated his loyalty to Judaism and to Judea on many occasions. Suggesting that he was not a champion of Judaism makes many of his actions simply unintelligible.

Herod's construction projects throughout the region of Palestine—aqueducts, cisterns, theaters, amphitheaters, shops, palaces, stadiums, protective walls, towers, and public buildings—strengthened Judea's economy. He improved trade routes, enlarged several harbors, and created new markets for dates, wine, olive oil, asphalt, and balsam. Other industries such as glass, perfume, and pottery made significant advances during his reign. Resettlement programs, agricultural development, and work relief brought the nation an unprecedented era of productivity. Interestingly enough, though possessing a large ego, Herod named only one site after himself, the Herodium, a palace complex in the barren Judean hills eight miles south of Jerusalem and three and a half miles east of Bethlehem.

As noted, tax relief as well as gifts of grain for his subjects following both natural disasters and sabbatical years helped the citizens of Judea to weather tough times. He apparently melted his own gold and silver jewelry into bullion for trade during economic crises. Herod even allocated food supplies to neighboring states in need. One of his concerns was directed toward the infirm and elderly. Herod's efforts to improve the quality of life in his kingdom also included efforts to enact new laws improving social justice while encouraging the application of the Torah in everyday life. Such actions won not only support from his subjects and the goodwill of his neighbors but also an international reputation of generosity and innovation.

Toward his non-Jewish subjects, Herod attempted to be fair. He demonstrated that it was possible for a Jewish king to remain on cordial terms with local pagans who lived in the Greek cities around and within Judea. The difficulties inherent in ruling two distinct groups of people within the region, Jews and non-Jews, cannot be overemphasized. Hostilities between the Jews of the Judean and Galilean hills, on the one hand, and the pagan inhabitants of Greek cities along the coastal plane and in the Decapolis of the north, on the other, went back to Hasmonean times. Such rancorous relationships posed significant challenges to Herod.

During the second and early first centuries B.C., the aggressive Hasmonean state had expanded over surrounding areas and suppressed the freedom of the city states such as Gaza and Ashkelon. The oppression was so severe that, when Pompey conquered the Jews and restricted their state to the hill country, the Greek cities greeted him as a liberator. The Hasmoneans found their Greek subjects immutably alien; unlike the hill peoples of Galilee and Idumea, attempts to convert them to Judaism proved totally ineffective.

As we have noted, Herod's attempts to steer a middle course between competing cultural communities were challenging if not outright daunting. His gentile subjects thought of him as a Jewish king; nevertheless, he supported non-Jewish citizens of the region in their rights and furnished funds to build Greek cities and temples. Further, his army was composed of both gentiles and Jews. This army not only checked rebellion from within but also protected the inhabitants of Judea from attack from without. Like the Romans, Herod attempted to establish public order in his nation by any means available. As a result, he believed that surveillance and secrecy were essential to maintaining security and stability.

Certainly, Herod encouraged the adoption of many aspects of Greek culture, even among his Jewish subjects. He and his artisans copied art and architecture from the surrounding cultures. Even Greek forms of architecture and decoration adorned the exclusively Israelite areas of the Jerusalem temple. Greek was widely spoken, though doubtless more so in cosmopolitan Jerusalem and other cities than in the Galilean and Judean countryside. For Herod, Hellenization had come about neither through imposition from outside, nor through the spontaneous adoption of Greek culture wholesale, nor through gradual assimilation, but through the deliberate integration of Greek elements to enrich the indigenous society and culture. Apparently, Herod amassed a sizable Greek library and surrounded himself with competent people, including Romans and Greeks, to help run the affairs of state and manage increasing resources.

We should recall that, during the Hellenistic and Roman periods, the leading families of the cities of Asia enjoyed greater wealth than ever before. The Herodian dynasty was one of these privileged families; and, as a result, Herod used his resources to move his influence beyond his own kingdom.

Herod donated funds to build facilities for festivals and games at Berytus, Damascus, Delos, Ptolemais, Sidon, and Tripolis. Inscriptions and monuments in Herod's honor were located in Athens, Chios, Cilicia, Cos, Lycia, Pergamum, Phaselis, and Samos. He helped improve public buildings at Antioch, Balanea, Byblus, Laodicia-on-the-Sea, Sparta, and Tyre. Herod built temples to Roma and Augustus in Caesarea,

Panias (Caesarea Philippi), and Sebaste. He reconstructed a temple in Rhodes.

Many studies of Herod's life emphasize his building activity for obvious reasons—they have endured, observable by even the most casual tourist and appreciated more easily than any other aspect of his career. They are stunning in any way one chooses to categorize them—size, location, or purpose. He was a remarkable patron, matching even Augustus and Marcus Agrippa, his only two rivals. The significant absence of any references to his architects suggests that Herod played a crucial and significant architectural role in his building programs.

Some feel that the palaces and fortress complexes reveal Herod's paranoia. He undertook Jewish projects as a purposeful plan to ingratiate himself with the religious element of his nation. In contrast, he pursued non-Jewish construction projects as a facet of his deep commitment to Hellenism. Whatever purpose these structures were intended to fulfill, they represent an ambitious enterprise, superbly implemented.

In spite of the many successes during his reign, Herod's last year was difficult and full of confusion, betrayal, and stress. Apparently for the New Testament authors Luke and Matthew, Herod's last days were significant for early Christians as an important historical reference point. Luke sets the historical stage of his Gospel by announcing John the Baptist's birth as follows: "There was in the days of Herod, the king of Judea, a certain priest named Zacharias, of the course of Abia: and his wife was of the daughters of Aaron, and her name was Elisabeth" (Luke 1:5). Matthew also identifies the historical setting of Jesus' birth in Judea: "Now when Jesus was born in Bethlehem of Judea in the days of Herod the king, behold, there came wise men from the east to Jerusalem" (Matthew 2:1).

Sometime between the arrival of the wise men and the murder of the children in Bethlehem (Matthew 2:16–18), Josephus records that it was widely announced that Herod was about to die (in his seventieth year, about 4 B.C.) (*Jewish Antiquities* 17.6.1). As in studies about his life, Herod's last sickness is surrounded by controversy. Various diagnoses have been suggested for his complaint. A very good case is made by Dr. W. Reid Litchfield of Brigham and Women's Hospital in Boston for type II (adult-onset) diabetes mellitus (personal correspondence, May 12, 1997). Whatever the cause for his last illness, Herod went to his winter palace at Jericho, where he distributed fifty drachmas to his soldiers and greater gifts to commanders and friends. There he died. Although he had ordered the executions of Jewish notables so that people would be in mourning when he died, the order was not carried out.

Whatever the truth may be about his last days and death, Herod's body was taken to the Herodium. Ironically, the burial place of one of the best documented personalities in the ancient world remains hidden to archaeologists today.

For Further Reading

David Noel Freedman et al., eds., *The Anchor Bible Dictionary*, 6 vols. (New York: Doubleday, 1992), s.v. "Hasmonean Dynasty," "Herod the Great," and "Herod's Building Program."

David B. Galbraith, D. Kelly Ogden, and Andrew C. Skinner, *Jerusalem: The Eternal City* (Salt Lake City: Deseret Book, 1996), 153–62.

Lester L. Grabbe, *Judaic Religion in the Second Temple Period: Belief and Practice from Exile to Yavneh* (New York: Routledge, 2000), 84.

Richard Neitzel Holzapfel, "King Herod," and John W. Welch, "Herod's Wealth," in John F. Hall and John W. Welch, eds., *Masada and the World of the New Testament* (Provo, Utah: BYU Studies, 1997), 35–73 and 74–83.

Peter Richardson, *Herod: King of the Jews and Friend of the Romans* (Columbia: University of South Carolina Press, 1996).

Emil Schürer, *The History of the Jewish People in the Age of Jesus Christ*, 3 vols., rev. ed. by Geza Vermes, Fergus Millar, and Matthew Black (Edinburgh: T & T Clark, 1973–87), 1:282–329.

Ben Witherington III, *New Testament History* (Grand Rapids, Michigan: Baker Academic, 2001), 51–61.

Part 2

Sacred Writings

CHAPTER 8

WHAT IS SCRIPTURE?

King Ptolemy watched as the Jewish sages filed into the palace reception room. He had inherited his Egyptian kingdom from his father, the founder of the Ptolemaic empire and former general to Alexander the Great. Unlike his warrior father, Ptolemy wanted to enrich his subjects in cultural and religious ways. Therefore, he had founded a library in Alexandria, which he hoped would come to possess copies of the most important writings ever produced by the human spirit. Long ago, he had heard of a venerable book of the Jews, a book that told of their history and laws and customs, a book that had infused unity and purpose into their people. Their book even talked of a time when Jewish ancestors lived in Egypt. He wanted a copy of that book for his library. But it was not written in Greek, the language that he himself spoke and wrote. Instead, it was in the ancient language of the Jews' ancestors, Hebrew. So through Eleazar, the high priest of their temple in Jerusalem, he had invited a group of Jewish scholars to Alexandria to translate their book into Greek. They had come. And for seven evenings he and they had engaged in a stimulating exchange of ideas about how a king should govern his subjects. This evening, as they had all agreed, the Jewish sages would begin the work of translating their sacred book into Greek. There were seventy-two of them.

Scripture consists of both sacred writings inspired by God and a person's state of mind. On God's part, sacred writing exists independent of whether anyone believes such writing to be divine or even important. On the human side, we must accept scripture as inspired and important before it can exert any meaningful influence in our lives. It has been so since the beginning when God taught His believing children to keep "a book of remembrance . . . according to the pattern given by [His own] finger" (Moses 6:5, 46). For those devoted to God's word during the intertestamental period, scripture was paramount in their lives, and, as we might expect, they were active in its promotion and dissemination.

The Hebrew Bible

The most important set of manuscripts that have survived from antiquity is that known as the Masoretic Text or Scripture. Written in Hebrew, these manuscripts form the basis for all translations of the Old Testament into other languages, including the King James Version (KJV). The Masoretic Scripture is an agreed-on or established text whose contents were accepted about A.D. 90 by a group of Pharisaic survivors of the horrible Jewish war with Rome that ended with the destruction of Jerusalem and its temple (A.D. 66–70). Meeting under the direction of Rabbi Yohanan ben Zakkai in a town called Jamnia (also known as Yavneh), which lies between Jerusalem and modern Tel Aviv, these Pharisees knew that their faith had to survive without their beloved temple. And the basis of that faith had to be their scripture. Because different versions of the biblical books were known in their society, as the discovery of the Dead Sea Scrolls has shown, they felt the need to agree on an official Bible. Though there was still much to do, such as finalizing the pronunciation and voweling of the Hebrew text—it was the later Masoretes (sixth–seventh centuries A.D.) who would finish these tasks at Tiberias on the Sea of Galilee—what the sages at Jamnia agreed on has come down to us as the Old Testament. Their decision cut off any possibility that other ancient Hebrew books might become part of the Old Testament, such as the book of First Enoch, which the people at the Dead Sea venerated and which the Epistle of Jude in the New Testament quotes as scripture (see Jude 1:14–15).

Before those dark, pressured days when Ben Zakkai and his associates felt a desperate need to settle on a Bible for their people, many of whom were by then scattered and enslaved, the books of the Hebrew Bible had circulated in a number of different forms, some of which were lost. Both Samaritans and Christians were using scriptural books that differed from theirs. They needed their own scripture. In fact, the Book of Mormon preserves the names of lost prophetic works such as those of Zenock, Zenos, and Neum (see 1 Nephi 19:10). The big issue for Ben Zakkai and his associates had to do with the differences in various passages that affected the basic meaning of the scripture. In their minds, such differences pointed up a pressing urgency to establish the text of scripture once and for all. They turned to a version of the books of the Old Testament that had been carefully copied by scribes for many centuries. This version would become known as the Masoretic Text and would become accepted to the exclusion of all others.

The Samaritan Pentateuch

Some differences appear in sharp relief in the Samaritan Pentateuch. This scripture rests on a very old set of documents that some scholars estimate reaches back to the days of the divided Israelite monarchy, before the Assyrians came to Samaria and conquered the city in 722 B.C. If this is the case, the ancient texts that underlie the Samaritan Pentateuch would date to the era of the only other known ancient collection of sacred texts, the plates of brass that the party of Lehi and Sariah carried to the New World (see 1 Nephi 3:1–3; 4:38). Everything changed about 100 B.C. The Samaritans, one of the groups that kept early biblical documents, made several decisions about their scriptural books that led to what we now call the Samaritan Pentateuch.

One of the Samaritans' decisions was to make their sacred

documents more easily understood to readers and hearers in synagogue services. Already, many of the expressions in the biblical books were difficult to understand because of their antiquity. As a result of this decision, modern readers observe changed expressions in the Samaritan Pentateuch that make the accounts more accessible to ordinary, devoted worshipers. The effort to make the scriptures more easily understood, in oral form, goes back to Ezra (see Nehemiah 8:1–8). A second decision was to keep only the Pentateuch as scripture—that is, the books of Genesis through Deuteronomy. Ever since the first Jewish exiles had returned from Babylon in 538 B.C., the exiles and their descendants at Jerusalem had treated the Samaritans as little more than gentiles, an act that created a wide social and religious chasm between Jews and Samaritans. The historical and prophetic books that the Jews venerated, such as First Kings and Jeremiah, spoke of Jerusalem as the worship center of the nation. But the Samaritans knew that the first place of worship that Joshua built after the Israelites had entered the promised land was atop Mount Ebal (Joshua 8:30–32). Moreover, Joshua had built a sanctuary there in accord with Moses' instructions (Deuteronomy 27:1–8; also 11:26–29). And Mount Ebal lay in their territory. Hence, the Samaritans turned their back on the scriptural books that spoke of Jerusalem as the proper place of worship. Not surprisingly, it is this very issue of the proper place of worship that the Samaritan woman raised with Jesus when conversing with Him next to the well of Jacob (John 4:20–23).

The Samaritans' third decision had to do with their modest temple, which their forebears had constructed on Mount Gerizim more than three centuries before Jesus' day, soon after 350 B.C. Mount Gerizim lies opposite Mount Ebal, south across the valley where Joshua had brought the Israelites to celebrate the ritual entry into the promised land (Joshua 8:30–35). In addition, the ark of the covenant had rested at Shiloh until the days of Eli the priest, when it was lost to the Philistines

(1 Samuel 4:1–11; 5:1). And Shiloh lay only a few miles south of Mount Ebal and Mount Gerizim. To the Samaritans, tradition seemed to be on their side. Hence, the Samaritans had erected their temple as a religious counterpoint to the reconstructed temple in Jerusalem. To solidify their claim to be the legitimate heirs of ancient Israel, they decided to make adjustments in how their scripture reads, defending Mount Gerizim as the true center of worship. For, as they knew, Moses had said that Mount Gerizim would be the place of God's "blessing" (Deuteronomy 11:29). Thus, they adjusted the sacred records. In one instance, the Samaritans changed the reference to future holy sanctuaries from "*all* places where I [the Lord] record my name" to "*the* place where I record my name" (Exodus 20:24; emphasis added). Such a change pointed to the Samaritans' one authorized sanctuary atop Mount Gerizim. Another adjustment is more vivid. Instead of pointing to Mount Ebal as the place where Joshua was to build the first sanctuary, the Samaritan Pentateuch says that Moses specified Mount Gerizim (Deuteronomy 27:4).

All of these decisions—making the scripture more understandable, opting to keep only the Pentateuch and discard the other records, and buttressing their worship center on Mount Gerizim—led to the creation of the Samaritan Pentateuch, which would guide the lives of generations of unborn Samaritans. It was a weighty set of decisions. We know that the adjusted passages affected how people read and understood scripture beyond the Samaritan community. For example, the Christian martyr Stephen declared that Abraham "came . . . out of the land of the Chaldeans . . . when his father was dead" (Acts 7:1–4), agreeing with the chronology of the Samaritan Pentateuch, which assigns Abraham's father a lifetime of 145 years rather than 205 (Genesis 11:32). As this example shows, the group of documents that had formed the sacred records of the Samaritans differed from other Hebrew records (the Dead Sea Scrolls also preserve variant readings). But the Samaritans' earliest holy books shared common ground with the particular Hebrew records that would form the basis for the earliest translation of the Old Testament books into a foreign language, that of Greek. We call this Greek translation "the Septuagint."

THE SEPTUAGINT

The Septuagint, which became the Bible for early Christian missionaries, including the Apostle Paul, is one of the few pieces from our scriptural heritage for which we have a story about its creation. For instance, there are stories behind the writing and editing of the book of Jeremiah and the Book of Mormon, but we do not know who wrote the books of Ruth and Judges. In the case of the Septuagint, though few accept the truthfulness of the account about its translation, we find ourselves in Egypt during the days of Ptolemy II Philadelphus, who ruled almost forty years, from 283/282 to 246 B.C. This Macedonian king was the founder of the famous Library of Alexandria, which was partially destroyed by fire in 48 B.C.

The word *Septuagint* comes from the Latin term for seventy (*septuaginta*) and is often abbreviated by the Roman numeral LXX. This number may derive either from the seventy elders of Israel known in Old Testament passages (for example, Exodus 24:1, 9; Numbers 11:16, 24–25) or, less certainly, from the number of Jewish sages who reportedly went to Alexandria at the request of King Ptolemy—seventy-two, six from each of the twelve tribes. According to the *Letter of Aristeas*, the king desired that the Alexandria Library obtain a copy of all the important books in the known world. After learning about the Bible and its antiquity, he corresponded with the Jerusalem high priest Eleazar and arranged for Jewish scholars skilled in Hebrew and Greek to travel to Egypt and undertake a translation of their scripture into Greek. According to Aristeas' account, each of the seventy-two sages produced a translation of the Pentateuch, which he then compared to those of his fellow translators.

Working easily together, they turned out a translation that was hailed by the Jews of Alexandria as well as by the king.

In contrast to this story, the most widely accepted reason for the translation of the Old Testament into Greek has to do with need. It seems certain that the large Jewish population of Alexandria—estimated to be about one million in Jesus' day—and of other places in the Mediterranean region needed a version of their scriptures that they could read. For, after Jews had migrated away from Palestine where they had learned to read their scriptures in Hebrew, their children grew up speaking and reading Greek while allowing their Hebrew skills to slip. Within a couple of generations, Jews in the Diaspora could no longer read their Hebrew Bibles. The effort to translate the biblical books into Greek helped meet a growing need for scriptures in their common language. The translation meant that Diaspora Jews had made an important decision. They no longer felt a compelling necessity to read scriptures in their original Hebrew language, a dimension of their scriptures that many Jews considered holy. In a word, need came to outweigh the time-honored custom of reading and reciting in the sacred Hebrew tongue. But this change did not occur readily. Evidence exists that Jews of the Diaspora, after losing their ability to read Hebrew, at first attempted to write the Hebrew sounds of their scriptures in Greek letters so they could read passages aloud during synagogue services. But because worshipers could still not understand the oral readings from the Bible, they felt the urgency to take the next step of translating the Bible into Greek.

We do not know why translators chose one version of the Hebrew Bible over another to serve as the basis for their translation. For, as studies have shown, in many passages the Septuagint differs in meaning and detail from what would become the Masoretic version of the Hebrew scriptures. For instance, the Septuagint version of the book of Jeremiah is about one-eighth shorter than the Hebrew text. At first, scholars assumed that the translator of Jeremiah was simply summarizing large, identifiable sections of the prophet's book. But the discovery of the Dead Sea Scrolls altered that view, for among the preserved biblical manuscripts was one copy of the Hebrew book of Jeremiah that agrees with the shorter Greek version of Jeremiah's book. In this light, it is obvious that the translators were faithful to their task of rendering their holy scriptures accurately into Greek. Why did the translators select the shorter version of Jeremiah rather than the longer? It is possible that the longer version was not available to them. We do not know. But we know that after the Septuagint had served Jewish congregations all over the Greco-Roman world for a long time, the Christians came along and everything changed.

When Christian missionaries began to proselytize in the Mediterranean world, they of course referred to the scriptures. As an example, Paul's pattern of preaching was to attend a synagogue service on the Sabbath day and, when he captured the attention of people there, to teach out of the scriptures (see, for example, Acts 13:14–43). And those scriptures in Greek-speaking Jewish congregations consisted of the Septuagint. As the New Testament attests, serious differences of opinion arose between Christian missionaries and local Jewish leaders over the meaning of certain scriptural passages. In time, the Christians had made such inroads within Jewish congregations that leaders had to rethink whether they wanted to continue to embrace the same scriptures that the Christians were appealing to when making converts of other Jews. In an astonishing turnabout, some Greek-speaking Jews eventually decided to retranslate the Hebrew Old Testament and to abandon the Septuagint, which, in their eyes, had become a Christian book. Two important retranslations of the Hebrew Bible still exist—those by Aquila and Theodotion. About A.D. 130, a gentile proselyte to Judaism named Aquila undertook a translation of the Old Testament into Greek. But his effort created a Greek version that was slavishly literal to Hebrew expressions. For Greek readers and speakers, it was almost unusable. About fifty years later, another gentile proselyte to Judaism named Theodotion made a Greek translation of the Bible that has stood the test of time. In fact, Christians embraced his work more wholeheartedly than did Greek-speaking Jews. As an illustration of the quality of his translation effort, his rendition of the book of Daniel has displaced the earlier Septuagint translation of that book.

Readers notice that Old Testament passages quoted in the New Testament often differ from what they find in the Old Testament. The reasons for these differences frequently have to do with the Septuagint. For instance, the Greek-speaking Luke quoted Isaiah 40:3 when describing the beginning of the ministry of John the Baptist. We read, "The voice of one crying in the wilderness, Prepare ye the way of the Lord, make his paths straight" (Luke 3:4). This version preserves virtually the same reading as the Septuagint. But the Hebrew rendition of this passage exhibits differences. In the King James Version, which goes back to the Hebrew Masoretic text, the passage reads, "The voice of him that crieth in the wilderness, Prepare ye the way of the Lord, make straight in the desert a highway for our God" (Isaiah 40:3). The contrast in readings appears in the final clause. The Hebrew preserves the phrase "in the desert," which the Septuagint drops, and the Hebrew term for "highway" is singular whereas the Septuagint translates the term into the plural "paths." Although the variants make little difference doctrinally, they point out the fact that Luke, who spoke Greek, appealed to the scripture version that he could read. A second instance points up mild doctrinal dissimilarities.

The Apostle Paul frequently quoted passages from the Old Testament. One that he cited in 1 Corinthians underscores his reliance on the Septuagint when writing to Greek-speaking members of the Church. We read, "For it is written [in scripture], I will destroy the wisdom of the wise, and will bring to nothing the understanding of the prudent" (1 Corinthians 1:19). As in the prior example, this quotation matches almost exactly the wording of Isaiah 29:14 in the Septuagint translation. The King James Version, resting on the Hebrew wording, renders the passage as follows: "The wisdom of their wise men shall perish, and the understanding of their prudent men shall be hid." We notice immediately the forceful sense in the Septuagint that God "will destroy . . . and will bring to nothing. . . ." It is His action alone that will abolish worldly wisdom and sophistication. To be sure, the Hebrew version bears this sense implicitly because Isaiah 29:14 begins, "Therefore, behold, I [God] will proceed to do a marvellous work." But the forms of the Hebrew verbs do not relay the powerful sense of God's action that the Greek verbs do.

THE TARGUMS

When Jesus stood in the Nazareth synagogue to read passages out of the book of Isaiah and then sat down to explain them, he was following an honored tradition of making the Hebrew scripture intelligible to Aramaic-speaking Jews (Luke 4:16–27). In their later written form, such commentaries on or rerenderings of the text of scripture are called Targums. The term *targum* comes from the Aramaic verb that means "to translate." Such efforts were intended to render the sacred records in a language that ordinary worshipers could understand—Aramaic rather than ancient Hebrew. This practice may have started as early as the days of Ezra, who arrived in Jerusalem about 428 B.C. We read that, in his day, the Levites "read in . . . the law of God distinctly, and gave the sense, and caused them [the worshipers] to understand the reading" (Nehemiah 8:8). The term translated "distinctly" in this verse can carry the meaning "with interpretation," which would make the point even stronger than the account already does.

The efforts to translate passages from the Hebrew books into the common Aramaic were first done in oral form. But eventually even this oral translation of scripture became rather fixed so that a person could not offer his or her own understanding of the passage under review. Hence, we can guess that Jesus' surprising explanation, which was not really a translation, may have caught a number of people in the synagogue off guard. Jesus, of course, read and then commented on passages in Isaiah. But the first of the targums that took firm shape and were finally committed to written form almost five hundred years after Jesus' time concerned the Pentateuch, because that part of scripture was a record of God's law to His people. Only later did the targums on the prophetic books achieve sufficient importance that they were written down. Even so, the targum of Jonathan ben Uzziel, who lived in the first century A.D., exhibited a tendency to interpret scriptural passages as pointing to the coming Messiah, including Isaiah 53. This is the very thing that Jesus was doing at Nazareth. The important point to notice is that people felt a deep need to understand God's words that had come to their ancestors and were preserved in scripture. To do so, they looked to those who possessed skills to render their sacred Hebrew books into a language they could understand. And they were not disappointed.

For Further Reading

Adolf Büchler, "The Reading of the Law and Prophets in a Triennial Cycle," *The Jewish Quarterly Review* 5 (1893): 420–68, especially 420–42; and 6 (1894): 1–73, especially 1–38, 51–60.

James H. Charlesworth, *The Old Testament Pseudepigrapha*, 2 vols. (Garden City, New York: Doubleday, 1983, 1985), 2:7–34.

David Noel Freedman et al., eds., *The Anchor Bible Dictionary* (New York: Doubleday, 1992), s.v. "Massoretic Text," "Samaritan Pentateuch," "Septuagint," and "Targum, Targumim."

Roland Kenneth Harrison, *Introduction to the Old Testament* (Grand Rapids, Michigan: Eerdmans, 1969), 211–43.

Emil Schürer, *The History of the Jewish People in the Age of Jesus Christ*, 3 vols., rev. ed. by Geza Vermes, Fergus Millar, and Matthew Black (Edinburgh: T & T Clark, 1973–87), 2:16–20; 3:474–504.

Qumran Cave Locations

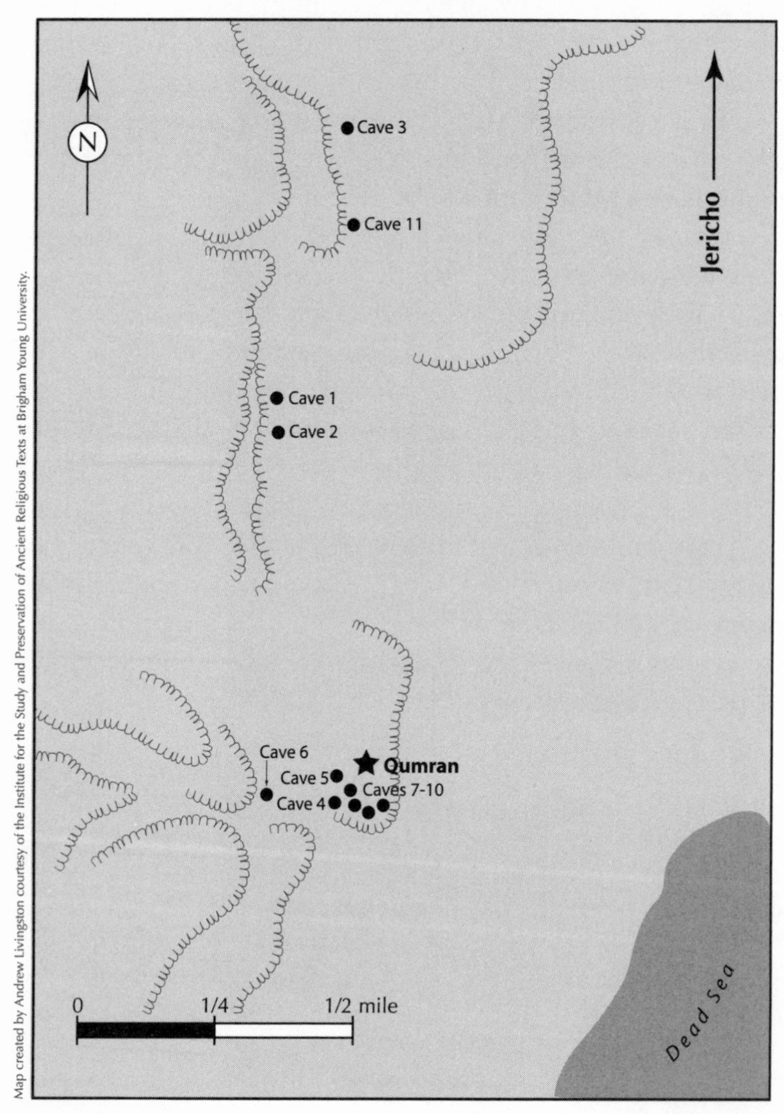

Map created by Andrew Livingston courtesy of the Institute for the Study and Preservation of Ancient Religious Texts at Brigham Young University.

CHAPTER 9

THE DEAD SEA SCROLLS

Two Ta'amireh tribe shepherds climbed the limestone cliffs above the shores of the Dead Sea searching for a stray goat. It was 1947, and events in the Middle East were about to explode, changing the political map of the region once again. However, these Bedouins were probably unaware of events on the horizon. What mattered on this day was the lost goat. One of them threw a rock into a large hole, hoping to scare the goat from its hiding place. Instead, they were frightened at the sound of a loud crash when the rock shattered something at the bottom of the cave behind the hole. They instinctively ran, but later in the evening, one of them, a teenager named Mohammed-ed-Dhib, thought that he should return and investigate; maybe they had come upon a hidden treasure at the cave. But instead of gold or silver, Mohammed found ten clay jars. Most of the jars were empty, but one of them did contain some leather scrolls that he could not read. These scrolls and others found shortly thereafter ended up in the hands of an antiquities dealer in Bethlehem, and the rest, as the saying goes, is history. The young shepherd could never have realized at the time that his discovery would change the maps of scholarship as much as the Arab-Israeli conflict at the time was changing the political maps of the region. In the end, the scrolls were a stunning treasure after all.

Since their initial discovery in 1947, the Dead Sea Scrolls have captured the hearts and minds of scholars and laypeople alike. Anyone familiar with the story of the coming forth of the Book of Mormon (see Joseph Smith—History 1:27–59), the

Church's teachings on the history of the Bible (see 1 Nephi 13 and Articles of Faith 1:8), and scriptural promises regarding ancient records still to be revealed in the future (see Doctrine and Covenants 107:57) should not have been surprised at the excitement within the Latter-day Saint community when the discovery was announced. Nor should others be astonished at our continued interest and involvement in the study, preservation, and publication of the Dead Sea Scrolls.

The importance of these textual discoveries on the northwestern shore of the Dead Sea can hardly be overestimated. Like the Apocrypha and Pseudepigrapha, these ancient texts open an important window onto the past, particularly for a period when the paucity of sources made it frustrating for students and scholars attempting to reconstruct the Jewish world during the intertestamental period. They also illumine the world of John the Baptist and Jesus, although it is doubtful that either of them spent time at the site where the scrolls were copied.

Following Mohammed-ed-Dhib's initial discovery of the cave (now known as Cave 1) containing scrolls and fragments in the spring of 1947, Bedouins and archaeologists located ten additional caves (known as Caves 2 through 11) between 1952 and 1956 near Khirbet Qumran (Arabic for "ruins of Qumran"). The caves are numbered in the order that scrolls were discovered in them, the Bedouins finding more scroll-bearing caves than archaeologists. Scrolls are identified by a strict system of numbers and letters. For example, the *Community Rule*, *Serekh ha-Yahad* in Hebrew, is 1QS (Cave 1, Qumran, Serekh Scroll), and the *Temple Scroll* is 11QTemple (Cave 11, Qumran, Temple Scroll), whereas 4Q252 refers to a fragment (Cave 4, Qumran, fragment number 252). The ruins of Qumran, located approximately ten miles south of Jericho and thirteen miles east of Jerusalem, are situated on the clay-limestone terrace adjacent to Wadi Qumran that runs just north of the ruins and that empties into the northwest corner of the Dead Sea.

The more than 850 texts found in the caves near Qumran are written in Aramaic and Hebrew, with a few in Greek (belonging to the Greek translation of the Bible, the Septuagint, with minor variations), mostly on leather (BYU professor Scott R. Woodward has identified gazelle, bovine, and ibex skin parchments). There are a few examples of manuscripts written on papyrus (for example, 9Q1) and, in one case, on metal, known today as the *Copper Scroll* (3QTreasure). Scribes wrote in black ink with an exception in the book of Numbers, in which several verses appear in red ink.

Most of the manuscripts are written with square Hebrew characters (Aramaic or Assyrian script), but a few manuscripts exhibit what scholars call the paleo-Hebrew script. Scholars discovered that multiple scribes worked on many of the manuscripts. The dating of the Dead Sea Scrolls ranges from before the community settled Qumran (usually identified as the Essenes; see chapter 15, "Essenes and Zealots") about the end of the third century B.C., and on into the first half of the first century A.D. It is not surprising that the community already possessed texts before founding their settlement at the Dead Sea, which is the best explanation for the existence of scrolls predating the settlement of Qumran.

The scrolls and fragments range in size and completeness. The *Temple Scroll* (11QTemple), the largest manuscript found at Qumran, is nearly twenty-nine feet long. Some of the smallest fragments with legible letters are no larger than a modern U.S. postage stamp. Nevertheless, all the material, whether complete texts or small fragments, are proving to be valuable for everyone's understanding of this period of history and the history of the Bible itself.

Most scholars believe that the Essenes mentioned by Josephus and other ancient authors are the group who collected, copied, and deposited the scrolls in the caves near Qumran, even though the name *Essene* does not appear in the texts themselves. Additionally, scholars believe that, since the major caches of scrolls and fragments were discovered in caves located within hundreds of yards of Qumran, the members of the community centered their spiritual lives at the Qumran complex. The ruins include a remarkable aqueduct system, supplying water for drinking and ritual immersions so important to the religious practices of the Essenes; a dining hall to accommodate the members of the group; and possibly a place where community members undertook manuscript production and copying. Since Qumran was the evident religious center of the group, it appears that members of the community lived in caves, huts, and tents beyond the stone buildings. Presumably they did so because the site was devoted to religious activities, such as worship, instruction, study, and ritual (even meals seem to have had a spiritual dimension to them). Since the earliest stages of Dead Sea Scroll research, scholars have acknowledged this connection with the caves, ruins, and scrolls.

In the face of advancing, menacing Roman troops during the Jewish revolt (A.D. 66–70), the community apparently hid their library in nearby caves in the summer of A.D. 68. Eventually, Qumran itself was destroyed by the Roman Tenth Legion, *Legio X Fretensis*, as the Romans moved to stamp out Jewish resistance in Judea after subjugating Galilee. The Essenes who once inhabited Qumran either were killed or abandoned the site; some may have joined other Jews at Masada in a last desperate attempt to defend themselves against the Roman army in A.D. 74.

Shortly after the destruction of Qumran, Roman soldiers established a military camp among its ruins, a camp that was apparently occupied until sometime shortly after the fall of Masada. Additionally, there is evidence that Roman soldiers at the time may have stumbled upon some of the manuscripts, long before Mohammed-ed-Dhib found the clay jars resting on the cave floor in 1947.

Types of Texts from Qumran

Hidden for nearly two thousand years, the scrolls and fragments found near Khirbet Qumran contain several types of texts. The most important types are the following:

Sectarian. The Essenes produced and transmitted these works for their own use. Such documents reflect their own rules and worldview. Previous to the 1947 discovery, most of what we knew about the Essenes was through the eyes of others. The most important manuscript in this category discovered at Qumran is the *Community Rule* (1QS), also known as the Manual of Discipline, of which additional fragments of at least ten manuscripts were found in Cave 4 (4Q255–64) and two small fragments (5Q11), as well as a text quoting the *Community Rule*, in Cave 5 (5Q13).

The central theme of this manuscript is that it was the Qumran community with whom God established his "New Covenant" as prophesied in Jeremiah: "And I will make an everlasting covenant with them" (see Jeremiah 32:37–41). Additionally, the *Community Rule* provides a description of the rite of covenantal renewal and the regulations that governed daily life.

What becomes clear from the Sectarian manuscripts and the biblical material discovered at Qumran (see below) are that the Mosaic Law was the most weighty center of concern and that a particular interpretation of the Law is what separated Essenes from other Jews (see chapter 15, "Essenes and Zealots").

Biblical. The Dead Sea Scrolls include examples of all the Old Testament texts, except the book of Esther. These documents represent about a third of the total material discovered. Although scholars hold various views about the absence of Esther, its exclusion may simply be coincidence.

The biblical material is priceless. It provides important information about the textual development of the individual books of the Bible and the canon itself (see chapter 8, "What Is Scripture?"). Specifically, the finds yielded copies of biblical books that are a thousand years older than previous known copies of the same books. This discovery allowed scholars to literally jump a thousand years of transmission history and to glean specific information regarding scribal practices, including spelling, corrections of text, and note and marginal insertions. In all cases, every biblical text discovered at Qumran is older than any witnesses to the same biblical text previously known.

Additionally, the biblical manuscripts demonstrate that the canon was not closed at this period of time. The community evidently considered a wide variety of religious writings to be inspired and authoritative, including those that eventually became part of the Old Testament. Among those not accepted by later generations are texts of at least three psalms previously unknown. The biblical manuscripts also exhibit variant readings that later Judaism may never have considered. For example, some variant manuscripts, written in Hebrew, are closer to the Greek Septuagint than to the Hebrew texts of what would become the Old Testament. The same can be said for the Samaritan Pentateuch, which disagrees at key points with the Hebrew Old Testament. These variant biblical manuscripts demonstrate that diverse forms of the Hebrew Bible were current during the first century B.C.

Finally, the fact that several books of the Hebrew Bible are well attested in many copies suggests that Essenes viewed some biblical texts as more important than others. For example, Deuteronomy (twenty-nine copies), Psalms (thirty-six copies), and Isaiah (twenty-one copies) were each found in multiple copies.

What is more, a number of commentaries upon biblical texts came to light in the discoveries. These commentaries provide another window onto the world of the Qumran community, as the members often correlated biblical passages with their own history.

Apocryphal and Pseudepigraphal. Among the scrolls and fragments are numerous examples of a wide range of religious texts that were generated during the intertestamental period but were not included in the Jewish canon (see chapter 10, "Apocrypha and Pseudepigrapha"). The importance of this discovery is twofold. First, previous to 1947, many of these texts were known in Greek, Ethiopic, or other languages, but not in the original language of composition. Second, among the Dead Sea Scrolls are previously unknown religious texts.

Halakhic. The Halakhah (Jewish laws) are important because they help us understand how different interpretations of the Law separated Essenes from other Jews (see chapter 18, "Jewish Law"). These differences focus on three separate but related issues: (1) the religious calendar (the Essenes differed from other Jews); (2) ritual purity as related to the temple, including the sacrificial system; and (3) laws regarding marriage relationships.

The most important manuscript in this category is the *Temple Scroll* (11QTemple), produced during the decades just before Jesus' birth. What immediately caught the attention of scholars when the *Temple Scroll* first appeared in 1977 was the first-person, direct address from God Himself. In the *Temple Scroll*, God focuses on the perfect temple, the perfect system of sacrifices, and the perfect society, including the enduring place of priests. We must remember that the people of Qumran rejected the priesthood and the temple in Jerusalem as being corrupt and therefore dwelt in the desert awaiting the building of a perfect temple to replace the one in Jerusalem. Apparently, the author of this scroll believed that he was recording God's vision of the perfect temple, which would be erected in heaven.

In some cases, the text closely follows what is contained in the Pentateuch and in First Kings regarding the temple and its services (the author brings together all the appropriate texts from the Bible, including from the prophets). There are, however, several instances wherein the *Temple Scroll* provides information not found in the Bible.

Although the first section of the manuscript is missing, the remaining portions of the text provide a discussion of almost every aspect of temple worship, including discussions on the various religious feasts associated with the temple; temple sacrifices; temple building and courts; temple furnishings, including the altars; and purity laws that govern the temple and worshipers.

The main differences between the *Temple Scroll* and the classical sources regarding the temple, including the Bible, Josephus, and the Mishnah (a collection of the "oral law" or teachings), are three: First, the architecture of the temple is decidedly different, and the area considered part of the temple precinct is enlarged to cover most of what was ancient Jerusalem, virtually making the whole city a part of the temple. Additionally, the *Temple Scroll* mandates additional religious feasts or holidays. Finally, the *Temple Scroll* requires additional steps for purifying people and animals to ensure the ceremonial purity of the temple.

Because the *Temple Scroll* is wide-ranging in the legal topics it addresses, its contents disclose much about both the Qumran community and their evident belief in continuing, current revelation. This group of Jews must have believed that the scroll represented God's own words, which, in many cases, adjusted the words of previous scripture.

Conclusion

The painstaking effort to assemble the fragments and scrolls took more than a decade (40,000 pieces representing some 584 manuscripts were found in one cave alone). The publication of scholarly editions and translations has taken more than fifty years—and is finally at an end. Latter-day Saints, including BYU professors Donald W. Parry, Dana M. Pike, David R. Seely, and Andrew C. Skinner, have contributed to the official publication series, *Discoveries in the Judean Desert*, published by Oxford University Press, with translations of material from the scrolls. Significantly, the discovery of the Dead Sea Scrolls has made at least four important contributions.

First, the Dead Sea Scrolls greatly enrich our understanding of the religious and social life of Judaism during several centuries for which few sources are available. Second, added with archaeological evidence discovered at Qumran and in the caves associated with the settlement, the Dead Sea Scrolls provide detailed information about one of the groups of Jews who, previous to the discovery, were known only through second- and third-hand sources. Third, the Dead Sea Scrolls provide a sketch of life from the pre-Maccabean period, for which sources have been very few. Fourth, the Dead Sea Scrolls reveal the fluctuating nature of the Hebrew Bible at the time, completely and significantly altering previously held ideas. All in all, the Dead Sea Scrolls attest to the rich variety of approaches to Jewish law, practice, and faith during the two centuries before the birth of Jesus of Nazareth.

For Further Reading

S. Kent Brown, "The Dead Sea Scrolls: A Mormon Perspective," *BYU Studies* 23, no. 1 (winter 1983): 49–66.

David Noel Freedman et al., eds., *The Anchor Bible Dictionary* (New York: Doubleday, 1992), s.v. "Dead Sea Scrolls."

Florentino García-Martínez, trans., *The Dead Sea Scrolls Translated*, 2d ed. (Leiden: E. J. Brill, 1996).

George W. E. Nickelsburg, *Jewish Literature between the Bible and the Mishnah: A Historical and Literary Introduction* (Philadelphia: Fortress Press, 1981).

Monte S. Nyman, "Other Ancient American Records Yet to Come Forth," *Journal of Book of Mormon Studies* 10, no. 1 (2001): 52–61.

Donald W. Parry and Dana M. Pike, eds., *LDS Perspective on the Dead Sea Scrolls* (Provo: Foundation for Ancient Research and Mormon Studies, 1997).

Shemaryahu Talmon, "The Emergence of Jewish Sectarianism in the Early Second Temple Period," in Patrick D. Miller Jr. et al., eds., *Ancient Israelite Religion: Essays in Honor of Frank Moore Cross* (Philadelphia: Fortress Press, 1987), 587–616.

John Trevor, *The Dead Sea Scrolls: A Personal Account* (Grand Rapids, Michigan: Eerdmans, 1977).

Geza Vermes, *The Dead Sea Scrolls: Qumran in Perspective* (London: SCM Press, 1994).

CHAPTER 10

Apocrypha and Pseudepigrapha

Joseph Smith leafed through his family-size King James Version of the Bible. There it was, the section titled "The Apocrypha." What was he to do with this section? The Lord had commanded him to make a translation of the Bible, and his Bible purchased in 1829 from E. B. Grandin's Bookstore in Palmyra contained this important collection of books. Joseph had all but finished his work on the Bible translation and had learned much from the time that he had dedicated to this "branch of [his] calling." The Lord graciously bestowed revelation after revelation, opening one spiritually rich vista after another during the process, beginning with an inspiring vision received in June 1830 (see Moses 1*) and continuing throughout the ensuing effort. Would this section of the Bible lead to similar spiritual insights? Did the Lord wish him to translate these books too? He would have to ask.*

Joseph Smith began working on his translation of the Bible (known today as the Joseph Smith Translation) in June 1830 (see the chapter heading to Moses 1). The work continued off and on over the next few years. In early March 1833, he was again working his way through parts of the Old Testament, and four months later the Prophet completed his work. Yet, when his scribe wrote "Finished on 2d day of July 1833," the Prophet still had not translated the books found in the section between the Old and New Testaments, called the Apocrypha.

Printed on its own signatures of sixteen pages each and in slightly smaller type, the Apocrypha was inserted at Phinney's bindery in Cooperstown, New York. In comparison to the other two sections of the Bible, the Old and New Testaments, this section was the smallest, consisting of only ninety-nine pages.

Sections	Chapters	Verses	Words
Old Testament	929	23,214	592,439
New Testament	260	7,959	191,253
Apocrypha	183	6,081	152,185

Joseph Smith, like most Protestants of his era, was uncertain about the value of the Apocrypha. While Anglicans in Great Britain and their counterparts in America, the Episcopalians, prescribed lessons on the Apocrypha, many other Protestants, particularly those with a Puritan background, opposed the Apocrypha's inclusion within the covers of the Bible. Amid such conflicting points of view, it seems only natural that Joseph ask the Lord whether he should translate it. The answer to his inquiry is found in the Doctrine and Covenants: "Verily, thus saith the Lord unto you concerning the Apocrypha—There are many things contained therein that are true, and it is mostly translated correctly; there are many things contained therein that are not true, which are interpolations by the hands of men. Verily, I say unto you, that it is not needful that the Apocrypha should be translated. Therefore, whoso readeth it, let him understand, for the Spirit manifesteth truth; and whoso is enlightened by the Spirit shall obtain benefit therefrom; and whoso receiveth not by the Spirit, cannot be benefited. Therefore it is not needful that it should be translated. Amen." (D&C 91).

This March 1833 revelation provided a guide to members of the Church in Joseph Smith's day for their study of this section found in their Bibles. Since then, however, most Protestant Bibles, including the King James Version adopted by The Church of Jesus Christ of Latter-day Saints today, no longer include the Apocrypha. The general inaccessibility of the Apocrypha since it was removed from the Bible during the nineteenth century has made it difficult for Latter-day Saints to study the "many things contained therein that are true," unlike members of the Church living during Joseph Smith's ministry.

The Greek term *apokryphon* means "hidden" and in the context of this discussion refers to the material that was originally printed between the Old and New Testaments in many Protestant Bibles, like the 1828 Phinney Bible that Joseph Smith used during his translation work in the early 1830s. (There is also a scholarly collection of New Testament Apocrypha containing material produced during the first four centuries A.D. See Hennecke and Schneemelcher, eds., *New Testament Apocrypha*, 2 vols. [Philadelphia: Westminster Press, 1963, 1965].) The books of the Apocrypha found in early Protestant versions of the Bible are described briefly in the Bible Dictionary published in the Latter-day Saint Edition of the King James Version of the Bible:

First Book of Esdras. An account of the religious reforms of King Josiah (640–609 B.C.) is contained in the First Book of Esdras along with the subsequent history down to the destruction of the temple in 587 B.C. It then describes the return of exiles under Zerubbabel and events that followed, of which we have another account in the books of Ezra and Nehemiah. Incidentally, Esdras is another form of the name Ezra. In Esdras 3:1–5:6 is a story that tells how Zerubbabel, by his wisdom as page of Darius, won the king's favor and obtained permission to restore the captive Jews to their own country. This section stands entirely independent of the canonical scriptures. Of the date of the compilation of the book we know nothing save that its contents were known to Josephus (born A.D. 38).

Second Book of Esdras (also identified as Fourth Ezra). This work contains seven visions or revelations vouchsafed to Ezra, who is represented as grieving over the afflictions of his people and perplexed at the triumph of gentile sinners. The book is marked by a tone of deep melancholy. The only note of consolation is the thought of the retribution that is to fall upon the heads of the gentiles who have tormented Jews. The references to the Messiah deserve special notice (7:28–29; 12:32; 13:32, 37, 52). Many scholars conclude that the book was composed in the first century A.D.

Book of Tobit. The story told in the book of Tobit is as follows. Tobit is a Jew of the tribe of Naphtali, living in Nineveh, and is a pious, God-fearing man who is very strict in his observance of the Jewish law. Trouble comes upon him, and he loses his eyesight. Later, he sends his son Tobias to fetch ten talents of silver, which he had left in the hands of his kinsman Gabael who dwells at Rages in Media. Tobias takes a traveling companion with him, who is in reality the angel Raphael. On the way, they stop at Ecbatana and lodge at the house of one Raguel, whose daughter Sara has through the evil spirit Asmodeus been seven times deprived of husbands on the night of wedlock. Tobias on the ground of kinship claims her in marriage, and her parents consent. By supernatural means, Tobias is able to expel the demon Asmodeus. During the marriage festivities, the angel Raphael journeys to Rages and obtains the money from Gabael. Tobias and his wife then return to Nineveh; and by further application to supernatural means, Tobias is able to restore his father's sight. Raphael, having revealed his true nature, disappears. Tobit breaks forth into a song of thanksgiving. He and his family end their days in prosperity. The story's general character seems to show that it was a writing in praise of a life spent in devout consistency with the Jewish law, even in a strange land.

Book of Judith. The book of Judith purports to describe a romantic event in the history of the Jews—that is, the destruction of the Assyrian general Holofernes by Judith, a rich and beautiful widow of Betulia. The historical contradictions in the story, as well as its general character, leave us no reason to doubt that it is a work of fiction, in which perhaps some traditional deed of heroism in early days has been worked up.

The Rest of the Chapters of the Book of Esther. The other chapters of Esther expand in greater detail the narrative of the canonical book of Esther. Their object is to illustrate God's gracious hearing of prayers and His deliverance of His people, the Jews, from the grasp of gentiles.

Book of the Wisdom of Solomon. Written in praise of "wisdom" and in condemnation of those who willfully rejected her, the Book of the Wisdom of Solomon purports to be King Solomon's address to the kings and rulers of the earth. Many scholars feel it is of first-century A.D. origin, in the Greek language. It shows traces of influence from Greek philosophy. The most famous passages are those containing the description of "the righteous man" (4:7–18) and the portrait of "wisdom" (chs. 7–9). The object of the book is to warn Alexandrian Jews against abandoning the religion of their fathers. This text teaches that the "wisdom" of the book of Proverbs, "the fear of the Lord," is the basis of all true happiness.

Wisdom of Jesus the Son of Sirach, or *Ecclesiasticus* (also known as Ben Sira). The only book in the Apocrypha to which the name of the author can be assigned is the Wisdom of Jesus the Son of Sirach, or Ecclesiasticus. In 50:27, he speaks of himself as "Jesus the son of Sirach of Jerusalem." We know nothing about him beyond what we learn in the prologue to the book. In style and character, the book resembles the canonical book of Proverbs. The greater part is occupied with questions of practical morality. Among its subjects are friendship, old age, women, avarice, health, wisdom, anger, and servants. The Song of Praise of the works of Creation (42:15–43:33) is a powerful and beautiful composition, and the eulogy of the nations' great men runs over the whole list of Old Testament heroes, the omission of Ezra, Daniel, and Mordecai being remarkable. The book was originally written in Hebrew and has come down to us in a Greek translation made by the author's grandson, who added a preface to it. This preface deserves special notice for its reference to the Jewish scriptures under the threefold title of "The Law, the Prophets, and the rest of the writings" (compare Luke 24:44). Some pages containing about twenty-three chapters in Hebrew were discovered at the Ben Ezra Synagogue in Old Cairo in 1896. The name *Ecclesiasticus* dates from the time of Cyprian, bishop of Carthage (A.D. 248–58). It has no connection with the Old Testament book of Ecclesiastes.

Book of Baruch. So-called because it purports to contain a work written by Baruch, the prophet, in Babylon, the book of Baruch takes readers to the fifth year after the destruction of Jerusalem by the Chaldeans. Most scholars believe that it was probably composed at a later date. Attached to the Book of Baruch is the Epistle of Jeremy, purporting to be a letter written by the prophet Jeremiah to the Jews who were being carried away captive to Babylon.

Song of the Three Children. The Song of the Three Children purports to be the song sung by Shadrach, Meshach, and Abednego (they are called Ananias, Azarias, and Misael in v. 66) when they were in the midst of the burning, fiery furnace.

History of Susanna. This is a story that describes how Daniel as a young man procured the vindication of Susanna from a shameful charge and won the condemnation of the two elders who had borne false witness against her.

History of Bel and the Dragon. In this short work, we find two more anecdotes related to Daniel. In the first, Daniel discovers for King Cyrus the frauds practiced by the priests of Bel in connection with the pretended banquets of that idol. In the second, we read the story of Daniel's destruction of the sacred dragon that was worshiped at Babylon. Both stories serve the purpose of bringing idolatry into ridicule.

Prayer of Manasses, King of Judah. For the most part, the

Prayer of Manasses, King of Judah, is a penitential prayer consisting of sentences and phrases taken from the canonical scriptures. There is little reason for the title that it bears.

First Book of Maccabees. The importance of the First Book of Maccabees for our knowledge of Jewish history in the second century B.C. can hardly be overstated (see chapter 4, "The Maccabean War"). It recounts with sharp detail the whole of the Maccabean movement from the accession of the Seleucid king Antiochus Epiphanes (175) to the death of Simon the Hasmonean (135). The chief divisions of this document from this stirring period are the persecution of Antiochus Epiphanes and the national rising led by the aged priest Mattathias, the heroic war of independence under the lead of Judas the Maccabee, and the recovery of religious freedom and Jewish political independence under Jonathan (160–143) and Simon (143–135).

Second Book of Maccabees. The Second Book of Maccabees deals with the history of the Jews during a fifteen-year span (175–160 B.C.) and therefore covers part of the period described in First Maccabees (see chapter 4, "The Maccabean War Breaks Out"). It is inferior to that book both in simplicity and in accuracy because legends are introduced with great freedom. However, this work strongly affirms the doctrine of the Resurrection and carries an appeal that Jews adopt the celebration of Hanukkah, a non-biblical festival that celebrates the rededication of the temple in 164 B.C.

History of the Apocrypha

The term *apocrypha* is technically a neuter plural adjective in Greek (its singular is *apocryphon*) that was made into a plural noun, much as we currently use the word *data*. Because the adjective *apocryphal* usually refers to some fictitious or unsubstantiated story, most people are wary about the contents of the Apocrypha. The general inaccessibility of these books has caused undue avoidance of the Apocrypha by many members of the Church of Jesus Christ.

Ironically, the term *apocrypha* originally carried the sense of "hidden" or "secret," indicating that some books were of such special and important status that it was unwise to make them available to the public at large. Later, the term, not the collection, took on a pejorative meaning when some early Christian fathers used it to refer to heretical books, those that were banned by the early Catholic Church. By the time of Jerome (A.D. 342–420), however, the term bore a neutral meaning, referring simply to those books found in the Septuagint (LXX), the Greek translation of the Old Testament, but not in the Hebrew canon. It is these extra texts that comprise the Apocrypha. Only later in Protestantism did the term begin to carry a negative connotation again. This time, however, it applied both to the fixed collection of Old Testament Apocrypha as well as other noncanonical texts in circulation.

The books of the Apocrypha are of Jewish origin, and they circulated in Palestine at the end of the Old Testament and the beginning of the New Testament periods. The original texts and subsequent early copies vanished in Palestine so that only Greek and Latin copies survived for more than a millennium. Except for the Wisdom of Jesus the Son of Sirach (see above), it was not until the important discoveries at Qumran between 1947 and 1956 near the Dead Sea that copies of some of the Apocrypha books were found in Hebrew or Aramaic. These early texts of the Apocrypha form part of the Dead Sea Scrolls.

For various reasons, and in some cases for unknown reasons, the books of the Apocrypha were not included in the Hebrew canon, established by the third century A.D. (The process had begun much earlier.) However, it would be incorrect to believe that some of the books of the Apocrypha were never considered as inspired or authoritative (canonical) by groups of Jews during this period. It appears that when these books, along with some pseudepigraphic texts (see below) were being composed, the Hebrew Old Testament remained fluid, at least among some segments of Jewish society.

Following the closing of the Hebrew canon, Jews generally did not take any special interest in these texts. It was not until the modern era that Jewish scholars began to study them for their own sake and for the important background they provide in understanding the period between the Old and New Testaments.

On the other hand, Christians have enjoyed a long and complex interaction with these books. When Jerome (A.D. 342–420) made his famous Latin translation of the Old Testament, completed in 384 and known as the Vulgate, he included these books, which he found in the Old Latin manuscripts and the Septuagint. However, he noted that he did not find these books in the Hebrew Bible. Jerome's translation and inclusion of these texts ensured that the books of the Apocrypha formed part of the Old Testament for the western Christian Church until the sixteenth century, the time of Martin Luther (1483–1546).

Like some others at the time, Luther felt that the Hebrew Bible reflected the true canon of Old Testament scripture, instead of the Latin Vulgate or the early Greek Septuagint. Additionally, when Luther's opponents quoted freely from the books of the Apocrypha to support such Roman Catholic doctrines as purgatory, prayers and masses in behalf of the dead, and the efficacy of good works for personal salvation, Martin Luther questioned the value of the Apocrypha and called them "uninspired." For him, it was imperative to determine which texts in the Vulgate were considered as authoritative in establishing doctrine and practice and which were not.

Luther and other Protestants reasoned that, since the books of the Apocrypha were not included in the Hebrew canon, they were spiritually inferior to the books of the Old Testament.

Protestants eventually took what might appear to be the next logical step, to physically separate these books from the Old Testament and form a third division of the Bible (the Old Testament, the Apocrypha, and the New Testament). By now, at least in Protestant circles, this collection of books became known as "*The* Apocrypha," distinguishing them from other known apocryphal works. The first Bible to publish these texts as a separate division or category was the Dutch language edition published in Antwerp in 1526.

When Luther completed his German translation of the Bible several years later in 1534, to the Apocrypha he added a preface: "The Apocrypha—that is, books which are not held equal to the Holy Scriptures, and yet are profitable and good to read." The practice of publishing the Apocrypha as a separate section in Protestant Bibles, with such a qualifying preface, continued well into the nineteenth century for many versions, but not all.

Miles Coverdale (1488–1568) printed the first English-language Bible in 1535. He followed the 1526 Dutch Bible and 1534 German Bible models by placing the Apocrypha in a section between the Old and New Testaments. When the King James Version was printed in 1611, however, the Apocrypha was printed without a preface. This was true of all subsequent editions of the KJV that included the Apocrypha.

During the intense counter-Reformation period, the Roman Catholic Church responded forcefully to Protestant attitudes toward the Apocrypha at the Council of Trent on 8 April 1546. The prelates attending this special church council stated that twelve of the fifteen works of the Apocrypha were, in fact, canonical (the Prayer of Manasseh and 1 and 2 Esdras were assigned to an appendix attached to the New Testament). This action officially made the books of the Apocrypha part of the Bible for Roman Catholics. In calling the twelve books of the Apocrypha deuterocanonical, Roman Catholics meant that, while they had been added to the canon later, they were nevertheless canonical in every sense of the word. From this time forward, Catholic usage of the term *apocrypha* came to refer to books of Jewish or Christian origin that are, or claim to be, from the biblical period but are not accepted as canonical by the Catholic Church (not the books of the Protestant Apocrypha). This often confuses people because Protestants and Catholics use the same term to refer to different texts.

Later, some Protestants took another pivotal step when they began publishing Bibles without the Apocrypha altogether. Over a long period of time and in diverse locations, Protestants debated about whether they should include the Apocrypha with the Bible. This debate was heated and divisive because some Protestants, as was the case with the Church of England for a period, punished printers who did not include the Apocrypha while other churches encouraged the elimination of the Apocrypha from printed Bibles.

Eventually, the famous and influential British and Foreign Bible Society in London announced in 1827 that it would no longer print the Apocrypha with the Bible and set a policy of withholding financial help to groups that did not follow their lead. Other organizations soon followed, including the American Bible Society, making it difficult to obtain a copy of the Apocrypha by the second half of the nineteenth century.

Despite changing attitudes toward the Apocrypha during the past five centuries, it has had a tremendous influence upon western literature, music, and art. For instance, the Second Book of Esdras provided Christopher Columbus (1451–1506) a text to convince the king and queen of Spain to provide him the financial help necessary to make his voyage of discovery in 1492. Moreover, the Apocrypha has given us several popular names, including Susannah (from which we get Susan, Susie, and so on). Finally, and probably most important, the Apocrypha offers a window onto the period connecting the worlds of the Old and New Testaments, helping bridge the gap between the two records.

Pseudepigrapha

As noted above, Protestants and Latter-day Saints consider the Apocrypha to be a fixed number of texts originally found in the Greek Septuagint, but not in the Hebrew Bible, transmitted through the Latin Vulgate to the English-language Bibles, including the 1828 Phinney Bible used by Joseph Smith. But this does not exhaust the matter.

Another group of texts, often identified as the Pseudepigrapha, stand outside the Apocrypha. Their designation as *Pseudepigrapha* is a modern invention. The Pseudepigrapha covers a wide range of texts representing a variety of ideas, literary genres, and styles as diverse as the Bible itself. Most important, there is no scholarly agreement upon which text should or should not be considered as part of this collection. Thus, the Pseudepigrapha is neither fixed nor canonical in any sense. From a Latter-day Saint perspective, our approach to these various texts should probably be guided by the same inspired instruction regarding the Apocrypha as the Lord outlines in Doctrine and Covenants 91.

The Greek term *pseudepigrapha* means "falsely attributed writings" and, like the term *apocrypha*, has various and often conflicting meanings. In our discussion, we use the term to refer to a modern collection of ancient texts generally dating from about 250 B.C. to A.D. 200. Scholars still argue about the exact content of this modern category.

Many of these texts were compiled or composed by Jews, some of whom probably believed they were recording the inspired word of God. A few others were compiled or composed by Christians who relied heavily upon Jewish sources, including oral and written traditions predating the destruction of Jerusalem in A.D. 70. All of them are influenced by the Old

Testament to some degree. And while in many cases they have come down to us under the names of ancient patriarchs and prophets, most of them were probably composed or compiled during the period noted above. Many scholars agree that some of the Pseudepigrapha are not pseudepigraphic. But even those texts that were purposely or accidentally attributed (falsely) to Old Testament personalities sometimes contain much older authentic material, dating from the Old Testament period. We think, for example, of parts of the Testament of Levi and the Testament of Joseph.

Like the Apocrypha, the Pseudepigrapha dates from the period when the Old Testament canon was still fluid and suggests that, for some Jews and certainly for some Christians, the texts were considered as inspired as the books of the Bible.

Apparently, the term *pseudepigrapha* was first used by the Christian author Sedation in the late second century to refer to New Testament period texts with false authorship attributions. The first attempt to collect pseudepigraphical material in an English translation was R. H. Charles's two-volume work, *The Apocrypha and Pseudepigrapha of the Old Testament*, published in 1913. Some seventy years later, James H. Charlesworth expanded Charles's classic work with another English translation in two volumes entitled *The Old Testament Pseudepigrapha.* This work contained fifty-two writings together with a long supplement and was released in 1983 and 1985.

Christians seem to have been more interested in these texts than their Jewish neighbors. Christians continued reading and quoting from the texts long after the Jewish community completely lost them. Ironically, these Jewish texts were preserved and transmitted mainly by Christians. While certainly not the only reason, the fact that the New Testament book of Jude quotes from the text now known as First Enoch (see Jude 1:14–15) and refers to a story from the Assumption of Moses, another pseudepigraphic text (see Jude 1:9–10), may suggest an early interest in these works by Christians that continued much longer in their circles than in Jewish ones.

In recent times, there has been a surge of interest in these books among scholars, partly because of the discovery of more and more ancient texts, including the Dead Sea Scrolls. Like the Apocrypha, texts that form part of the modern collection of the Pseudepigrapha were found in the caves at Qumran, including First Enoch, Jubilees, and the Testaments of the Twelve Patriarchs. Additional texts, unknown to scholars before their discovery at Qumran, were also found, including those associated with the life and ministry of Daniel, David, Ezekiel, Jacob, Jeremiah, Joseph, Levi, Naphtali, Noah, and Samuel.

To a limited degree, Latter-day Saints continue to be fascinated by these texts, particularly as a result of the research and publications of Hugh Nibley and others, as they demonstrate the diversity and richness of the Jewish and Christian traditions in antiquity beyond what has been preserved in the Old and New Testaments. While we must refrain from attempts to "prove that the Church is true" from these ancient texts (such attempts often fail when we are confronted by passages within the same texts that contradict modern prophetic teachings and practices in the Church), we can certainly benefit from their study because they reveal a world almost forgotten by formative Judaism and Christianity. And in cases where the texts contain things "that are true," we can enrich our understanding of the people and places made holy by the presence of God's prophets, teachers, and His Only Begotten Son so that we, through study, faith, and the Holy Spirit, "shall obtain benefit therefrom" (see D&C 91:5).

CONCLUSION

Both the fixed collection of books identified as the Apocrypha and the growing collection of texts identified as the Pseudepigrapha provide a real link between the Old and New

Testament worlds and, in some cases, offer overlapping views of people, places, and events during this most important period. Instead of a "dark age" between the Old and New Testaments, the Apocrypha and Pseudepigrapha show us a period of intense turmoil and rich religious development. These sources demonstrate that, despite successive conquests by Persians, Greeks, and Romans, the Jews of Palestine continued to live their religion and died to defend it. Nevertheless, these texts also reveal the conflict and struggle among Jews to define their self-understanding and the role of God in their lives.

For Further Reading

R. H. Charles, ed., *Apocrypha and Pseudepigrapha of the Old Testaments*, 2 vols. (New York: Oxford University Press, 1913).

James H. Charlesworth, ed., *The Old Testament Pseudepigrapha*, 2 vols. (Garden City, New York: Doubleday, 1983, 1985).

David Noel Freedman et al., eds., *The Anchor Bible Dictionary* (New York: Doubleday, 1902), s.v. "Apocrypha" and "Pseudepigrapha."

C. Wilfred Griggs, ed., *Apocryphal Writings and the Latter-day Saints* (Provo, Utah: Brigham Young University Religious Studies Center, 1986).

Edgar Hennecke and Wilhelm Schneemelcher, eds., *New Testament Apocrypha*, 2 vols. (Philadelphia: Westminster Press, 1963, 1965).

Kent P. Jackson, "Joseph Smith's Cooperstown Bible: The Historical Context of the Bible Used in the Joseph Smith Translation," *BYU Studies* 40, no. 1 (2001): 41–70.

Bruce M. Metzger, ed., *The Apocrypha* (New York: Oxford University Press, 1977).

———, *An Introduction to The Apocrypha* (New York: Oxford University Press, 1963).

R. J. Zwi Werblowsky and Geoffrey Wigoder, eds., *The Oxford Dictionary of the Jewish Religion* (New York: Oxford, 1997), s.v. "Apocrypha and Pseudepigrapha."

CHAPTER 11

PROPHECY AND APOCALYPTICISM

Malachi stood up from his seat. He had been sitting a long time. His faithful scribe was writing the last few words that the prophet had dictated. Malachi himself was surprised at the depth of the spiritual impressions that had come to him. The Lord was obviously concerned with the state of current affairs among His covenant people. That concern had manifest itself in the warnings and accompanying promises about hypocrisy at the temple and about tithing. But what Malachi had not expected were utterances about the far-off future—prophecies of the coming of the Messiah as the Lord's messenger and of the last days. It was more than a curiosity for him that he felt inspired to mention Elijah in connection with children and fathers, for, as he knew from the old records preserved among his people, those records did not mention anything about Elijah's family, either parents, wife, or children. But Malachi knew he had been inspired to dictate those words about Elijah and the tying together of families. What he did not yet know was that he would be the last to receive prophetic inspiration until the coming of a messenger to God's temple four hundred years hence, a messenger of whom he had just learned.

The successful Babylonian attack on Jerusalem in 587 B.C. had left a gaping hole in the minds and hearts of those who survived. War always does, especially when it results in utter defeat. We can almost hear survivors asking, "Has not God promised through His law and His prophets that Jerusalem would be His shining light and that He would hang His lamp in the temple? Did not those promises mean that God would protect and shelter His holy city and His people? What has gone wrong?" More fundamentally, people asked, "Is God really there? And if He is really there, is He powerless to stop ruthless kings such as Nebuchadnezzar who command their soldiers to slaughter, destroy, and pillage?"

Prophecy

It is a matter of record that God had tried to forewarn His people of an impending doom. More than a hundred years before, Isaiah had warned the "house of Jacob . . . which swear by the name of the Lord . . . but not in truth, not in righteousness" that they ran a calamitous risk because, he said, "Thou art obstinate" (Isaiah 48:1, 4). "There is no peace," he declared, "unto the wicked" (48:22). God knew that a bleak day would arrive when His people would say, "The Lord hath forsaken me, and my Lord hath forgotten me" (49:14). For the exiles, that day had come.

A few decades before Nebuchadnezzar's arrival, Jeremiah had even been more specific. Because the people of Judah were "not valiant for the truth" and because they proceeded "from evil to evil," God would "make Jerusalem heaps . . . and . . . the cities of Judah desolate." Moreover, God forewarned that He would "scatter them also among the heathen . . . and . . . send a sword after them" (Jeremiah 9:3, 11, 16). Since the day of the city's demise at the hands of the Babylonian soldiers, life had completely changed.

Of course, God had promised through both Isaiah and Jeremiah that better days would eventually come. For example, Isaiah wrote about the exiles, "Go ye forth of Babylon, flee ye from the Chaldeans, . . . say ye, The Lord hath redeemed his servant Jacob. And . . . he led them through the deserts" (Isaiah 48:20–21). Through Jeremiah, God declared, "Behold, the days come, saith the Lord, that I will make a new covenant with the house of Israel . . . and I will bring them again unto this place. . . . And I will make an everlasting covenant with them, that I will not turn away from them" (Jeremiah 31:31; 32:37, 40).

Naturally, the spirit of prophecy did not end with Jeremiah—and his contemporaries—who had warned about the fall of Jerusalem. We know that this spirit continued after the return of the exiles from Babylonia. For in 520 B.C., Haggai pled in the name of God that people in Jerusalem rebuild the temple. They had reinhabited the city almost twenty years previously but had been content to rebuild their own homes while letting the temple "lie waste" (Haggai 1:4). The prophet revealed that, because of this neglect, people "have sown much, and bring in little." What is more, God had "called for a drought upon the land, . . . and upon that which the ground bringeth forth" (1:6, 11). Quoting God's words, Haggai prophesied that there was a simple solution to citizens' troubles: "Thus saith the Lord of hosts; Consider your ways. Go up to the mountain, and bring wood, and build the house [the temple]; and I will take pleasure in it" (1:7–8).

A year or so later, in 519, God moved Zechariah to utter a series of prophecies that pointed to the coming Messiah. For instance, we think of Zechariah's words about the Messiah-King "riding upon an ass" into Jerusalem (Zechariah 9:9; Matthew 21:1–7). What was different was a series of visions, much like those of the earlier Ezekiel and Daniel, wherein Zechariah beheld symbolic scenes that an angel had to explain because of their unusual character (Zechariah 1–6). In these visions, many scholars and students have detected what they now call "apocalypticism," which we explain below.

We know of one more Old Testament prophet whom God inspired about 450 B.C. His name was Malachi, the same whose book the Risen Savior chose to quote from to an audience of Israelites in the New World (see 3 Nephi 24–25). Malachi was a rough contemporary of Nehemiah and Ezra. Besides admonitions about a dulling laxity at the temple and an ungrateful refusal to pay tithes, as well as promises of Elijah's coming, Malachi shows knowledge of a group who "feared the Lord" and had evidently banded together for spiritual support (see Malachi 3:16–18). This group may have anticipated those who would arise later and attempt to live the Mosaic law more devotedly than others in their society. Malachi's prophecies are best known, of course, for God's pledge to send "Elijah the prophet before the coming of the great and dreadful day of the Lord" to "turn the heart of the fathers to the children," and vice-versa, so that God would not "smite the earth with a curse" (4:5–6). After Malachi, there was a prophetic silence. What took its place?

Interpretation

From all appearances, a number of individuals and movements sought to fill the silence. While we do not follow a chronological sequence here, we first note that a spirit of rationalism grew up. It was not the type of appeal to reason seen in the Greek world that, in time, discounted God and His influence. Instead, it was an attempt to make sense out of the world in light of a close, reasoned examination of the law of Moses. During the intertestamental period, a feeling began to blossom that almost any person could study and come to understand the Law. In the era before the fall of Jerusalem, teaching the Law had been the responsibility of the priests and Levites (Deuteronomy 33:10). Now a cadre of scribes rose up—men who wanted to understand and teach the Law.

As we note in the following chapter, one of the titles that Ezra carried, "the scribe," was a badge of honor and a designation of sacred trust. To be sure, Ezra was also a priest, and he thus combined two functions in his role as reformer. But after Ezra had introduced his reforms on the basis of a careful reading of the Mosaic law, someone after him had to preserve the Law in its written form and to interpret it, as Ezra had. Since there were no prophets to undertake either of these tasks, they were taken up by people who attempted to understand the world and how it affected people's lives. They evidently tried to apply common sense to the stipulations of the Law so that it became a helpful tool for the ordinary person. We suspect that, like most groups who were just starting, the scribes drew suspicion upon themselves because they were pushing into an area that had once been the sole possession of Levites and priests. Seen from this angle, theirs was a bold move. We further suspect that, in time, they began to appear less like nonconformists and more like responsible citizens. After all, as the spirit of prophecy began to diminish after the exile, descending on only three known prophets, there was a need for someone to step in and offer social guidance on the only basis that was left, the Mosaic law. The scribes filled this need. But they were not alone.

It seems reasonable that the learned voice of the scribes would be heard mainly in times of relative tranquillity when the law of Moses could be applied straightforwardly to daily concerns of the former exiles, to domestic and agricultural and ritual matters. In contrast, we ask, what sorts of voices would people want to hear in crises when they faced, say, the horrors of war or the miseries brought on by despotism? The answer to that question lies at the base of most studies on apocalypticism. Primarily, the people needed voices of comfort, for their lives had been shattered. They desperately needed someone to offer assurances that God was still in charge and would bring events to His own appointed end. Such assurances would bring hope that God had a plan, no matter how stormy events might become, and that He would carry it out.

APOCALYPTICISM

The modern term *apocalypticism* (there seems to have been no ancient term to describe this phenomenon) derives from the opening of the book of Revelation. There we read, "The Revelation of Jesus Christ, which God gave unto him" (Revelation 1:1). The Greek word translated "Revelation" in this line is *apokalypsis*. It means literally an "off-covering," that is, the removing of a covering to reveal what is hidden or unknown. Thus, apocalypticism is a form of revelation. This quotation from the book of Revelation also tells us that such revelation came from God Himself through Jesus Christ, underscoring its thoroughly divine origin and transmission. In addition, as this verse also tells us, one major purpose of the disclosure is "to shew unto [Jesus'] servants things which must shortly come to pass" (1:1). This kind of revelation uncovers the future, letting its recipients know of coming events and of God's plans to bring about His aims within them. Hence, for believers, such a disclosure offers the hope that God is in charge and will watch over His people, no matter what.

Concerning written forms of apocalypticism, the literature tied to this phenomenon exhibits links to scripture, even though its heyday fell chiefly during and after the intertestamental period. On the basis of what a variety of sources preserves, there are a few common characteristics of apocalypticism. We have already touched on several—those of comfort, hope, and God's plan. Let us turn to other main features.

Vision

As in the case of the early chapters in the book of Zechariah, which include elements of apocalypticism, the prophet or seer receives divine information in a dream or vision. Of course, such visions often include spoken instructions. But the main part of the experience is visual. Although some images are familiar to the recipient, many are unfamiliar because they are highly symbolic or portray events that have not yet occurred. We immediately think of Nephi's vision filled with images he did not fully understand. As a result, he needed help in comprehending what he was seeing; he needed a guide (1 Nephi 11–14).

Interpreting Angel

One common characteristic of apocalyptic visions is an accompanying angel who helps the seer to understand. The first vision of Zechariah makes this point. When the prophet beheld "a man riding upon a red horse, and he stood among the myrtle trees" with other horses, Zechariah asked, "What are these? And the angel that talked with me said unto me, I will shew thee what these be" (Zechariah 1:8–9). Perhaps notably, the prophet Daniel seems not to have needed an angelic guide for his visions. His book, as will become clear, also exhibits links to apocalypticism. But in a work tied to Enoch, which was composed in its current form by the first century A.D. but whose parts go back much earlier in time, a number of angels accompany Enoch in a series of visions. In one instance, Enoch asks about chains that he sees manufactured in a fiery valley: "I asked the angel of peace who went with me, saying: 'For whom are these chains being prepared?' And he said unto me: 'These are being prepared for the hosts of Azâzêl [Satan], so that they may take them and cast them into the abyss of complete condemnation" (1 Enoch 54:4–5).

Ecstasy

In the context of apocalypticism, the term *ecstasy* refers to an out-of-body experience or to a change of location so that the vision might occur. We know of such instances from scripture, as with the Apostle Paul and with the Savior's disciples in the New World (2 Corinthians 12:2–3; 3 Nephi 28:15). In the book of Revelation, John simply reports that he was "in the spirit," a phrase that carries the same meaning (Revelation 1:10; 4:2; etc.). Enoch "was high and lifted up, even in the bosom of the Father" for his vision, and Nephi found himself on "an exceedingly high mountain, which [he] never had before seen" (Moses 7:24; 1 Nephi 11:1). Similarly, in an apocalyptic text that was composed in its final form in the second century B.C. but that rests on earlier accounts we believe to be authentic, Levi records that in a dream he was on "a high mountain" when "the heavens were opened, and an angel of God said unto [him], Levi, enter. And [he] entered from the first heaven" (Testament of Levi 2:5–7). The author of Second Baruch, a Syriac text dating to the first century A.D. but preserving earlier traditions, describes himself "standing upon Mount Zion" near Jerusalem when "a voice came from the [celestial] height and said unto [him], 'Stand upon thy feet, Baruch, and hear the word of the mighty God'" (2 Baruch 13:1–2). After Baruch obediently arose and proved his loyalty by further actions, a series of visions unfolded to him (22:1; 36:1; 53:1; 55:3).

SECRECY

The information that apocalypses impart is often termed "hidden" or "secret." Because of the spiritually sensitive nature of divine communications, the recipient receives instructions either to seal the record of the information—almost always the seer keeps a record—or to reveal it only to the trustworthy. The example of the Brother of Jared illustrates this point: "The Lord said unto him: Write these things and seal them up; and I will show them in mine own due time unto the children of men. . . . And . . . they were forbidden to come unto the children of men" (Ether 3:27; 4:1). We read a similar set of instructions in Second Esdras, a work composed in Hebrew about A.D. 100 but whose roots reach back into the intertestamental period. The accompanying messenger says to Esdras—or Ezra—about his vision, "Thou alone hast been found worthy to learn this mystery of the Most High—Therefore write all these things that thou hast seen in a book, and put them in a secret place; and thou shalt teach them to the wise of the people, whose hearts thou knowest are able to comprehend and keep these mysteries" (2 Esdras 12:36–38). At times, the sacred nature of the dream or vision is self-evident, and the seer therefore refuses to share its content, as we read in the Testament of Levi: "I hid this [dream] . . . in my heart, and told it not to any man on earth" (Testament of Levi 8:19).

The End of Time

The history of the earth is divided into distinct eras, one that concerns the earth's temporal history and one that deals with the world to come. This final era is often called the *eschaton*, a Greek term that means "last." God is in charge of both ages. The current period is full of trials and wickedness, and Satan seemingly possesses unlimited power. In contrast, God ushers in the age to come wherein the faithful, those who have overcome the world, become part of His kingdom. It is the promise of this future world that offers believers the hope that sustains them through persecutions and allows them to face even death. That God is in charge of both eras, and will triumph in the end, is shown in a vivid dream of King Nebuchadnezzar, who saw "a stone [that] was cut out without hands." In the king's dream, this divinely cut stone then "smote the image [of worldly kingdoms] upon his feet . . . and brake them to pieces" (Daniel 2:34). Moreover, the stone, which represents God's kingdom, "shall never be destroyed: and . . . it shall break in pieces and consume all these kingdoms, and it shall stand for ever" (2:44). Here we see plainly the two eras as well as God's control over both of them. In a similar vein, to the guiding angel of his visions, Esdras declares prophetically about the end of this world that "the age which is not yet awake shall be roused, and that which is corruptible shall perish" (2 Esdras 7:31). Likewise, the angel who accompanies Enoch in his vision quotes God as saying, "I will transform the heaven and make it an eternal blessing. . . . And I will transform the earth. . . . And I will cause Mine elect ones to dwell upon it: But the sinners and evil-doers shall not set foot thereon" (1 Enoch 45:4–5). All such views of the end of time offer to believers the comforting assurance that God is ultimately in control.

Essene Hopes

Among those who clung to the hope that apocalyptic works offered, we single out the Essenes of Qumran. Their distant origins began in the terrors of the severe crisis of Hellenism that precipitated the Maccabean War. Even after this war that liberated the temple, struggles with the Seleucid Greeks continued. The dark mists of Hellenism must have seemed to create a permanently cloudy day. Then, when the Hasmoneans finally broke the country free of Seleucid interference, the Hasmoneans showed themselves to be little better than the former masters, visiting war and destruction on neighboring tribes and countries and squabbling endlessly among themselves over position and power. When the Romans' mighty grip squeezed the life out of the Hasmoneans' old family quarrels, the new Roman representatives subtly discolored temple and religious affairs, adding burdens of taxation and fostering a wealthy class that was ceaselessly seeking favors from the new overlords. None of this stream of events could have seemed hopeful to the monks at Qumran. To them, the priests and officials of Jerusalem seemed hopelessly corrupt. The course of events in their minds did not exhibit a pattern of ups and downs but instead was plunging into an ever-deeper abyss of spiritual and moral depravity. As a result, one of the few shafts of light to penetrate the unrelieved gloom came from the pages of apocalyptic books. So the Essenes dedicated themselves in part to preserving and recopying such works. Multiple copies of the books of Daniel and First Enoch among the Dead Sea Scrolls attest to this fact.

Of the Essenes' own compositions, no recovered text from the Dead Sea constitutes an apocalypse, complete with a vision or the like. But several of their compositions breathe the air of apocalypticism. For instance, the *War Scroll* (1QM) sets out the rules for the final military engagement between the sons of light and the sons of darkness, framing it as the last battle that will bring the final era, the age of wrath, to an end and usher in the reign of God. As an aid, during this war the heavenly hosts are to mingle with the sons of light, the earthly combatants. According to the *Community Rule* (1QS), the sons of light—the Essenes—saw themselves as living in a world that was constantly contested by the "Prince of Light" and the "Angel of Darkness." For Essenes, only the intervention of God, introducing a new age, would overcome falsehood and bring forth righteousness. Though we could cite further examples, it is sufficient to point out that one of the major underpinnings of Essene life, besides a strict adherence to Mosaic law, was the hope promised through apocalypticism.

Ancient Apocalypticism

Naturally, Daniel and Zechariah and Nephi were not the first prophets to see visions adorned with symbols or filled with information about the future. We mention a few earlier prophetic accounts to illustrate that the visions characterizing apocalypticism, a fixture of the intertestamental period, also found a place in much-earlier sacred literature. For example, Enoch saw not only the weeping of God but also the days of the Messiah and the end of time (Moses 7:27–29, 47, 66–67). Joseph of Egypt beheld the coming of Moses, who appeared just a few generations later than himself, and then "saw [Lehi's] day." In a series of divine disclosures, Joseph next learned about "a choice seer" whom God would raise up "in the latter days" to restore "the knowledge of [God's] covenants" (2 Nephi 3:4–21). In his turn, Moses beheld alternatively in vision both God and

Satan as well as "the world and the ends thereof" (Moses 1:2, 8, 12–14, 27–29). We could discuss others, such as the Brother of Jared, the youthful Solomon, and Isaiah (Ether 3:11–16; 1 Kings 3:5–15; 2 Nephi 11:2; Isaiah 6:1). But we have made the point.

A handy list of Old Testament passages that share some or most of the apocalyptic characteristics that we have noted includes the following:

Isaiah 24–27 and 60–63. The prophet predicts events at the end of time when the wicked will suffer justice and those who have looked for God's delivering hand will see it in His judgment and in the resurrection; Jerusalem shall be adorned again, and the restoration of all shall take place.

1 Nephi 11–14. The vision opens with the Messiah, "the Lamb of God," and His virgin mother and closes with the vanquishing of the mother of harlots and her evil empire; along the way, Nephi beholds the rise and fall of nations, including the one that grows out of his own descendants.

Ezekiel 40–48. Ezekiel views the heavenly temple of the last days and learns of the rites that authorized priests will perform within its walls; he also beholds the healing of the salty Dead Sea and witnesses his people living in peace with others in the land.

Daniel 2 and 7. The visions include both the establishment of the kingdom of God in the last days, "a stone [that] was cut out without hands" (Daniel 2:34), and the destruction of wickedness before the coming of "the Ancient of days" and "the Son of man" during the distant millennium (7:9, 13).

Zechariah 1–6 and 9–14. The people of Zechariah's society, including the high priest Joshua and the governor Zerubbabel, represent individuals of the last days who will lead out in bringing about the victory of righteousness over evil and the restoration of their people to their proper inheritance; the Messiah will return to the Mount of Olives and heal His people.

If we are to trust the majority of modern studies about

apocalypticism, all of these segments of scripture arose because of some crisis in Israelite society. Therefore, there existed a need to offer the comforting assurance that God was still in charge and was caring for his faithful flock. In part, that may be true. In the case of Nephi, his family was fleeing just before God brought down the Babylonian hammer on Jerusalem. In the cases of Ezekiel and Daniel, Nephi's contemporaries who had been taken to Babylonia as hostages, the hammer had already fallen, and the kingdom of Judah had suffered its fatal blow. But the matter is not so clear for Isaiah and Zechariah. Their words about the future of their people and the future acts of God are pure prophecy and seem independent of any perceived crisis in their societies. It is possible, of course, that works such as First Enoch and Fourth Esdras reached back to earlier heroes and the assurances embedded in their visionary experiences because of severe difficulties, such as the Maccabean War. But we go too far if we suggest that apocalyptic expressions arose solely from social and emotional needs connected with national or spiritual crises.

Conclusion

It is important to notice that, following the intertestamental period, Jesus Himself appealed to expressions that are at home in apocalypticism. Because these expressions were familiar to His audience from an earlier age, they helped Him communicate more effectively with His hearers and add emphasis to His teachings. Besides the Revelation of John, one of the most important New Testament passages that deals with the same kinds of topics is Matthew 24, Jesus' sermon to the trusted members of the Twelve on the Mount of Olives. This sermon is preserved among several sources—Matthew 24, Joseph Smith—Matthew, and Doctrine and Covenants 45:16–59. In it, Jesus focuses not only on the historic period immediately following His resurrection but more especially on events at the end of time, including "the Son of man coming in the clouds of heaven with power and great glory" (Matthew 24:30). Perhaps less noticeably but certainly just as important are Jesus' statements throughout the Gospels wherein He identifies Himself with the Son of Man of earlier apocalyptic expectation. For instance, concerning His appearance at the end of time, He warned, "Be ye therefore ready also: for the Son of man cometh at an hour when ye think not" (Luke 12:40). In addition, His prophecies that He would arrive suddenly and unexpectedly at the end of time "as the lightning" or as the floods "in the days of Noe [Noah]" connect with the apocalypticism of an earlier day (Luke 17:24, 26). However, it is not merely an issue of unexpected suddenness in these examples but also a matter of a complete reorientation on this earth when its inhabitants move from this age to the age to come.

Outside of such works as First Enoch and Second Esdras, the largest and most comprehensive apocalyptic work is the book of Revelation. This text alone tells us that the Apostles received inspiration in the form of apocalypticism. This work, of course, focused on the future, on "things which must shortly come to pass" (Revelation 1:1). Because the book of Revelation seems to be at least partly a critique of the Roman regime at the time, the question arises whether such works were generally critical of governments under which Jewish people lived, whether foreign, as the Seleucid Greeks, or native, such as the Hasmonean priest-kings. We cannot arrive at a definitive answer. Often, the circumstances that surrounded the final composition of an apocalyptic work remain unknown. And though apocalypticism is critical of earthly systems that coddle wickedness, this alone does not mean that all apocalyptic works are always radical in some way. On the contrary, their insistence on God's victory at the end of time is a positive affirmation that the created order will end up in the place where God intends it to go. There is reason to hope and, ultimately, to rejoice in God's plan for this earth. This is the message of apocalypticism.

For Further Reading

R. H. Charles, ed., *The Apocrypha and Pseudepigrapha of the Old Testament*, 2 vols. (Oxford: Oxford University Press, 1913), vol. 2.

James H. Charlesworth, ed., *The Old Testament Pseudepigrapha*, 2 vols. (New York: Doubleday, 1983, 1985), vol. 1.

Keith Crim et al., eds., *The Interpreter's Dictionary of the Bible*, suppl. vol. (Nashville: Abingdon Press, 1976), s.v. "Apocalypticism."

Florentino García-Martínez, *The Dead Sea Scrolls Translated*, 2d ed. (Leiden: E. J. Brill, 1996).

C. Wilfred Griggs, ed., *Apocryphal Writings and the Latter-day Saints* (Provo, Utah: Brigham Young University Religious Studies Center, 1986).

Edgar Hennecke and Wilhelm Schneemelcher, eds., *New Testament Apocrypha*, 2 vols. (Philadelphia: Westminster Press, 1963, 1965), 2:581–600.

Daniel H. Ludlow et al., eds., *The Encyclopedia of Mormonism*, 5 vols. (New York: Macmillan, 1992), s.v. "Apocalyptic Texts," "Prophecy," "Prophecy in Biblical Times," "Scripture: Scriptures," "Seer."

Geza Vermes, *The Dead Sea Scrolls in English*, 4th ed. (New York: Penguin Books, 1995).

Part 3

The Faithful

CHAPTER 12

Priests, Levites, and Scribes

King Herod sat listening to the high priest whine about the difficulty of functioning in his office without more help from the royal house. The man was named Ananel, and he came from Babylon. Herod had appointed him only two years before. Ungraciously, the priests in Jerusalem had objected to the appointment of this man. Then a thought occurred to Herod, a wonderful thought that would allow him to escape the seemingly endless run of troubles that he faced from the priests. He had been looking for a way to control them because, more than any other group of people in his Jewish kingdom, they were a threat to him. Yes, now he knew what he would do. He would take custody of the ceremonial clothing in which the high priest was always parading around the temple grounds. Herod knew the clothing was essential to the high priest's performance of ceremonies during the important holy days of the calendar. But if he held these garments in his chambers between those events, where the high priest could not don them at any other time, he could hold the high priest and the others in check. Looking directly at Ananel, the king commanded, "Take off your robe."

From the days of the decree of King Cyrus of Persia (538 B.C.), priests and Levites stood at the top of the governing structure of life in the land of Judah. This situation arose because the Jerusalem temple and its altar formed the center of people's lives. More than any other institution that tied back to the period before the exile in Babylon, the temple represented continuity with the Israelites' past, a visible symbol that their God had not completely forsaken them. It is to the credit of the priests and Levites that they kept the sacred ceremonies and sacred calendar largely intact from the period before the exile to the era that followed. This would not be the case, of course, after the fall of the temple to the Romans in A.D. 70. The permanent loss of the temple meant not only that sacrificial worship came to a halt but also that the priests and Levites ceased to perform their services for fellow worshipers. As a matter of record, much of what we know about sacrificial practices and special holidays during the intertestamental period comes to us from other Jewish literature and the Mishnah (ca. A.D. 200).

Even before the exiles returned following Cyrus' edict of 538 B.C., evidence from the Bible indicates that the altar of the broken temple was in use among the ruins of the city (see Jeremiah 41:5), for the Babylonian army had not captured and deported all the people in the countryside or those who fled elsewhere for safety (Jeremiah 40:7, 11–12). In this light, it is reasonable to assume that Levites and perhaps a few priests remained behind to officiate at the now-humbled site of Solomon's altar. But when a group of exiled priests and Levites returned, the situation changed.

As we might expect, the chief issue concerned genealogy. After all, if a man was not a member of either the tribe of Levi or the family of Aaron, he could not function in any capacity in the temple (see Leviticus 8; also Deuteronomy 10:8–9). The most sacred performances on behalf of fellow Israelites were literally in their hands, and their hands alone. Hence, those who claimed to be priests but could not prove their ancestry were "put from the priesthood" (Ezra 2:62). For the priests, ancestry had to run back to the sons of Aaron, and the high priest was himself to be a descendant of Aaron's oldest son, serving in his office for life. Since the days of King Solomon, a high priest named Zadok and his descendants had served as priests and high priests (1 Kings 1:38–39; 2:35). Zadok's genealogical descendants continued in temple service until the time of King Zedekiah, the last king of Judah, whereupon they were taken with others to Babylon. When Cyrus issued his edict, the person with the right to the office of high priest was a man named Jeshua, or Joshua, who returned to Jerusalem with the former exiles (Ezra 2:1–2, 36). Jeshua reestablished the priesthood line at the site of the old sanctuary, whose damaged altar was still standing. Because of his position, he was involved in rebuilding the altar and in the initial but failed effort to rebuild the temple itself (3:2, 8–13). Over time, Jeshua's descendants and others of the priests would come to play the most important roles in their society, not only as head of the temple but also as head of the local government under the supervision of the current, dominant power in the region.

One of Jeshua's most challenging tasks was to regularize temple services. Another important step was to reconstitute the former twenty-four courses of priests, each of which would serve at the temple twice a year (1 Chronicles 24). A person who would later be affected by this arrangement was Zacharias, father of John the Baptist and a member of the course of Abia, which, being the eighth course, served at the temple during the eighth and thirty-second weeks of each year (1 Chronicles 24:10; Luke 1:5). Evidently, Jeshua divided the members of the four returning priestly families into the required twenty-four courses for temple service, an organization that persisted into the New Testament period until the fall of the Jerusalem temple to the Romans in A.D. 70 (Ezra 2:36–39). In addition, he must have divided the returning Levites similarly (Ezra 2:40), for Levites assisted the priests in their semiannual rotations. The descendants of the "singers" and "porters" and "Nethinims," or servants who assisted the Levites (Ezra 2:41–43), would be joined to and identified with the Levites by the New Testament period.

So how did the priests, and particularly the high priest, come to play such a prominent role in the post-exilic era? The simplest answer comes in three parts. First, because the temple was the most important and enduring institution in the new Jewish society, its leaders and functionaries naturally came to play a leading role in the city. Second, the Persian office of governor of Judah did not continue. The first appointee was Sheshbazzar in 538 B.C., followed by Zerubbabel, who, after a gap, was succeeded by Nehemiah in 440 (Ezra 5:14; Haggai 1:1, 14; Nehemiah 2:5–9). There is no evidence that anyone succeeded Nehemiah. Third, the priests enjoyed a royal commission. When Cyrus announced his edict, he specifically said that returnees were to "build the house of the Lord God of Israel . . . which is in Jerusalem" (Ezra 1:3). Naturally, those who would take charge of "the house of the Lord God" were the priests. Making this status even firmer, Ezra "the priest" came to Jerusalem bearing a royal commission (Ezra 7:6, 11–26).

In light of these three observations, it becomes clear why priests rose to such a lofty prominence during the post-exilic age. There is a further point. During the earlier days of Moses, priests and Levites had been singled out as arbiters of disputes, as judges of crimes, and as teachers (Deuteronomy 21:5; 33:10). With the death of Nehemiah and thereby the effective loss of a governor who could stand as arbiter and judge, it was natural for the priests and Levites to take over old tasks that were theirs by scriptural injunction. In addition, as Ezra demonstrated in his role as both priest and royal scribe, priests were to appoint "magistrates and judges" as well as to "teach . . . them that know . . . not" (Ezra 7:25).

Our third point above, which has to do with royal commissioning, was a blessing for the priests and for the people they served. But eventually it became a curse. How so? During the period of the Persian empire and for much of the Hellenistic era that followed (538–168 B.C.), the priests and their associates functioned normally and without interference. The ready acceptance of their position in Judean society appears brightly in two stories that are apocryphal, at least in large measure. Even so, these stories underscore the status that the priests and Levites enjoyed for hundreds of years. The first has to do with the coming of Alexander the Great to Jerusalem. According to the story repeated by Josephus, when Alexander saw the priests and other temple officials coming out of the city to meet him, dressed as they were in white and gold and purple vestments, he dismounted and paid respect to the high priest (*Jewish Antiquities* 11.8.4–5). While almost no one takes this account seriously, it still underscores the point about the station of the priests and their colleagues in the Jewish society at the beginning of the Hellenistic age. The timing of the second narrative falls about fifty years later and concerns the appeal to the Jerusalem high priest by Ptolemy II, king of Egypt (285–246 B.C.), to send scholars to Alexandria who could translate the Old Testament from Hebrew into Greek. This story appears in a text known as the *Letter of Aristeas*. Admittedly, while the record exhibits legendary characteristics, it goes a long way in underlining the respect that the high priest typically drew to himself as the one who spoke on behalf of others in society, particularly the elite. This pair of stories contrasts sharply with what came next.

Beginning with the second century B.C., priests, and particularly the high priest, found themselves treated in a much less dignified manner. On the one hand, the treatment was partly the fault of individual priests. On the other, the political climate had changed. As noted earlier, in 198 B.C., Antiochus III wrested control of Palestine from the Ptolemies of Egypt, who had ruled that area for just over a century. Antiochus was the king of the Greek-oriented Seleucid empire and, by all accounts, was himself a decent ruler. But in 188 B.C., at a battle at Apamea, a town that lies in western Syria, the Romans defeated the army of Antiochus and put his people under heavy monthly tribute. Thereafter, the Seleucid rulers were desperate for cash. Beginning with Antiochus IV (175–163 B.C.), who was an enthusiast for Greek culture and religion but was in deep need of funds, the high priesthood went up for bid. In 174 B.C., while Onias III, the last of an unbroken succession of descendants of Zadok to serve as high priest, was out of town, Onias' brother Joshua, who preferred to be called Jason, promised King Antiochus money to make him the high priest in place of his brother. Antiochus agreed, and Onias had to remain in exile away from his beloved Jerusalem. The world of the priests had changed.

Jason was a thoroughgoing Hellenist who encouraged people in the city to adopt Greek ways. Almost overnight, people became for or against the high priest. Before that moment, they had faced the question of how much Greek culture they would allow into the city and into their institutions and lives. But now the issues were different. In the end, Jason fared no better that his brother Onias. In 171 B.C., a man named Menelaus outbid Jason for the job of high priest. The king deposed Jason and awarded the office to Menelaus, another enthusiast for Greek ways. In the person of Jason, people at least were served by a high priest of the family of Zadok. But Menelaus was not of that family and was even of a doubtful priestly lineage. The line of Zadok was broken. When Onias' son, Onias IV, saw that there was no hope to recover the office of high priest for his family, he went off to Egypt, where Ptolemy VI permitted him to establish a temple in Leontopolis, a city in the middle of the Nile Delta.

We have noticed before that perhaps the most crucial turn came in 168 B.C. Prior to that year, Menelaus had been guilty of looting treasures from the temple to pay off the promised bribe to King Antiochus. He had even helped Antiochus strip gold leafing from the facade of the temple. Then, in 168, Antiochus invaded Egypt, likely looking for sources of money with which to pay Rome. He was confronted there by a Roman official named Popilius Laenas, who ordered him out of the country. Popilius drew a circle in the dirt around Antiochus and told him that he had to "decide in there" whether he would withdraw. Rome was by this time consolidating its power in the eastern Mediterranean and was not humored by Antiochus' reckless actions in places valued by Rome such as Egypt, which was a major source for grain. On his part, Antiochus had spent a few years in Rome as a youth and knew the military might of this new power. He withdrew in shame. During his humiliating retreat, he learned that Jason had recaptured Jerusalem, forcing Menelaus out. It was more than Antiochus could bear. Returning home and reinforcing his army, his general Apollonius descended vengefully on Jerusalem the next year. Apollonius slaughtered citizens and desecrated the temple. He forced people to eat pork under penalty of death and installed different priests who offered pigs on the altar as sacrifices. The king withdrew the promises made by his father long ago, including the stipulation that the priests would not have to pay taxes. People seethed but could do nothing. Fortunately, a family of priests was willing to resist. But their resistance led to further changes.

The family of Mattathias, a priest, lived in the town of Modein, which lies west and north of Jerusalem on the way to Caesarea. When Seleucid soldiers showed up in their town and tried to force a man to offer a sacrifice of a swine, Mattathias killed the man and the commander of the soldiers and fled with his five sons (1 Maccabees 2:1–28). Thus began the Maccabean War, which took its name from Mattathias' third son, Judas Maccabee. In time, Judas became the leader of the insurrection and drove the Greeks out of much of the country. In December 164 B.C., the priests of Jerusalem rededicated the temple, establishing the festival of Hanukkah in the process. But the issue of who should serve as high priest was not yet settled. In fact, the one person who could trace his ancestry back to Zadok, Onias

IV, withdrew to Egypt. In 161 B.C., after a failed Seleucid attempt to regain Jerusalem, a man named Alcimus was appointed to serve as high priest. He was a compromise candidate whom both the Hellenists in the city and the nationalists who supported Judas Maccabee would accept. Though he was not of Zadok's family, he was a descendant of Aaron. His ascent to the position was a hopeful first step. Unfortunately, it would falter.

Alcimus died two years later. His allegiance to the Seleucids had stained his term of service, particularly his treachery in executing sixty people who had come to seek peace with his aid (1 Maccabees 7:12–18). The office went unfilled for the next seven years. By then, the Hasmonean family, the family of Judas and his brothers, held a firmer control on the countryside. Certain Seleucid Greeks were ready to deal. In a trade for support, Alexander Balas, then a pretender to the throne of the Seleucid kingdom, conferred the high priesthood on Jonathan, Judas Maccabee's successor and younger brother. At the Feast of Tabernacles in 152 B.C., Jonathan appeared in public wearing the garments of the high priest. That high and holy office had now come to one who was a member of the Jehoiarib course of priests (see 1 Chronicles 24:7). Jonathan was a descendant of Aaron but not of Zadok. What is more, his new office had come to him from a foreigner.

Jonathan died nine years later, in 143 B.C., and his older brother Simon succeeded him both as the leader of the nationalist party, which was almost the same as head of state, and as high priest. Jonathan had held the office until the end of his life, as high priests had done in previous eras. Simon would too. But Simon evidently sensed that receiving the high priesthood with the blessing of a foreign power was wrong. So after he had pushed out the Seleucid Greeks for good in 141, a popular gathering of his countrymen in September of the next year declared Simon "high priest forever" (1 Maccabees 14:41). The office of high priest was now securely within the Hasmonean family and, for the first time in centuries, had received the enthusiastic and sanctioning approval of the people of the land.

Here matters remained for the next sixty-five years. The senior member of the Hasmonean family would serve as both head of state and as high priest. Notably, beginning with Aristobulus (104–103 B.C.), the ruling member of the family took the title "king." The only change came during the reign of Alexandra Salome (76–67 B.C.), who, because she was ineligible to serve in a priesthood office, appointed her son Hyrcanus II as high priest, an office that he held until her death. When Salome died, Hyrcanus' younger brother Aristobulus II revolted and seized the high priesthood and kingship. With the ensuing civil strife, the office of high priest became the spoils of war, held by the brother who happened to control Jerusalem at the time. Aristobulus' moment in the sun came to a halt when Pompey captured the city in 63 B.C. and stripped him of both his kingship and his elevated rank as high priest. With Roman help, Hyrcanus now reacquired his priesthood position. Less than eighty years after Simon sought the approval of his people, the office once again became the gift of a foreign power, a fact underscored in 47 B.C. by Caesar's actions of reaffirming Hyrcanus in his high priestly role and conferring on him the title of ethnarch. But Hyrcanus and his family would never regain the title "king."

Events of 40 B.C. did not help the dignity of the priests. The Parthians, the new power in the East, invaded Palestine and placed the son of Aristobulus II, a man named Antigonus, on the throne of Judea and conferred on him the office of high priest. Antigonus thereupon made certain that his aging uncle Hyrcanus would never officiate in the temple again. He mutilated Hyrcanus' ears, knowing the biblical regulation that a priest must be physically unblemished to serve (Leviticus 21:16–24). The Parthians also narrowly missed capturing

Herod, whose father and older brother had been supporters of Hyrcanus. Herod fled to Rome, where he was nominated and confirmed by the Senate as the new client-king of Palestine. He would have to force out the Parthians; he was equal to the task. When he finally wrested control of Jerusalem in 37 B.C., he brought the priests under his control and changed fundamental aspects of the high priesthood.

In a surprising twist, Herod reached outside the priesthood ranks of Jerusalem and appointed a Babylonian named Ananel to be the high priest. Herod's mother-in-law, Alexandra, who was herself of the Hasmonean family, disapproved and urged her son-in-law to appoint her young son Aristobulus to the high priesthood. Herod deposed Ananel after two years and installed his seventeen-year-old brother-in-law. Aristobulus' time in office lasted less than a year when he died by drowning. The tongues of rumor held that Herod was ultimately responsible for the young high priest's death. He would be the last Hasmonean to hold the office. Herod brought Ananel back. It was 34 B.C. The whole affair was beginning to resemble a three-ring circus, yet the switching would continue.

It is uncertain when or how Ananel the Babylonian left office. But we know the name of his successor, Jeshua (Jesus) ben Phiabi. With Jeshua's arrival, we see a pattern begin to emerge that would continue beyond Herod's lifetime. The chief Roman official in Jerusalem would hand the office of high priest to a person who belonged to one of a few prominent families of priests. Between Jeshua's appointment and the fall of the city about a hundred years later (A.D. 70), two other members of his family would be elevated to the position of high priest. The family that produced Annas and his son-in-law Caiaphas, known from the New Testament gospels, would see no fewer than eight high priests, none apparently serving until his death. Jeshua's term came to an end when love and politics intervened.

Herod fell in love with a beautiful young woman named

Mariamne from a prominent priestly family in Alexandria. He looked around for a way to reward his potential father-in-law, Simon son of Boethus, a reward that would allow Herod to marry a commoner. Simon was a priest who occasionally served in Jerusalem. In 23 B.C., after deposing Jeshua, Herod conferred the high priestly office on Simon. This man presided over the beginning of the renovation of the temple that began in the winter of 20/19 B.C., an effort that would last eighty years. Simon served for eighteen years, until 5 B.C., but not to the end of his life. Herod, who was by then suffering from the disease that would take his own life, deposed Simon because he became suspicious that his wife, Simon's daughter Mariamne, had concealed knowledge of a plot to poison him. Even so, five other high priests would come from Simon's family.

Herod then appointed a Jerusalemite priest named Matthias who, tragically, incurred ritual uncleanness the night before he was to conduct his first Day of Atonement service. To add to Matthias' woes, Herod came to suspect that he was secretly involved in removing a golden eagle that Herod had placed atop one of the temple's gates. A few months later, in March of 4 B.C., Herod deposed him in favor of a man named Joazar, brother of his now-divorced wife Mariamne. In this unusual turnabout, the family of Simon son of Boethus now had its second member in the high priestly office. Within weeks, Herod was dead. But the rotating of the high priesthood would continue under Herod's son Archelaus, who came to power as the ethnarch of Jerusalem (4 B.C.–A.D. 6). Within his nine years, Archelaus would appoint two more high priests and depose Joazar, only to reinstall him later. Following Archelaus, it was a succession of Roman governors who would try their hands at Jewish religious affairs, appointing and deposing high priests of the temple. The humiliation continued.

To make matters even worse, during the years of Herod's reign and beyond, he and his successors in governmental office kept custody of the high priest's ceremonial robes. Each time the high priest needed to dress in his robes for an important holiday, he had to go to the ruler and ask for them. By this device, Herod and the others kept the high priest and his associates under their control. Of course, they were willing to give the robes to the high priest. The robes were even handed over seven days in advance of the Day of Atonement and of the three major festivals (Feast of Tabernacles, Passover, and Pentecost). It was the principle of the thing that rightly aggravated the high priest and his followers. Only in A.D. 36, when Vitellius was serving as Roman governor, did this practice change so that the high priest retained custody of his own ceremonial robes.

Those who served with the high priest were, of course, fellow priests. But there is one officer who is worth singling out, the captain of the temple who stood next to the high priest in rank. We learn of this person and his subordinates, "captains of the temple," in the New Testament Gospels as well as from other sources (see Luke 22:4, 52; John 18:12). It is not clear whether deposing a high priest meant that the captain of the temple was also replaced. What is clear is that the captain had charge of order within the temple and its grounds. His subordinates were equivalent to a temple police force, a function that was filled largely by Levites during Jesus' ministry. At all important events that occurred in the temple, the captain stood next to the high priest, usually at his right side, an indication of his status. If, for example, the high priest read from scripture during a synagogue service, the head of the synagogue handed the scroll to the captain who then handed it to the high priest. Such a practice reminds us of Jesus reading from the scripture in the Nazareth synagogue (Luke 4:16–20). Perhaps as a symbol, no one stood between the minister and Jesus to hand the scripture to Him. The minister had direct access to Jesus without going through an intermediary.

Besides the high priest's responsibilities as head of the temple and its services, he also served as head of the Jerusalem Sanhedrin. There were seventy members of this body. The high priest was the seventy-first. As a result of his position, the priests always controlled the calendar and the deliberations. No one else, including the many Pharisees in the Sanhedrin, was in a position to manage its agenda.

At the outbreak of the Maccabean War, those who felt that some of their fellow Jews had gone too far in embracing Greek ways supported the goal of ridding the country of Seleucid influences that sustained Greek culture and had led to the terrible situation in the capital city. With the temple stripped of its treasures and the horrific slaughter of many of its citizens by the general Apollonius, matters had become intolerable. As a result, those with anti-Greek feelings threw their support to the war effort of Judas Maccabee and his brothers. This support generally continued through the years that Judas' brothers, Jonathan and Simon, led out in the struggle against the Seleucid rulers. But as soon as their Hasmonean successors began reaching for more territory and influence by use of military force, beginning with John Hyrcanus, Simon's son (134–104 B.C.), people began to withdraw their support and seek other paths for sustaining their way of life. It is in this era particularly that we begin to see clearly for the first time the emergence of opposition groups such as the Pharisees and the Hasidim.

Scribes

The titles that Ezra carried to Jerusalem—"Ezra the priest, the scribe" (Ezra 7:11–12)—point to one of the important developments that occurred in Jewish history, the rise of the scribes. As we have noted, in earlier times, it had been the duty of the priests and Levites to teach their fellow Israelites (Deuteronomy 33:10). We suspect that the priests and Levites who returned from the Babylonian exile involved themselves in this sacred task. But their lack of success, for whatever reason, appears in the reforms Ezra introduced. His effort to teach the Law to his people meant that earlier priests and Levites had failed. Moreover, as a scribe, Ezra stood as an example for others. In the decades that followed, there arose a group of people who sought to understand and teach the Law in a way that made sense in people's lives. And when priests became lax about their teaching duties in the era that followed Alexander the Great, there were others who saw an important role in preserving and then trying to understand the scriptural heritage of their people. These scribes became the guardians of the Law and influenced how common folk came to regard its precepts. In addition, their approach was to make a more rational system, a more relevant or sensible framework for understanding God's word from the past. It is Jesus son of Sira, writing about 180 B.C., who lets us know that scribes were an already well-established group who had gained high respect in the broader Jewish community (Ecclesiasticus 38:24–39:11).

We could see these scribes as usurping the place of the priests and Levites whose scriptural duty was to teach their people, but someone had to perform this important function. And the priests and Levites seem to have sidestepped their obligation. The new caste of scribes, of course, could never replace those who served at the temple because, by lineage, only priests and Levites could sacrifice and minister in the sacred rites of the holy place. But in the teaching aspect, there seemed to be room for others who were willing to study and come to understand the Law, for the Law carried its own enticement for people to study it. Those who were so inclined became the forerunners of the powerful scribes whom we meet in later generations, including the time of Jesus and John the Baptist.

For Further Reading

F. F. Bruce, *New Testament History* (Garden City, New York: Anchor Books, 1972), 56–68.

First Maccabees, Second Maccabees, and Ecclesiasticus, *The Apocrypha* (New York: Oxford University Press, 1977).

Joachim Jeremias, *Jerusalem in the Time of Jesus* (Philadelphia: Fortress Press, 1969), 147–221.

Stephen E. Robinson, "The Setting of the Gospels," in Kent P. Jackson and Robert L. Millet, eds., *Studies in Scripture, Volume Five: The Gospels* (Salt Lake City: Deseret Book, 1986), 10–37.

Emil Schürer, *The History of the Jewish People in the Age of Jesus Christ*, 3 vols., rev. ed. by Geza Vermes, Fergus Millar, and Matthew Black (Edinburgh: T & T Clark, 1973–87), 2:227–91, 322–25.

Victor Tcherikover, *Hellenistic Civilization and the Jews* (Philadelphia: Jewish Publication Society, 1959), 117–265.

CHAPTER 13

HASIDEANS, PHARISEES, AND SADDUCEES

Alexander Janneus struggled for breath. Next to him sat his devoted and capable wife, Salome Alexandra. Janneus had spent many of his years as priest-king of Judea expanding his small kingdom, often in a ruthless manner. And even though his father had been sympathetic to the views of Pharisees at one point in his life, in a fit of anger a few years past, Janneus had ordered the crucifixion of eight hundred of them. He believed they were partly responsible for a revolt against himself that led to the Seleucids of Syria joining the fray against him. His act was horrible, he knew, both because of what he had done and because he had adopted the terrible method of execution employed by pagan peoples. His faith taught that death, when imposed by society, should be merciful and quick. For years, his conscience had tortured him because of his act. Now, turning his head slowly toward his wife, he whispered, "You must help to undo my acts against the Pharisees. Please bring them into your confidence. Listen to their ideas. They have the interests of our people in their hearts."

Every society includes in its numbers those who harbor strong feelings about religious and moral behavior. It was no different for ancient Jewish society. The people who supported Nehemiah and Ezra stand out, particularly those who took offense at religious laxity (Ezra 9:1–2; 10:1–4). We learn that, about the same time, the Lord identified certain people to Malachi who had evidently banded together in an effort to preserve what was sacred and important: "They that feared the

Lord spake often one to another: and the Lord hearkened, and heard it, and a book of remembrance was written before him for them that feared the Lord, and that thought upon his name. And they shall be mine, saith the Lord of hosts, in that day when I make up my jewels; and I will spare them" (Malachi 3:16–17).

We do not know whether these people kept their identity and persisted. But they apparently tried to record the names of one another in "a book of remembrance." The point is that they found one another and entered into a noble, common cause together.

Hasideans

Because of a lack of sources, there is a gap of almost two hundred years before we stumble onto another group who possessed similar ideals and led out in strictly keeping the Sabbath and in other acts of devotion. They first appear in the narrative of the book of First Maccabees, which, when describing the beginning of the Maccabean War, records that "a company of the Hasideans, mighty warriors of Israel," joined the family of Mattathias the priest in resisting by violent means their Greek overlords who sought to force Greek ways into their lives. Each of these people "offered himself [to fight] willingly for the law." (The name for these people, Hasideans, is related to the Hebrew term that means "loving kindness.") The event that had driven the Hasideans into Mattathias' camp was a savage attack on some of their numbers during a Sabbath, an attack led by the Seleucid Greek general Apollonius, who slaughtered scores of Hasideans and their families who were hiding in caves for safety. In retribution, these people lashed out initially at fellow Jews who sympathized with the Seleucid government's aims "and struck down [Jewish] sinners in their anger and lawless men in their wrath." It was then that the sons of Mattathias convinced the Hasideans that, in times of war, it was acceptable on the Sabbath day to pick up one's weapons and defend oneself (1 Maccabees 2:29–44).

Throughout the first three years of the war, until the rededication of the temple in 164 B.C., and even beyond, these Hasideans maintained their soldierly support for the Hasmonean family, whose members were leading out against the Seleucids—Mattathias had died and his middle son Judas Maccabee carried on the struggle. But when it came time to make peace, they swept to the front of the line of those pining for peace: "The Hasideans were the first among the sons of Israel to seek peace" (1 Maccabees 7:14). For their good intentions, they paid a horrible price. They seemingly misjudged the Hellenizing high priest Alcimus, who had been appointed by the Seleucids. In an inexplicable act, Alcimus and the Seleucid governor executed sixty of the Hasideans, a horror that galvanized them against any form of Greek culture (1 Maccabees 7:16–18).

The Hasideans thereafter continued to support the Hasmoneans until Jonathan, the younger brother of Judas Maccabee, accepted the role of high priest in 152 B.C. As we have noted, though a descendant of Aaron and therefore a priest by birth, Jonathan had actually received his office from one of the pretenders to the Seleucid throne, a man named Alexander Balas. The Hasideans' chief objection to Jonathan's new office arose from the fact that he was not a descendant of Zadok who had served King Solomon. The descendants of Zadok had held the high priests' dignity in an unbroken line until 171 B.C. when a man named Menelaus, himself of dubious priestly ancestry, had bribed the Seleucid king Antiochus IV to oust the scoundrel Jason who was of the proper lineage but had bribed his own way into office in the place of his brother. In a way, the hesitancy of the Hasideans in supporting Jonathan as high priest was of minor significance because a few years before, the real heir to the high priesthood, Onias IV, had gone off to

Egypt, where Ptolemy VI allowed him to found a Jewish temple in Leontopolis in the central delta region. But when Jonathan's older brother Simon inherited the office of high priest and was subsequently accepted by an assembly of fellow Jews in 140 B.C. as "high priest for ever, until a trustworthy prophet should arise," everyone, including the Hasideans, joined in supporting Simon (1 Maccabees 14:41–49).

Beyond this point, we lose track of this group. Presumably, if they had remained together, the Hasideans would have approved the rest of Simon's time in office. Then, his son, John Hyrcanus, came to power in 134 B.C. There is little in the latter's leadership that would have kept the allegiance of people who were loyal to the Law. Because the Seleucids to the east had fallen on hard times, there was a power vacuum. Within it, Hyrcanus sought to add territories to his domain by military might, subjugating the Idumeans in the south and the Samaritans and a portion of Galilee in the north. It is about this time that we first hear of the Pharisees.

PHARISEES

Some scholars have tied the origin of the Pharisees to the Hasideans, but that link cannot be demonstrated. It is Josephus who first draws our attention to them, noting that the Pharisees greatly influenced John Hyrcanus. That would be difficult to believe if the Pharisees were simply refurbished Hasideans who would likely have opposed Hyrcanus' policy of military expansion. Whatever the case, Pharisaic influence on Hyrcanus was short-lived. At a banquet hosted by Hyrcanus, he invited his Pharisaic supporters—probably lower- and middle-ranking bureaucrats—to be candid and express any criticism. While most praised the king, a certain Eleazar sharply criticized Hyrcanus' mother, which the others rejected. But the seed had been sown. A Sadducee acquaintance of Hyrcanus, Jonathan by name, seeking to establish his own group in a better light, seized the occasion and eventually brought about a rupture between Hyrcanus and the Pharisees (*Jewish Antiquities* 13.10.5–6).

Because the Pharisees were already a force by the time Hyrcanus came to power, we must seek their origins in the preceding decades. But nothing in ancient sources indicates what circumstance may have brought the first group of adherents together. We assume that their early representatives participated in the Maccabean War, which began in 167 B.C. But it is impossible to say more. To be sure, the Pharisees may have been an offshoot of the Hasideans. But what occasion might have driven them apart remains unknown. For their part, Pharisees eventually came to base their fellowship chiefly on Sabbath and festival observances, as well as on food laws. Food laws, of course, concern how one renders foods ritually clean and also how one tithes them, all in an effort to turn Pharisaic homes into virtual temples, even though Pharisees were not typically of the Levite tribe. It seems reasonable that early Pharisees would have placed value on these aspects of life as well. In the case of the Hasideans, there is nothing in the few sources about them that would point to food laws as an important aspect of their lives, although they could have been. Thus, we conclude that the two groups probably originated separately. Even so, they both held the law of Moses in highest esteem. We can say with some confidence that, because Alexander Janneus' execution of eight hundred Pharisees in 88 B.C. did not drive the Pharisees apart, this terrible act probably injected the glue that held the group together for years to come.

The term *Pharisee* may go back to a Hebrew word that means "separatist." On this view, the term may well point to an occasion when Pharisees separated themselves from the Hasmonean rulers, perhaps beginning with John Hyrcanus. Another possibility is that the word *Pharisee* derives from the Hebrew verb "to expound" and points to them as expounders of the law of Moses. Whatever the case, they remained a force within the society long past the Maccabean era and well beyond the fall of Jerusalem and its temple in A.D. 70. The Pharisees continued on as the rabbis of later ages, and the Judaism of late antiquity was the child of Pharisaic teachings and ideals.

Josephus calls the Pharisees one of the four major "sects" or "schools" of his society (the Greek term is *haireseis*). The others were the Sadducees, the Essenes, and the "fourth philosophy" that was the Zealot movement. These groups were not sects or schools in the modern or even ancient senses. Unlike among the priests and Levites, membership was not a matter of lineage. Each of the four groups held to a set of distinctive teachings to which adherents pledged allegiance, although it remains unknown how people pledged that allegiance and thus became members of one or another group except the Essenes (see chapter 15, "Essenes and Zealots"). Pharisees were not a school in the Greco-Roman sense of students who surrounded a prominent teacher and assented to his basic views of life. The Jewish groups, like the Pharisees, were more intense, more committed to the views they held. For them, their teachings not only led to a distinctive way of life but were life itself. And all such teachings fit within the framework of the law of Moses and the scriptures. Further, all of life was played out within the larger Jewish community. On this level, one's Israelite ancestry was crucial. The only exceptions were those who allowed themselves to absorb gentile ways in the Diaspora.

When we read Josephus' account of Pharisaic beliefs, we have to remember that he was a Pharisee who sought to portray them in a warm light, even though he was born into a family of Hasmonean priests. From him it becomes clear that Pharisees believed in a life after death, complete with judgment and resurrection. Further, in their view, angels and spirits inhabit the heavens. They also believed in a divinely guided fate that steered the world toward God's planned destiny and thereby limited a person's free will (see *Jewish Antiquities* 18.1.3; *Jewish*

War 2.8.14; also Acts 23:6–10). Further, they held that Moses received two laws on Mount Sinai, one that he wrote down and one that he passed on orally. It is this latter, the source of "the tradition of the elders," that Jesus and His disciples objected to (Matthew 15:2; Mark 7:3). For Pharisees, this oral tradition was the real governing influence in how a person was to understand the Law; and, in the view of the Pharisees, they had received the oral law from Moses himself (see *Mishnah* Pirke Aboth 1.1).

Although Josephus marks the Pharisees as the most powerful group in his society, holding influence over the majority of the populace, it is evident that over time there were few who rose to positions of power either under the Hasmonean priest-kings or under Herod and his Roman successors. In this light, we should probably see Pharisees as middle-level bureaucrats and small business owners who, because of their views on religious matters, sought to influence social and political policies in a direction that would support and even enshrine their own teachings. Because of their position in the middle of their society, they were indeed well placed to influence others who occupied the spots next to them in the social spectrum, the poor and the moderately wealthy.

Beginning with the elevated status accorded to them when Alexandra Salome was head of state, they enjoyed a major role in the Jerusalem Sanhedrin. This position also afforded them a platform from which they could collectively effect changes that accorded with their views, for on the political front they did seek to make changes, acting as a political-action group. From what we can learn, they were neither reclusive nor outlandish in their public behavior. As a result, their group temperament was well suited to obtaining the favors they desired, particularly from Jewish officials who would have known them and their interests. The case would have been different when they approached foreign officials. The concerns of Pharisees—food laws and religious observances—did not involve the kinds of behavior that would come to the attention of Roman overlords unless, for instance, someone tried to force a Pharisee to break the Sabbath or the like, an act that would have elicited a strong reaction. The Pharisees' concerns centered chiefly in their own homes and out of the sight of others.

Sadducees

In the case of the Sadducees, we know much less. In the first place, we learn about them and their beliefs from people outside their group. Not one written source has survived from antiquity that can be attributed to Sadducees, whereas the Mishnah and a host of other Jewish sources preserve an extensive record of Pharisaic teachings. Josephus is our main source for understanding the Sadducees, and he held them in low regard. What is more, modern scholars are divided over questions of the Sadducees' origins and their political and religious status.

The meaning of the term *Sadducee*, it seems, might throw light on the origins of this group. But it does not. We simply do not know when or why they became a group that could and did exercise influence in Jewish life, although scholars have made educated guesses. Some believe that the word *Sadducee* goes back to the Hebrew *tzaddik*, a word that appears, for example, in the *-zedek* of the name *Melchizedek* and means "righteous." In this view, the term would mean something like "righteous one." But others believe that *Sadducee* derives from the name *Zadok*, the name of the man who served Solomon as high priest, and thus points to an order or fellowship of priests. There is no firm way to determine which view is correct, though the latter view, which ties the name to the high priest Zadok, is more likely, as we shall see.

Because the Sadducees evidently made up the majority of the Jerusalem Sanhedrin, they are identified in large measure with the priests who served in the temple (see Acts 5:17).

Moreover, they were among the aristocracy of Jerusalem. Their wealth alone would have given them significant power. But when we add their status as priests, we see that they stood on two platforms, as it were, from which they could exercise influence: wealth and priestly status. But Josephus cautions us against seeing their wealth and status as strengths in their relationship with the general population. On the contrary, he holds that these aspects of their lives diminished their popular influence. They found themselves forced to cooperate with the Pharisees to implement public-policy decisions (see *Jewish Antiquities* 18.1.4; *Jewish War* 2.8.14).

Like the Samaritans, the Sadducees held only the Pentateuch—that is, the first five books of the Old Testament, rejecting the oral law trumpeted by the Pharisees—to be fully sacred scripture. Therefore, only the principles, rituals, and sacrifices that God had enjoined on His people through the patriarchs and Moses were essential to maintaining a proper relationship with Him and His people. Unlike the Pharisees, Sadducees seem not to have accepted the historical and prophetic books as canonical. As a result, they taught that the soul is extinguished at death. Hence, in their belief, there is no judgment and no heaven or hell. Nor for them was there to be a resurrection, a stance that they exhibited in their classic question to Jesus about marriage in the next life and in Paul's famous hearing before the Sanhedrin (Matthew 22:23–33; Mark 12:18–27; Luke 20:27–40; Acts 23:6–10). Further, for them there were no angels or divine spirits in the heavens (Acts 23:8). In addition, they embraced the concept of free will, teaching that all that happens in the world is a result of individual choice. Such teachings offer a background to understanding an unusual receptiveness among these people. Though most of them were priests and were therefore constantly surrounded by reminders at the temple that they needed to preserve their sacred religious traditions, they were apparently open to the influences of the Greek way of life, with its emphasis on education and ennobling art. Because they believed in no eternal consequences for mortal actions, there was no apparent inner restraint on what they might accept outside of their own culture and religious lives.

Unlike the Pharisees, whose numbers and teachings continued in strength beyond the fall of Jerusalem and the temple to the Romans in A.D. 70, the Sadducees disappeared. For the majority of them who were priests, their chief reason for existing evaporated with the loss of the temple. In addition, their important place in the political and social life of the Jewish community dissolved when there was no longer a central hub for that life. Their connections to the common people, who survived the disaster, were nil. We hear of the Sadducees no more.

For Further Reading

F. F. Bruce, *New Testament History* (Garden City, New York: Anchor Books, 1972), 69–81.

First Maccabees and Second Maccabees, *The Apocrypha* (New York: Oxford University Press, 1977).

David Noel Freedman et al., eds., *The Anchor Bible Dictionary* (New York: Doubleday, 1992), s.v. "Hasideans," "Hasidim," "Pharisees," and "Sadducees."

Joachim Jeremias, *Jerusalem in the Time of Jesus* (Philadelphia: Fortress Press, 1969), 228–32, 246–67.

Stephen E. Robinson, "The Setting of the Gospels," in Kent P. Jackson and Robert L. Millet, eds., *Studies in Scripture, Volume Five: The Gospels* (Salt Lake City: Deseret Book, 1986), 10–37.

Emil Schürer, *The History of the Jewish People in the Age of Jesus Christ*, 3 vols., rev. ed. by Geza Vermes, Fergus Millar, and Matthew Black (Edinburgh: T & T Clark, 1973–87), 2:381–414.

CHAPTER 14

SAMARITANS

Sanballat sat astride his mule. It was a two-day ride from Samaria to Jerusalem. In recent months, he had made the trip several times. This time he was going to visit Jerusalem officials in an attempt to persuade them—again—to let his people join them in their effort to rebuild the temple. Indeed, the prior temple had been sacred to his ancestors, the people of the northern kingdom of Israel. So far, those who had returned from Babylon had resisted his entreaties, even his threats. They were an arrogant bunch, even though they lived in heaps of rubbish and partly rebuilt homes. It had become clear that they thought of themselves as a purer race of Israelites than his own people. But he hoped that one more effort on his part would bring an unparalleled opportunity to his people to participate in restoring God's house among them. He looked down on the bobbing head of his mount and, with his heels, urged the mule to move faster. Sundown was approaching.

The origin and history of the Samaritans appear to be straightforward. But they are not. Most questions arise on the basis of information preserved in the Old Testament. One key passage, which draws everyone's attention, has to do with the loss of the northern Israelite tribes following the destruction of the capital city Samaria in 722 B.C. by the Assyrian King Sargon II (722–705 B.C.) (see 2 Kings 17:22–41).

The Assyrian empire, along with Egypt, had been a major force in the ancient Near East for more than two centuries before its army besieged and then destroyed Samaria. According to Sargon's record, he carried off 27,290 captives and, in accordance with Assyrian policies, relocated them to other places within his kingdom. He replaced these people from "the cities of Samaria" with others from "Babylon, and from Cuthah, and from Ava, and from Hamath, and from Sepharvaim" (2 Kings 17:24). These people brought their own gods to worship. But when "the Lord sent lions among them, which slew some of them," they appealed to the Assyrian king for help in learning how to placate "the God of the land," namely, Jehovah (17:25–26). Then "one of the priests whom they had carried away from Samaria came and dwelt in Beth-el, and taught them how they should fear the Lord" (17:28). Beth-el, of course, had been a sanctuary city for the Israelites of the northern kingdom (1 Kings 12:25–29).

There were two results. First, the people who had replaced the Israelites "in the cities of Samaria" eventually "feared the Lord"—that is, they learned how to worship Him properly. On the other hand, they "served their own gods" (2 Kings 17:24, 32–33). Hence, the citizens of the kingdom of Judah to the south came to distrust them as fellow worshipers of Jehovah because they "served their graven images" (17:41). The second result concerned the subsequent ethnic makeup of the populace in the region north of Judah, which was mixed. There is good reason to believe that the Assyrians left many of the northern Israelites in their villages and towns, in contrast to citizens of "*the cities* of Samaria" whom they deported (17:24; emphasis added). After all, King Sargon claimed to relocate fewer than thirty thousand people. And the total population must have exceeded that figure, even accounting for the casualties resulting from the Assyrian attack. Thus, over time, members of families and clans—both the new move-ins and the natives—married one another and brought into being generations whom the people of Judah saw as an impure race.

But is this the whole story? We must remember that the

people seen in this harsh light were descendants of the tribes of Ephraim and Manasseh, who inhabited the region north of Jerusalem. We observe first that, according to the book of Jeremiah, Israelites from this area were still coming to the broken altar in Jerusalem after Nebuchadnezzar's army had destroyed the city in 587 B.C., 135 years after the fall of Samaria. We read that "there came certain from Shechem, from Shiloh, and from Samaria, even fourscore men, . . . with offerings and incense in their hand, to bring them to the house of the Lord" (Jeremiah 41:5). Apparently, these eighty men were exercising a right of worship that they and their forebears had enjoyed in Jerusalem. Moreover, there seems to be no stigma attached to their presence at the altar. On the contrary, they felt that their attendance would be welcomed. Apparently, none among the priestly authorities officiating at the altar in those bleak days refused them opportunity to worship on grounds that they were somehow not true Israelites. Their self-perception that they were fully of the house of Israel seems to lie behind the later offer by people from the north to join in rebuilding the temple (Ezra 4:1–3).

There is a second point that arises from the Book of Mormon. Nowhere in the narrative of 1 and 2 Nephi do we hear that Lehi and Sariah and their family were excluded from the temple because they were of the tribe of Manasseh and were from the north. Naturally, both Lehi and Sariah may have been able to trace their complete ancestries back to purely Israelite progenitors. Even so, it seems clear that genealogical questions had not yet raised their heads in the case of people who hailed from the region where the Assyrian king had settled non-Israelites three or four generations before. Those questions would become crucial only after the return of the Jewish exiles from Babylon.

One of the most compelling evidences that Samaritans of the north enjoyed reputations as Israelites, at least in the eyes of some Jews in the south, is the fact that at least two sons of high priests married daughters of Samaritan governors. In each case, the name of the governor was Sanballat. From all appearances, this name seems to have been passed from father to son for three or four generations within the governor's family. In the first instance, we read that during Nehemiah's second term of office, probably about 430 B.C., he expelled "one of the sons of Joiada, the son of Eliashib the high priest" who had married Sanballat's daughter (Nehemiah 13:28). Although this marriage may have been political—intended to cement relations between the people of Jerusalem and Samaria—it is also apparent that the family of the high priest saw nothing objectionable in marrying a son to a Samaritan daughter. The second case comes to us from Josephus. Not long before Alexander the Great came to Palestine in 332 B.C., the high priest's brother, a man named Manasseh, married a daughter of the governor of Samaria. By this point, Ezra's reforms had been in place for almost a century, including the stipulation that Jewish people not marry outsiders. As we might expect, leaders in Jerusalem later hounded Manasseh out of their society. But we should not miss the point that, even in the social and religious climate of the day, the high priest's family ventured to marry one of their sons to a Samaritan girl (*Jewish Antiquities* 11.7.2; 11.8.2).

In all of this, it seems that the central issue concerns people's perceptions of one another. On the side of those who came back from exile in Babylon, most saw Samaritans as at least semiapostates who had married gentiles. As a result, they disapproved of them. On the other side, the remnants of the tribes of Manasseh and Ephraim saw themselves as Israelites, entitled to the same blessings that God had promised their common forebears, Abraham, Isaac, and Jacob. Somehow, these two peoples never did reconcile their differing perceptions, even though they both embraced the celebrations mandated by the law of Moses and both revered its words.

These perceptions of one another—in some cases, misperceptions—appear in the name "Samaritans." It occurs once in the Old Testament and is attached to idolatry, making it a term of derision (2 Kings 17:29). From all appearances, the name was given them by outsiders—namely, the people of Jerusalem and Judah. For their part, as Josephus reminds us, the Samaritans preferred to be known as "descended from Joseph" (*Jewish Antiquities* 9.14.3). In fact, the name *Samaritans* derives from the Hebrew word *shāmerīm*, which means "keepers"—that is, keepers of the Law. Thus, in its far-off origins, the name *Samaritans* may have to do with an honored profession of scribes who watched over and preserved the law of Moses.

As we have seen, the Samaritans' relationship with their distant Jewish relatives defined in large measure who they were. The question Who is an Israelite? stood at the forefront of tensions that surged and ebbed over centuries of time. As noted previously, the Samaritans' first real clue that the returning exiles would not embrace them came in the exiles' rebuff of their offer in 538 or 537 B.C. to help rebuild the altar and temple on the spot where the Samaritans had evidently been worshiping for more than fifty years (Ezra 4:1–3). The second moment of tension came when Nehemiah began work on the walls in 445. Relations grew strained enough that the Samaritans even threatened to take military action against people in Jerusalem, although matters seem never to have come to that pitch (Nehemiah 4:7–8). A third instance doubtless arose when Ezra obliged all in Judah to divorce their foreign spouses, probably in 428 B.C. There must have been Samaritan spouses among those who were forced to depart. And the pain and anger in Samaritan families following this action would have been intense, giving rise to a hardening of already-strained relationships.

Evidence that relationships were strained in the fifth century when Nehemiah and Ezra were active appears in the

Elephantine papyri from Upper Egypt. Within the preserved texts are letters both to the leaders of Jerusalem and to those in Samaria asking for help in building a Jewish temple in Upper Egypt. The fact that the Egyptian Jews addressed letters to leaders of both groups hints strongly that the members of the Jewish garrison at Elephantine were aware of sharp differences between the two communities.

But the Jews of Jerusalem were not the only source of challenges for Samaritans. On the positive side, we presume that Samaritans lived rather peaceably and well during the years of the Persian hegemony (538–333 B.C.). The Persians seem to have appointed a regular succession of local governors in Samaria. At times, these governors had responsibility for Judah; at other times, they did not. Then came Alexander, and Samaritan life began to fill with extreme challenges.

When Alexander finally razed the impregnable island city of Tyre in 332 B.C., everyone in neighboring lands took note. As we have observed, Josephus tells us that the Samaritans thereafter supplied troops for Alexander's foray into Egypt. Everything seemed fine. Then, inexplicably, the Samaritans turned against Alexander's newly appointed governor, a man named Andromachus, and killed him. In reprisal, Alexander sent troops against the city of Samaria, destroying it and forcing survivors to flee. He resettled Macedonian colonists from his home area in Samaria, and the city thereafter remained chiefly Greek. Concerning the Samaritan refugees, a cave in the area has yielded the skeletal remains of some two hundred people—men, women, and children—who died by suffocation when Alexander's soldiers evidently built fires at the entrance of the cave and filled it with smoke. The cave has also yielded legal papyri, called the Samaria papyri, that offer a glimpse into Samaritan life of the fourth century B.C.

Some survivors of Alexander's reprisal traveled southeast to the base of Mount Gerizim, where they refounded the city of

Shechem. It was about this time that the Samaritans built their temple on this mountain. Although archaeologists have not identified the remains of this structure, and they therefore presume that the building was modest in size, Josephus relates that it was built to keep the priest Manasseh from divorcing his Samaritan wife, the daughter of Sanballat, whom we mentioned earlier. Josephus also places the building of the temple in the period just before Alexander arrived (*Jewish Antiquities* 11.8.2). Whatever the case, the Samaritans were quite aware of the high and holy significance of the general locale. For instance, they knew that in this place Abraham had received a revelation from God and, as we have seen, that the conquering Israelites had erected their earliest sanctuary here in the land of Canaan (Genesis 12:6–7; Joshua 8:30–35). It is interesting in this context to note that the Samaritan woman whom Jesus met at Jacob's well wanted to talk about "the [sacred] place" of worship on Mount Gerizim (John 4:20).

According to Judges 9:37, the area of Shechem was known as "the middle of the land" or "the center of the land." Significantly, the Septuagint adds weight to this notion by translating this expression as "navel of the earth." This concept, known in other ancient religious traditions as well, in effect says that a connection exists between heaven and earth in this place, something like what Jacob discovered at Luz or Bethel. As a matter of fact, a person builds altars and makes solemn and sacred covenants in such places (see Genesis 28:10–22; 35:6–7). Hence, there are reasons that the Samaritans would venture to build a sanctuary away from Jerusalem, though they had likely been worshiping at the Jerusalem sanctuary in modest numbers even after the exiles had rebuilt the temple. Evidently, the need for a temple had not arisen beforehand. The fact that the Samaritans chose to build their own temple in the later fourth century indicates that relationships with their Jewish cousins had gone especially sour.

Little is known about Samaritan fortunes during the century of Ptolemaic control over Palestine (301–198 B.C.). We assume that life went on rather normally, as it seemingly did among Jews. But after the conquest of the region by the Seleucid King Antiochus III in 198, matters began taking a downward turn. Samaritans found themselves caught in the same Hellenistic grip as the citizens of Jerusalem. As with the Jews, the Samaritans must have seen many of their traditional ways come under subtle attack from those in their society who favored the ways of the Greeks. Hence, when Antiochus IV (175–163 B.C.) undertook the Hellenizing of the Jews, he also forced Greek culture onto the Samaritans, who, surprisingly, acquiesced more readily than their Jewish cousins. What is unclear is whether the Samaritans accepted Antiochus' demand that they rededicate their temple to Zeus willingly or unwillingly. According to 2 Maccabees 6:2, in 167 B.C., the Samaritans were forced to rededicate their temple, as were the people of Jerusalem. In contrast, according to Josephus, the Samaritans petitioned Antiochus to allow them to name their temple in honor of Zeus (*Jewish Antiquities* 12.5.5–6). Whatever the case, the Samaritan temple on Mount Gerizim thereafter bore the name of Zeus until its destruction by the Jewish leader John Hyrcanus in 128 B.C. The Samaritans did not attempt to reconstruct their temple, although they maintained a worship site on the mountain.

It seems apparent that the attack by the forces of John Hyrcanus in 128 was the final blow that severed relations between Samaritans and Jews. In addition, any good feelings would not have survived Hyrcanus' second attack in 107 B.C. when he devastated the Samaritan countryside. We wonder whether Hyrcanus' anger arose in part because the Samaritans had not returned their temple to the worship of Jehovah as the Jews had done after Judas Maccabee liberated the Jerusalem temple in 164 B.C. In the bitter Samaritan view, "the Jews have no dealings with the Samaritans" (John 4:9). Such a state led to Samaritans' refusing hospitality to Jesus and His disciples (Luke 9:52–53). Worse than that, and possibly in reprisal for Hyrcanus' acts, Samaritans later attacked Jewish pilgrims and even desecrated the Jerusalem temple on one occasion (*Jewish Antiquities* 18.2.2; 20.6.1).

Although relationships worsened with people in Judea, and even in Galilee, Samaritans shared basic values with the people of Qumran, who were the keepers of the Dead Sea Scrolls. It is not clear whether Samaritans cultivated relations with Qumranites, but they held common beliefs. Most suggestive of at least an indirect tie is the discovery in Cave 4 at the Dead Sea of a fragmentary text of Exodus whose readings agree with the Samaritan Pentateuch, the scripture of the Samaritans (4QpaleoExod^{m}). As with all Israelites, both groups observed the Sabbath and practiced circumcision on the eighth day. But both groups adopted certain practices and distinctive views about themselves that converge. For example, both groups called themselves "the sons of light" to underscore their special status before God. Each venerated Moses as the most important of God's past prophets. Both placed a high emphasis on Moses' prophecy in Deuteronomy 18:18 about a future prophet who would lead God's true people. Neither group celebrated the Jewish festivals of Purim and Hanukkah, which were late additions to the Jewish sacred calendar and had not been mandated by the Old Testament. Both groups followed a rather complex calendrical reckoning of holy days that rested on both the sun and moon, whereas the calendar used at the Jerusalem temple rested chiefly on seasonal observations of the moon alone.

In light of all of this, how should we view the Samaritans? In part, their Jewish cousins misunderstood them. In part, they misunderstood the Jews. Throughout the entire intertestamental period, the most bracing question that grew directly out of their relationship with Jews was, Who is an Israelite? As for

Samaritans, they saw themselves as fully Israelite, even in the era when many adopted Greek ways and allowed their temple to serve the worship of Zeus. There are hints that Jesus and, later, His followers held Samaritans in high esteem, even though, as mentioned, on at least one occasion Samaritans refused hospitality to Jesus and His disciples simply because they were on their way to Jerusalem (Luke 9:52–53). It is telling that, after the Savior's resurrection, one of the first destinations for His disciples was Samaria (Acts 8:4–17). In fact, in the Savior's charge to the eleven before his ascension, He directed them to go to Samaria (Acts 1:8). Further, in at least two accounts from the Gospels, Jesus held up Samaritans as examples to His hearers. The first consists of Jesus' parable of the Good Samaritan, who, when others refused to aid a helpless and beaten man, "went to him, and bound up his wounds, . . . and took care of him" (Luke 10:30–35). The second arises in the story of Jesus' healing of ten lepers. He was traveling "through the midst of Samaria and Galilee," presumably along the common border area. When He and His disciples "entered into a certain village, there met him ten men that were lepers." As Mosaic law required, the ten "stood afar off" while they begged Jesus to "have mercy" on them. He did, and "they were cleansed." As the ten skipped off to show themselves "unto the priests," as the Law demanded, one "turned back" and "fell down on his face at [Jesus'] feet, giving him thanks." The man "was a Samaritan." Not seeking to hide the fact that the man was a Samaritan, for Jesus called him "this stranger," He said to the man in the hearing of His followers, "Thy faith hath made thee whole" (Luke 17:11–19). From these accounts we can draw three conclusions. First, the Samaritan was as concerned as the other lepers to follow the requirements of the Mosaic law. Second, Jesus held Samaritans in the same esteem that He held fellow Jews. Third, the kind of faith that invites the blessings of heaven is not limited to geography or ethnicity. And Samaritans serve as prime examples of these principles in these New Testament stories.

For Further Reading

John Bright, *A History of Israel*, 3d ed. (Philadelphia: Westminster Press, 1981), 269–76, 360–457.

Keith Crim et al., eds., *The Interpreter's Dictionary of the Bible*, suppl. vol. (Nashville: Abingdon Press, 1976), s.v. "Gerizim, Mount," "Samaria," "Samaria Papyri," "Samaritan Pentateuch," "Samaritans," and "Shechem (City)."

David Noel Freedman et al., eds., *The Anchor Bible Dictionary* (New York: Doubleday, 1992), s.v. "Gerizim, Mount," "Palestine, Administration of," "Samaria (City)," "Samaritan Pentateuch," "Samaritans," and "Shechem (Place)."

Joachim Jeremias, *Jerusalem in the Time of Jesus* (Philadelphia: Fortress Press, 1969), 352–58.

Martin Noth, *The History of Israel*, 2d ed. (New York: Harper & Row, 1960), 253–69.

Stephen E. Robinson, "The Settling of the Gospels," in Kent P. Jackson and Robert L. Millet, eds., *Studies in Scripture, Volume Five: The Gospels* (Salt Lake City: Deseret Book, 1986), 10–37.

Emil Schürer, *The History of the Jewish People in the Age of Jesus Christ*, 3 vols., rev. ed. by Geza Vermes, Fergus Millar, and Matthew Black (Edinburgh: T & T Clark, 1973–87), 2:15–20, 160–64.

Shemaryahu Talmon, "The Emergence of Jewish Sectarianism in the Early Second Temple Period," in Patrick D. Miller Jr. et al., eds., *Ancient Israelite Religion: Essays in Honor of Frank Moore Cross* (Philadelphia: Fortress Press, 1987), 587–616.

CHAPTER 15

Essenes and Zealots

Judas stood at the window looking out westward at the distant Sea of Galilee. He had just come from the synagogue of Gamla on the other end of town. His Pharisaic friend, Zadok, and others were with him, listening to the news from a man who lived in Damascus. The winter rains had made the canyon below a carpet of green and had filled the streams that converged at the west end of the hilltop town. The sight should have been one of promise and gratitude for the coming growing season. Instead, Judas felt rage creeping into his heart. The messenger was telling him and his associates that the new Roman governor of Syria was about to begin a census in the region—a census that would serve as the basis for taxing people. Judas knew that such an act would take freedom from his people. As the messenger finished, Judas turned to the others and said, "We have to stop the census, even if it means violence and costs us our lives." The year was A.D. *6*

Under the right circumstances, people with conservative and liberal views will rise within a society and seek ways to influence its policies and social directions. During the period between the writing of the Old and New Testaments, two very conservative groups appeared who took broadly different paths toward both temporal and spiritual salvation. Those two were the Essenes and the Zealots. The Essenes adopted a path of intensely personal approach to spirituality, which, as we might expect, had a limited public impact on the larger society. By contrast, the Zealots stirred the fires of a hot nationalism that sought to bring in the kingdom of God by a violent struggle against Roman overlords.

Essenes

Essenes are one of the few Jewish groups, outside of Christians and Pharisees, for which there is an abundance of contemporary sources. This is all the more so if we adopt the now general view that the people who produced and preserved the Dead Sea Scrolls were Essenes. From our perspective, the heavy weight of evidence identifies the two groups, the Dead Sea people and the Essenes, as one. And we shall treat them as identical.

The earliest reference to Essenes comes from the pen of Josephus and ties to the era of the Maccabean War (167–164 B.C.) and its aftermath (*Jewish Antiquities* 13.5.9). It was a turbulent age, and it spawned a number of movements, including the Hasideans and the Pharisees. The origin of the Essenes remains obscure, though, like the Pharisees, they may have originated within the Hasidean movement. Concerning the name *Essene*, some have concluded that it comes from a word that means "pious." It is true that some ancients perceived members of the movement as especially religious in their devotions. Others have thought that the name may go back to a term that means "healers." The issue is unresolved, although Essenes enjoyed a reputation among other Jews for their healing skills with medicines and herbs.

As we have pointed out previously, from all we can learn, the founder of the Essene movement—an enigmatic figure who was himself a priest and is known only as the Teacher of Righteousness—opposed Jonathan Maccabee. Jonathan received the high priestly office in 152 B.C. from a pretender to the Seleucid throne, a man named Alexander Balas. In the mind of the Teacher of Righteousness, Jonathan, though from a family of priests, did not possess the proper ancestry back to

Zadok, the high priest who had served in the days of Solomon. Moreover, Jonathan received his high rank as part of a deal wherein he would support Alexander Balas' claims to the Seleucid royal dignity. It was a case of foreign politics piloting religious affairs. From that point on, according to texts preserved among the Dead Sea Scrolls, the Teacher and his followers labeled the high priest of the temple in Jerusalem as the "Wicked Priest," an evident reference to Jonathan and, presumably, his successors. In their continuing opposition to the temple priesthood, the Essenes differed from their compatriots the Hasideans, who eventually reconciled themselves to the Hasmoneans as high priests, the first of whom was Jonathan.

In this connection, the Essenes viewed the temple and its functionaries as impure. Hence, unlike Jewish Christians during the first century (see Acts 2:46–47), they did not participate in services at the temple, though they willingly sent the offerings required by scripture. As we have seen, one of the other dimensions of their worship that pushed them even further from the temple is the fact that the Essenes followed a different calendar. Events at the temple occurred on dates fixed by the lunar calendar then in use. In contrast, the Essenes followed a calendar based chiefly on the sun. As a result, the Essenes celebrated festivals on days when other Jews were working and vice versa. By this means, Essenes and their followers conveyed the notion that the rest of the people were apostate in their observances of holy days. To keep themselves pure from the tainting influences of fellow Jews who resided in towns and cities, the main group of Essenes withdrew to a hill on the northwest edge of the Dead Sea and there established a community where they could wait in purity for the Messiah and His prophet who would precede Him.

Actually, these people came to believe in two messiahs, one from the house of Aaron and one from the house of David. The earliest sources tell us that the Essenes' messianic hope was centered in the priests, the descendants of Aaron. For some reason, the Teacher and his followers did not adopt the customary view that the Messiah would be a political figure. Perhaps offense at Jonathan's acceptance of the high priesthood, wedding it to his position as head of state, led Essenes to abandon hope in a Davidic deliverer. As time went on, apparently, instead of changing their view that a messiah would come to them from among the priests, they came to believe that two messiahs would appear, one from Aaron and one from David as noted in the *Community Rule* (1QS).

Also, prior to the appearance of the messiahs at the end of time, "the Prophet" was to come. This person, who would fulfill Moses' prophecy about "a Prophet from among their brethren," would come as a forerunner, as an Elijah (Deuteronomy 18:18). We immediately think of John the Baptist, as well as questions about the identity of John and Jesus, with "that prophet" whom people were expecting (John 1:21; 6:14; 7:40).

Before the coming of the Prophet and the messiahs, the followers of the Teacher were to prepare themselves through ritual and moral purity. This preparation was not easy. Josephus, who gave a long description about Essenes and their way of life because of his admiration for them, tried in his youth to follow the rigors of the Essenes and had to give up. It becomes clear from his description that, in their approach to life, the majority abstained from marriage, preferring to augment their numbers either by adopting young people and training them or by accepting people who wanted to join them. But becoming an Essene was not easy (see *Life* 2; *Jewish War* 2.8.2–13).

The Essenes formed a fellowship chiefly of men who held all property in common and lived under councils made up of three priests and twelve laymen. Those who wished to join made their intent known to the leaders of the community at the Dead Sea. Leaders issued three items to potential members: a white robe, a white apron or girdle, and a trowel with which to take care of latrine needs. With these items, potential members began a one-year trial period. At the end of one year, leaders of the group reviewed each initiate's performance and decided whether to let the person continue into a second trial period of two more years. If the person was allowed to continue, he received permission to participate in the ritual of the daily bath. If all worked well thereafter, that person was admitted into full membership at the end of three years and could eat the common meals with the group. The oaths that a new member swore about eating only foods prepared within the community meant that a person who left the Essene fellowship would literally starve to death. Before the midday meal, members bathed. Each of the two daily meals involved the whole community and began with a blessing over the food, which priests in the group had carefully prepared in accord with ritual requirements. Membership also involved a strict observance of the Sabbath day, not taking care of any personal needs on that day. In addition, each individual gave up all property to the group, including daily earnings if he was a craftsman, in effect taking a vow of poverty. Worldly goods were a distraction. So that such distractions did not become concerns, one person was appointed to oversee the financial and property matters of the community and to meet the needs of members as they arose. This person was a bishop of sorts.

One of the most intriguing aspects of the Essenes' life had to do with marriage. Actually, it appears that most remained unmarried. But Josephus informs us that, besides the main group who lived celibate lives, some married and lived in towns and villages scattered through the countryside. The moral code for married members was as strict as for those at the Dead Sea. In addition, like the monks, they helped one another by pooling their resources and efforts.

Those who lived away from the main center were to gather in groups of no fewer than ten for worship. The person who led them in praying and reading scriptures was a priest. This practice differed from Jesus' later view: "Where two or three are gathered together in my name, there am I in the midst of them" (Matthew 18:20). As we have noted, none of them participated in temple services. Instead, they engaged in observances that were, in their eyes, more spiritually effective than those performed by corrupt priests. Of course, they believed that, in the end, the impure priests would be cast out and God would cleanse His house for proper worship. It was not as though they had left the temple behind in their hopes and prayers. It still played a major, though future, role in their practice and belief. After all, they could not follow completely the law of Moses without some participation in temple activities, even if it was delayed.

Although we cannot be exhaustive in reviewing all of the Essenes' beliefs, several others draw our attention. First, these people believed in a hierarchical system of angels who inhabit the heavens and whose names they were not to reveal, treating them as sacred and secret. Second, more than any other Jewish group, the Essenes believed in a predestined world. For them, God's providence was the decisive, guiding force among humankind. Third, they believed that a person's soul inherits a bodiless eternity. In their view, there was no resurrection. On the contrary, according to Josephus, they considered the body as a tomb. Fourth, within the Dead Sea Scrolls, it becomes apparent that these people were decidedly anti-Ephraimite. For instance, in a commentary on Psalm 37:14–15 (4Q171), the descendants of one of the Essenes' opponents, called "the liar," are said to be the "wicked of Ephraim and Manasseh." In a commentary on Nahum 2:13 (4Q169), the "city of Ephraim" is used as a euphemism for apostates, "those who seek smooth things during the last days." In their opinion, the legitimate ruling class would come from the house of David, not from one of the Joseph tribes. Finally, the Essenes gained a reputation for revelation and prophecy. One illustration, as we have observed, is the *Temple Scroll*'s (11QTemple) rewriting of Old Testament instructions for building the temple into more direct commands from God. As a further example, an Essene named Menahem met the youthful Herod and predicted that Herod would become king of the Jews. When Herod in fact had brought the land of Palestine under his control, he summoned this same Menahem, who thereupon predicted that Herod would rule another twenty or thirty years. This pair of encounters led Herod to hold the Essenes in highest esteem (see *Jewish War* 2.8.2–13; *Jewish Antiquities* 15.10.5). What he does not seem to have known was their plan for war at the end of time.

From the *War Scroll* (1QM) found at the Dead Sea, it has become clear that the Essenes believed that, if they purified themselves properly before God, He would help them throw off the yoke of the Romans, whom they called "Kittim." In an elaborate description of final warfare, we read of a series of seven major battles during a six-year period, which will lead to the defeat of the Kittim and a cleansing of the land of Israel. During the seventh or sabbath year, the temple will function properly. Over another thirty-three years, the other heathen nations will suffer defeat. All the defeated people are called "the sons of darkness." Those who bring about this celestial victory are "the sons of Light," whose camps will be purified of outsiders, including women and children. In their pure state, they will be in a position to usher in the kingdom of God on earth. In this view of the final battles, it is the Essenes and no one else who will stand worthy of assisting God in His terrestrial triumph.

As a matter of fact, as archaeology shows, the end for the Essenes at the Dead Sea came in A.D. 68 when a Roman force under General Placidus, attacking towns and villages in the area of Jericho, destroyed the settlement (see Josephus, *Jewish War* 4.7.6). Either the Essenes abandoned the settlement and fled for safety, leaving the buildings for the Zealots who tried to resist the Romans, or they themselves tried to put up a fight and were routed. It seems apparent that, at this moment of alarm, many of the Dead Sea Scrolls were hidden in caves where they were later found, beginning in 1947.

ZEALOTS

The Zealots were Josephus' fourth "philosophy" or sect. Of the Jewish groups he discusses, the Zealots drew his unconditional spite. He saw them as the real cause of the terrible destruction of the country by the Romans in the war (A.D. 66–74). It was chiefly the Zealots who fanned the flames of revolt, and Rome responded with horrific force, laying the country waste and enslaving thousands of its citizens. Most scholars believe that the formative moment for the Zealots came in A.D. 6 when Quirinius, then Roman governor of Syria and Palestine, carried out a census after Rome had deposed the tyrannical Archelaus, son of Herod and the ethnarch of Judea. A man named Judas, who came from the hilltop town of Gamla east of the Sea of Galilee, led out in an armed resistance because he perceived that the census, undertaken for the purposes of taxation, would mean that he and fellow Jews would lose the few freedoms they then enjoyed. To illustrate, the issue of freedom from foreign rule, which was the number one concern of the Zealots, lay behind the question addressed to Jesus during the last week of His life, "Is it lawful to give tribute to Caesar, or not?" (Mark 12:14). Moreover, in the book of Acts, the famous teacher Gamaliel refers to Judas: "[There] rose up Judas of Galilee in the days of the taxing, and drew away much people after him" (Acts 5:37). Clearly, this man and his movement were well known.

If truth be told, passion for freedom from foreigners' grip raised its fiery eyes long before A.D. 6. The question had haunted Jews since at least the time of Antiochus IV (see chapter 4, "The Maccabean War Breaks Out"). The terrifying events during his reign sharpened the realization about what a dominating foreign power could do. For some, like the family of Mattathias of Modein and his sons, freedom was more precious than life itself. The example of these Maccabean freedom fighters, who finally threw off the Seleucid yoke, had shined for more than 150 years as a bright light for lovers of liberty such as Judas. To be sure, the Romans were much more powerful than the Seleucids. And Judas of Gamla miscalculated his enemy. Even so, he bore the name of the most famous of the Maccabee family members, Judas. In his turn, he would confer on one of his sons a name from that family—Simon. It appears that Judas was patterning his life and that of his family after those earlier freedom fighters. In fact, the family passion for the struggle against Rome and its representatives began a generation earlier.

As we have noticed, before 47 B.C., Judas' father, a man named Hezekiah, had led a resistance movement in Galilee against the new rulers, the Romans. The youthful Herod, then the chief military officer of the territory, caught Hezekiah and executed him. Because prominent people in Jerusalem, presumably members of the Sanhedrin, greeted the news with undisguised disappointment, Hezekiah and his movement apparently enjoyed a base of support throughout the country (*Jewish War* 1.10.4–8). Then it was Judas' turn. Forty years after the execution of his father, upon news of the death of Herod in 4 B.C., Judas raided the armory in Sepphoris, the capital of Galilee, which lay three miles northwest of Nazareth. His daring action may have been secretly connected with other uprisings around the country that flared at the same time, although the evidence is not firm. In any event, these small-scale revolts pulled into Palestine the Roman legate Varus and two legions from Syria to deal with them (*Jewish War* 2.4.1; 2.5.1). Even though we cannot know whether the uprisings were coordinated, it is highly probable that Judas' act was an early Zealot effort to try to win freedom.

Liberty was not the only ideal these people embraced. At the doctrinal heart of their enterprise stood the conviction that God was their only master, a concept that they found in the commonly recited *Shema'*, "Hear, O Israel: The Lord our God is one Lord" (Deuteronomy 6:4). They stoutly refused to call any person "master" and would die rather than do so. A second tenet held that scripture offered a perfect model for acceptable, zealous action before God: it was the righteous action of Phinehas, grandson of Aaron. For when the apostate Zimri was consorting with the Midianite woman Cozbi, Phinehas took their lives. He thus "turned [God's] wrath away from the children of Israel" because "he was zealous for [God's] sake among them" (Numbers 25:1–15). Phinehas had saved the day. Judas and his associates, particularly his close friend Zadok the Pharisee, also wanted to save the day and usher in the kingdom of God.

The concept of zeal for God found expression in Hebrew and Aramaic words that were equivalent to the Greek *zēlōtēs*. In Hebrew, these people called themselves *qannā'īm*. They also applied the Aramaic equivalent *qan'anayyā* to themselves and their adherents. It is such a term that lies behind the name of Jesus' eleventh Apostle, "Simon the Canaanite" (Matthew 10:4; Mark 3:18). This name does not mean that Simon descended from the early Canaanite people who inhabited the land before the Israelite tribes displaced them. His name has to do with the Zealot movement, as Luke properly reminds us, referring to him as "Simon called Zelotes" (Luke 6:15). Evidently, this Apostle had earlier associated himself with the Zealots and therefore stood for an intense zeal toward God as well as for freedom from foreign oppression. Even his name Simon may tie back to Simon Maccabee, a son of Mattathias who helped lead the Jews to freedom from Seleucid domination. In this light, Simon the Canaanite is the one Apostle who must have already possessed strong religious and political views at the time of his call.

As we have noted, Josephus despised the Zealots. He had lived through the war with Rome and seen the terrible suffering that descended on his people. He held the Zealots and their kind responsible for the suffering, calling them "robbers." Actually, the term that he chose, the Greek word *lēstēs*, also appears in the account of the condemnation of Jesus and the freeing of the man named Barabbas, who is called "a robber" (John 18:40). It becomes clear from Luke's recounting that this man had been cast into prison "for a certain sedition made in the city [of Jerusalem]" (Luke 23:19). Hence, Josephus' term for these people seems to point to a political side of their activity rather than merely to the criminal, although Josephus probably had both senses in mind.

There was another term that Josephus frequently wrote to describe a group whom he linked to the Zealots and the war with Rome: the *sicarii*. Early on, these people distinguished themselves as assassins. They carried a distinctive knife that they folded into their robes and that is called in Latin *sica*, meaning "dagger." They targeted not only Roman officials but also Jewish notables who seemed to foster the status quo or, worse, to side with the Romans. Their technique was to get close to their target in a crowd, stab the person, and then melt into the crowd as panic erupted at the discovery of the murder.

Though the origins of the Zealot movement reach back to a period before the ministries of Jesus and John the Baptist, the end came afterward. It was Zealots who took over the ill-fated defense of Jerusalem against the Roman siege. According to Josephus, the people then within the city suffered horribly at the Zealots' hands. Though many Zealots fled to Egypt after the fall of the city, the movement died with the burning of the temple in August of A.D. 70. As the temple went up in flames, the Zealots lost their one precious symbol of God's presence in their midst. For the *sicarii*, the end came at Masada. Under the leadership of Eleazar ben Yair, a kinsman of Judas of Gamla, the *sicarii* who garrisoned Masada failed to hold out the Roman force that besieged them. Their passion for freedom ran so deeply that they took their own lives rather than allow themselves to be taken prisoners and sold into slavery. The ends of their lives brought an end to the intense energy that had fueled the movement.

For Further Reading

F. F. Bruce, *New Testament History* (Garden City, New York: Anchor Books, 1972), 82–121.

David Noel Freedman et al., eds., *The Anchor Bible Dictionary* (New York: Doubleday, 1992), s.v. "Essenes," "War Rule," and "Zealots."

Kent P. Jackson, "Revolutionaries in the First Century," in John F. Hall and John W. Welch, eds., *Masada and the World of the New Testament* (Provo, Utah: BYU Studies, 1997), 129–40.

Stephen E. Robinson, "The Setting of the Gospels," in Kent P. Jackson and Robert L. Millet, eds., *Studies in Scripture, Volume Five: The Gospels* (Salt Lake City: Deseret Book, 1986), 10–37.

Emil Schürer, *The History of the Jewish People in the Age of Jesus Christ*, 3 vols., rev. ed. by Geza Vermes, Fergus Millar, and Matthew Black (Edinburgh: T & T Clark, 1973–87), 1:379–82; 2:550–90, 598–606.

Shemaryahu Talmon, "The Emergence of Jewish Sectarianism in the Early Second Temple Period," in Patrick D. Miller Jr., et al., eds., *Ancient Israelite Religion: Essays in Honor of Frank Moore Cross* (Philadelphia: Fortress Press, 1987), 587–616.

Geza Vermes, *The Dead Sea Scrolls in English*, 4th ed. (New York: Penguin Books, 1995).

John W. Welch, "Legal and Social Perspectives on Robbers in the First Century," in John F. Hall and John W. Welch, eds., *Masada and the World of the New Testament* (Provo, Utah: BYU Studies, 1997), 141–53.

Part 4

Spiritual Light

CHAPTER 16

MESSIANIC HOPES

The sun was blazing overhead, and Yosi the scribe yearned for shade. The temperature had risen higher than the day before. It was so hot that nature seemed paralyzed. Only the water moving slowly through the canals that the Essenes had built seemed to have the will to move in this unbearable heat. The world around Yosi seemed barren. He entered the shelter of a room and prepared his pen. The ink well was full and the parchment was ready, so he began carefully copying the text before him. This process was a sacred duty and a privilege. Others were making pots, and still others were curing animal hides so that he could continue his work. He and his brothers were the "Sons of Light," and they had withdrawn to this desolate wilderness to prepare for the time when the "community" would return to Jerusalem and eventually establish the ideal temple, replacing the polluted one that stood there now. They would replace the corrupt priesthood, too, and they would officiate there, acting as the true priests of the Lord. As Yosi carefully copied the words before him, he knew that he was living in the end of times and would see the fulfillment of the prophecies that he copied so carefully onto the parchment: "A sovereign shall not be removed from the tribe of Judah. While Israel has the dominion, there will not lack someone who sits on the throne of David. For 'the staff' is the covenant of royalty and the thousands of Israel are 'the feet' until the messiah of justice comes, the branch of David. For to him and to his descendants has been given the covenant of royalty over his people for all everlasting generations, which he has observed." When Yosi was finished, another person placed the sacred text in a clay jar that, eventually, would be hidden in a nearby cave, above the Dead Sea, to be retrieved at the conclusion of the war with the Romans, a war that was the beginning of the end for the present world.

Complex and *uncertain*—these words best describe the colorful and sometimes blank tapestry of beliefs about the coming Messiah. In no other dimension of intertestamental spiritual life did disagreements run so deeply. What is more, a lack of sources on this most fundamental belief cripples modern investigators who seek to restore the blank spots in the tapestry. Further, the blank spots impair the abilities of those who seek to behold the grand sweep of this Messianic tapestry, creating insoluble difficulties in interpreting the interrelationships of its multicolored parts. For example, what does it mean that the Sadducees apparently espoused a view of salvation that excluded the Messiah? How did the author of the book of Jubilees and the composers of the Testaments of the Twelve Patriarchs arrive at a view of a priestly messiah, whereas the Essenes of Qumran came to believe in two messiahs?

In short, no clearly defined concept regarding the Messiah existed. Even within those groups who held on to a Messianic hope, there were diverse concepts about the role and person of the Messiah, one view at times contradicting another. For instance, for some groups, the messianic hope was connected with the house of David, a Messiah king, so to speak. Others championed a Messiah son of Aaron, a priestly messiah, as we have noted. Additionally, other Messiah-like figures, who are not referred to by the actual term *Messiah*, were nevertheless among the currents of messianic hope manifesting themselves in this era.

For those who embraced some type of messianic hope, that hope was almost always grounded in the Old Testament. While these concepts bore many similarities to one another, there were striking differences, even when concepts went back to the same passages of scripture. Naturally, some of these differences grew out of appeals to differing scriptural texts. (Confusion was so great that even Josephus, at the end of the first century A.D., came to believe that messianic passages actually referred to a gentile human agent [see *Jewish War* 6.312–15]. Instead of the Messiah descending *from* Jacob, the Messiah was appointed *while in the land* of Jacob, referring to Vespasian's acclamation by his troops as the new Caesar while in Judea during the Jewish war.)

Finally, we notice that these groups often adapted their interpretations, and therefore their concepts, of the Messiah as historical circumstances changed. Such adaptations provided them new ways of interpreting Old Testament prophecies. This tendency to reinterpret messianic allusions in the Old Testament made it possible for certain groups to ignite new messianic hopes from time to time. Here we think of the failed attempt by an unidentified Egyptian Jew to liberate Jerusalem from the Romans, as some believed the Messiah would—an act that led to the slaughter of thousands (see Acts 21:37–39; Josephus, *Jewish Antiquities* 20.8.6; *Jewish War* 2.13.3–5).

The Hebrew Bible

The Hebrew noun *Messiah* derives from the verb "to anoint (with oil)" and means "the one who has been anointed" or "the anointed one." The associated verb describes that sacral action of "anointing" kings (1 Samuel 9:16; 10:1; 16:12–13; 2 Samuel 2:4; 5:3; 1 Kings 1:34, 45; 19:15–16; 2 Kings 9:6; 23:30), priests (Exodus 40:13, 15; Leviticus 8:12; 21:12; Numbers 3:3), and prophets (1 Kings 19:16; Isaiah 61:1). The term also refers to the patriarchs (Psalm 105:15; 1 Chronicles 16:22).

The Old Testament text preserves the word *Messiah*, "anointed (one)," also in reference to officials or individuals:

1. High priests, "the anointed [Messiah] of God" (Leviticus 4:3, 5, 16; and probably also Daniel 9:25–26).

2. Kings, "the anointed [Messiah] of the Lord" (1 Samuel 2:10, 35; 9:16; 16:3; 24:6; 2 Samuel 12:7; 1 Kings 1:34). The title included not only the kings of Israel and of Judah but also Cyrus of Persia (Isaiah 45:1).

3. Prophets of the Lord (1 Kings 19:16).

The person thus anointed became sacrosanct. To harm or even to curse such a person was a capital offense (see 2 Samuel 19:22). The anointed David, whom King Saul wanted to kill, refused on two occasions to slay the anointed-but-now-rejected Saul. Finding Saul resting in a cave, David said to his men, "The Lord forbid that I should do this thing [slay] unto my master, the Lord's anointed, to stretch forth mine hand against him, seeing he is the anointed of the Lord" (1 Samuel 24:6). On another occasion, David and Abishai found Saul asleep in the bottom of a trench, at which point Abishai said to David, "God hath delivered thine enemy into thine hand this day: now therefore let me smite him. . . . And David said to Abishai, Destroy him not: for who can stretch forth his hand against the Lord's anointed, and be guiltless?" (1 Samuel 26:8–9).

These accounts illustrate that Israelites held a concept in which human agents were anointed and set apart by God to fulfill certain responsibilities among His people. Besides this, there was a messianic hope that waxed and waned through the centuries, often depending on the circumstances that people faced. One of those circumstances had to do with prophetic inspiration.

During the period between Malachi and Matthew, it appears that no one spoke in the name of the Lord until the time of John the Baptist. Certainly, there were individuals and groups, such as the community at Qumran (see chapter 15, "Essenes and Zealots"), who would have argued that they spoke or wrote in God's name. But while some of the devout must have carried a portion of the Spirit of the Lord, people were largely left to interpret the words of God on their own, some with more success than others. For example, when life turned sour, some would dream, sing, and write about a messiah whom they hoped would come in their own time. Such hopes, expressed in records from this period, confirm the antiquity of the messianic expectation found in the Old Testament, a dimension of scripture that some scholars have been too quick to dismiss.

The Intertestamental Period

Two major obstacles confront readers trying to outline the contours of the messianic hope during the intertestamental period. First, sources from the early part of this era, from about 400 B.C. until about 175 B.C., are limited and therefore make it difficult to ascertain the general outline of messianic hopes in Judaism. Scholars have made too much of the fact that comparatively little information exists regarding a messianic hope during this early period. The paucity of evidence for messianic hopes does not mean they did not exist. It simply means we cannot often gauge the actual level of messianic hope or the exact form that such hopes took. Even many New Testament scholars dismiss the New Testament as evidence for messianic expectations for this period.

Second, the difficulty of dating sources from the later period, from the beginning of the Maccabean era about 175 B.C. through the middle of the first century A.D., makes it almost impossible to sketch out trends along historical lines. Nevertheless, we shall see that there is much to discover about messianic hopes during this period that helps to bridge the gap between the Old Testament and the New.

Background

A resurgence of messianic hope ran among Jews after the exile, based on prophecy and influenced by current historical realities. For example, a wave of messianic hope arose when Zerubbabel, the grandson of former King Jeahoiachin, returned to Judah about 520 B.C. The book of Zechariah is the best source for this new wave of messianic hope. Certainly, Zerubbabel's efforts to rebuild the temple at Jerusalem only heightened this expectation because many associated the building of the temple with Davidic kingship, which was part of the messianic hope. The tie of David to the temple, of course, arose from the fact that Solomon, David's son, built the first temple.

Because Zerubbabel descended from David through Jeahoiachin, there may have been those who believed that Zerubbabel might reestablish the triumphant Davidic kingdom. But there is no evidence that he attempted to do so, especially in light of Jeremiah's prophecy that no one from Jeahoiachin's family would ever establish the Davidic dynasty (see Jeremiah 22:24–30). Yet the expectation, whether merited or not, of a reestablished Davidic dynasty as part of a new independent nation may partially explain the high Samaritan concern with Zerubbabel's efforts to rebuild the temple and its altar in Jerusalem.

Matters become more complex with the messianic expectations featured in Zechariah 1–8. Here, the messianic hope also includes a priestly messiah. Scholars generally agree that these texts talk about two specific, anointed servants of the Lord: a new Davidic messiah and a priestly messiah (see Zechariah 4:11–14). Both Zerubbabel, the successor to the Davidic royal line, and Joshua, the high priest, play a central role in this story and may at one time have been viewed as the possible expected anointed leaders. But when Zerubbabel failed to establish the Jews as an independent nation, many had to rethink their messianic hope, which resulted in its transformation. In the end, this hope was given a pronouncedly future focus. Yet many saw the reestablishment of the temple and a functioning high priest as the first step in God's plan to save Israel.

The Hasmonean Dynasty

The period of severe persecution under Antiochus IV (see chapter 4, "The Maccabean War") naturally cultivated a fertile ground for a renewed messianic hope. Yet the militarily successful Hasmoneans, a priestly family, did not live up to the messianic hopes of some Jews, specifically because they did not belong to the house of David, an aspect that was rooted in the Old Testament. Indeed, when the prophet Nathan came to David, he spoke the following, brimming words: "Thine house and thy kingdom shall be established for ever before thee: thy throne shall be established for ever" (2 Samuel 7:16). But not everyone in this era saw the house of David as the grand key to Israel's future.

The author of the book of Jubilees (see chapter 10, "Apocrypha and Pseudepigrapha"), a work most likely composed during the Hasmonean period, offered to readers an alternative possibility without declaring null and void the Old Testament promises to the tribe of Judah and the dynasty of David. The book points plainly to the divine promises given to the tribes of both Judah and Levi (see Jubilees 31). However, it becomes clear that Jubilees accords the tribe of Levi a more important status than Judah, which can be explained only by the fact that the Jewish people were released from Antiochus IV's deadly excesses by a priestly family, the Hasmoneans. Further, more was said about the important role of priests, and it came from an unexpected source, the prophet Malachi.

Several scholars believe that the promise made in Malachi 2 regarding a covenant with Levi was the basis for the development of the Levite messianic traditions during the intertestamental period: "My covenant was with him [Levi] of life and peace: and I gave them to him for the fear wherewith he feared me, and was afraid before my name. The law of truth was in his mouth, and iniquity was not found in his lips: he walked with me in peace and equity, and did turn many away from iniquity. For the priest's lips should keep knowledge, and they should seek the law at his mouth: for he is the messenger of the Lord of hosts" (Malachi 2:5–7).

Of course, some voices in the land of Judah criticized the priestly Hasmonean dynasty (see chapter 15, "Essenes and Zealots"). One such criticism of the Hasmonean rule appears in the Psalms of Solomon.

The Psalms of Solomon

Composed about the middle of the first century B.C., the Psalms of Solomon are not only anti-Roman but also contain strong anti-Hasmonean sentiments, contrasting the promised Davidic rule and the kingdom of God with the current Hasmonean rule: "Lord, you chose David to be king over Israel, and swore to him about his descendants forever, that his kingdom would not fail before you. But for our sins, sinners rose up against us, they set upon us and drove us out. Those to whom you did not make promise, they took away from us by force; and they did not glory your honorable names. With pomp they set up a monarch because of their arrogance; they despoiled the throne of David with arrogant shout, but you, O God, overthrew them, and uprooted their descendants from the earth" (Psalms of Solomon 17:4–7).

Here, the early promise given to David through the prophet Nathan receives emphasis (see 2 Samuel 7:16). This connection to David seems to be the most consistent expression of the messianic hope during this period.

The Dead Sea Scrolls

Just as the discovery of the Dead Sea Scrolls (see chapter 9, "The Dead Sea Scrolls") brought to light important texts from the dark caves near Qumran, their translation and publication have shed a bright light on anti-Hasmonean attitudes that arose during this period, resulting in a plethora of messianic interpretations, including a pro-Levi concept.

Like the book of Jubilees, the Dead Sea Scrolls highlight the promise given to the house of David. Since the Essenes lived under the Hasmoneans as well as under Herod, the positive emphasis on the Davidic messiah may have been one way to make points about the illegitimacy of both dynasties. Yet the Essenes at Qumran, like the author of the book of Jubilees, apparently expected a Messiah son of Aaron. Several texts from the Qumran community express a belief that the final leadership of the kingdom of God will rest in the hands of a Messiah ben Aaron coupled with a Messiah ben Israel. While there is scholarly debate over the interpretation of some of the texts that support that interpretation, the *Temple Scroll* (11QTemple) makes the messianic descendant of Levi superior to the Messiah of Israel: "And the high priest shall offer the burnt offering of the Levites first, and after it he shall offer the burnt offering of the tribe of Judah" (*Temple Scroll*, XIII 9–10).

While Jews in Palestine were considering their unique messianic hopes, other Jews living beyond the boundary of their ancestral homeland had their own ideas.

The Sibylline Oracles

The Sibylline Oracles were produced over a long period of time. However, a section quoted below is believed to have been produced during the second century B.C. by Jews living in Egypt. The passage tells of a messianic figure who is human: "And then God will send a King from the sun. Who will stop the entire earth from evil war. Killing some, imposing oaths of loyalty on others and he will not do all these things by his private plans but in obedience to the noble teachings of the great God" (Sibylline Oracles 3:652–56).

Most scholars believe that this messianic figure refers to Ptolemy VI (180–145 B.C.), a gentile king who was known for his good relations with the Jews. There is also a possible connection to the Bible, at least with the concept that the Lord could anoint a "gentile" to accomplish His work. In this vein, we notice Isaiah 45:1, where Cyrus is identified as the Lord's "anointed."

Other Figures

As noted earlier, messianic hopes were connected not only to the House of David but also to a Messiah ben Aaron or a priestly messiah. Additional messianic figures who do not carry the actual title *Messiah* also appear in texts from this period, usually based on earlier biblical allusions. Some of these are the "Servant of the Lord" (see Isaiah 40–53), the "Son of Man" (see Daniel 7), and God's "Messenger" (see Malachi 3:1). In most cases, literature from the intertestamental period generally provides a collective interpretation of passages referring to the Jews and not to an individual when discussing suffering. And while 2 Maccabees 7:6, 18, 33–38 suggests that death (martyrdom) will end Israel's suffering (persecution in this particular case), there seem to be few examples of any person or group during this period who suggest that a suffering Messiah must die for the sins of Israel.

Though there have been sensational public announcements by irresponsible people about one messianic belief or another from the intertestamental period, scholars have been careful in drawing conclusions from allusions in the sources. Yet the seemingly endless discussions have not brought forward even the vaguest consensus about the parameters and meanings of references to the messianic hope. This lack of consensus underlines the difficulties that face students who seek to understand and interpret the kaleidoscope of hopes centered in a messiah.

Conclusion

No chapter in this book better highlights the absence of the prophetic voice during this period of Jewish history than this one dealing with various messianic hopes that surfaced in the intertestamental period. Most Jews and Christians accept what the author of the book of First Maccabees implied in his own narrative—that prophecy had ceased after Haggai, Zechariah, and Malachi. And while some Jews believed that prophecy would return shortly before God's ultimate victory over evil, there is no evidence that a prophet raised his voice again among the Jews until the coming of John the Baptist.

The lack of a prophet, it seems, best explains the incoherent picture that emerges regarding the messianic hope. It seems certain that any specific knowledge about the birth, death, and resurrection of a Savior-Messiah, revealed previously through ancient prophets such as Enoch (see Moses 7:53–57) and Lehi (see 1 Nephi 10:4–11), had largely been lost before the Jews returned to the land of Judah from exile.

A careful reading of the New Testament suggests that even among Jesus' most intimate disciples, a correct understanding of the Messiah's mission was seriously lacking. Although many Jews of the time expected a descendant of David to establish a throne, he was to be a human agent anointed by God's Spirit, much like the ancient judges on whom the Spirit of God fell and who delivered Israel from her enemies (see, for example, Judges 3:9–10).

In the case of Jesus' disciples, even after three years of preparation by Jesus himself, the disciples seemed unprepared to correctly interpret the fateful last days of Jesus' ministry in Jerusalem. Only after the resurrection, coupled with the Risen Lord's own teachings from the messianic texts found in the Law, the prophets, and the psalms (see Luke 24:44–46), did the disciples begin to grasp the mission of the Savior-Messiah. With the reception of the gift of the Holy Ghost on the day of Pentecost, the disciples were endowed with a special ability to open the scriptures and provide a correct interpretation of key messianic passages.

The Jewish writings from the intertestamental period provide only a limited set of perspectives on the dynamic religious experience within which the concept of a messianic hope was reborn and redefined into several distinct ideas. While these distinct ideas are rooted in the Old Testament, the historical context of each new interpretation allowed the group or individual who espoused it to go beyond and in some cases deemphasize or overemphasize certain prophetic texts beyond what God had intended.

For Further Reading

James H. Charlesworth, *The Old Testament Pseudepigrapha*, 2 vols. (Garden City, New York: Doubleday, 1984).

David Noel Freedman et al., eds., *The Anchor Bible Dictionary* (New York: Doubleday, 1992), s.v. "Egyptian, the" and "Messiah."

Florentino García-Martínez, "Messianic Hopes in the Qumran Writings," in Donald W. Parry and Dana M. Pike, eds., *LDS Perspectives on the Dead Sea Scrolls* (Provo, Utah: Foundation for Ancient Research and Mormon Studies, 1997), 115–75.

Lester L. Grabbe, *Judaic Religion in the Second Temple Period: Belief and Practice from the Exile to Yavneh* (New York: Routledge, 2000), 271–91.

Richard Neitzel Holzapfel, *A Lively Hope: The Suffering, Death, Resurrection, and Exaltation of Jesus Christ* (Salt Lake City: Bookcraft, 1999).

———, "The Hidden Messiah," in *A Witness of Jesus Christ: The 1989 Sperry Symposium on the Old Testament* (Salt Lake City: Deseret Book, 1990), 80–95.

Antti Latto, *A Star Is Rising: The Historical Development of the Old Testament Royal Ideology and the Rise of the Jewish Messianic Expectations* (Atlanta: Scholars Press, 1997).

D. Kelly Ogden, "Messianic Concept and Hope," in Daniel H. Ludlow, ed., *Encyclopedia of Mormonism* (New York: Macmillan, 1992), 893–94.

Gaye Strathearn, "A New Messianic Fragment (4Q521) from the Dead Sea Scrolls" (M.A. thesis, Brigham Young University, 1992).

M. Catherine Thomas, "From Malachi to John the Baptist: The Dynamics of Apostasy," in Kent P. Jackson and Robert L. Millet, eds., *Studies in Scripture, Volume Five: 1 Kings to Malachi* (Salt Lake City: Deseret Book, 1993), 471–83.

Yigael Yadin, ed., *The Temple Scroll* (Jerusalem: The Israel Exploration Society, 1983), 2:104–5.

CHAPTER 17

FEASTS AND FESTIVALS

A small company of devout Jews was walking to Jerusalem. Climbing along dusty footpaths and ancient roads, the group joined others who were making their way to the Holy City for one of the most important of Jewish holidays—the Passover. When they reached the top of the Mount of Olives, they caught their first glimpse of Jerusalem, a thrilling and long-awaited sight. The group naturally and instinctively looked beyond the walls of the city to the temple itself. Here was the jewel and heart of Jerusalem and of the Jewish nation—the holy temple. They were fulfilling the commandment: "Three times thou shalt keep a feast unto me. . . . Three times in the year all thy males shall appear before the Lord God" (Exodus 23:14, 17). Here they would worship the Lord God and stand in His presence.

One of the first objectives of those who returned from captivity in Babylon was to rebuild the temple (see chapter 2, "Jerusalem Arises from the Ashes"). Once the Jerusalem temple was completed in 515 B.C., it formed the centerpiece of Jewish life until it was destroyed again during the revolt against Roman occupation in A.D. 70. As before the exile, so during this period people worshiped primarily through sacrifices that consisted of the slaughter, roasting, and eating of animals. Additionally, people expressed their devotion to God through offerings of bread, fruit, grain, and incense at the temple.

Thus, Jews from around the Mediterranean world came to the Holy City for pilgrim festivals in the autumn and spring to make sacrifices and present offerings. But this was not all. They also came to the temple to make and renew covenants, to participate in prayer, to sing hymns of praise and supplication, and to stand on sacred ground in the presence of the Lord. Both Jews of the Diaspora and those living in the land of Judah, along with proselytes and sympathizers, supported the temple priesthood and maintained the temple through the half-shekel payment each year and, in many cases, through additional contributions.

Sacrifices and Offerings

One of the central features of the temple was the system of sacrifices and offerings (see Leviticus 1–7), offered only at the temple in Jerusalem, only at set times, only in certain ways, and only by the priests. The regulations governing this system are set forth in great detail in Leviticus, Numbers, and the last chapters of Ezekiel. The book of Leviticus describes five types of sacrifices:

1. The burnt offering, sometimes identified by the Greek designation "holocaust" (see Leviticus 1; 6:8–13).
2. The meat offering, sometimes referred to as the meal offering (see Leviticus 2; 6:14–18).
3. The peace offering (see Leviticus 3; 7:11–21).
4. The sin offering (see Leviticus 4:1 to 5:13; 6:24–30).
5. The trespass offering (see Leviticus 5:14 to 6:7; 7:1–10).

The ritual slaughter of bulls, goats, and sheep was sacred principally because the Lord had commanded it. The exact meaning that priests and worshipers saw in these sacrifices cannot be reconstructed with certainty because the texts basically provide us with details about how they were to be performed rather than a discussion of their symbolism. Of course, as we have noticed, at the temple people were to present the additional offerings of thanksgiving and offerings for temple maintenance as well as pay for the redemption of their firstborn children.

Feasts and Festivals

The sacred calendar was punctuated with a series of special holidays, some of which required all Jewish males to make pilgrimage to Jerusalem and all of which entailed special rituals and ceremonies at the temple. People celebrated each of these temple festivals with various of the five sacrifices noted above, making the altar of the temple a very busy place. These holidays were days of covenant-making and renewal and were celebrated with sacred acts such as fasting and specific readings from scriptures. In this connection, one of the most important holidays in the sacred calendar, since it occurred so frequently, was the Sabbath.

The Sabbath

Jews observed the Sabbath as a time to remember God as the creator of the universe and as the Redeemer of Israel who delivered His people from the bondage of slavery and from death. Following the example of the Lord during creation, the covenant people were to rest from their daily labors on the seventh day of the week. The beginning and ending of the Sabbath, from dusk to dusk, was indicated at the temple by the sounding of trumpets.

Priests celebrated the Sabbath at the temple by doubling the daily burnt offerings—four lambs instead of two. But the host of sacrifices brought by individuals was not permitted. In addition to the two doubled burnt offerings, the priests removed the old shewbread, which was then reverently eaten, and set out twelve fresh loaves on the table of shewbread while making an incense offering.

Five Festivals

Besides the Sabbath, the Mosaic Law identified five special holidays or festivals to be observed during the year (see Leviticus 23):

1. Passover (*Pesah*), or the Feast of Unleavened Bread, held in the spring, usually in March or April.

2. Pentecost (*Shavu'ot*), or Weeks, held in the summer, fifty days after Passover, usually in May or June.

3. New Year (*Ro'sh ha-Shanah*), in the fall, usually in September or October.

4. The Day of Atonement (*Yom Kippur*), or Day of Fasting, fell in the fall, usually in September or October.

5. Tabernacles (*Sukkot*) occurred in the fall, usually in September or October.

Passover

The Passover feast began with a sacred meal. This meal commemorated the Lord's deliverance of Israelite slaves from the angel of death, which killed all of the firstborn in Egypt and led to the deliverance of the slaves from bondage. God revealed the details of the meal, details that are recorded in Exodus 12. On the tenth day of the first month (Nisan), an unblemished male lamb was chosen. On the fourteenth day, participants were to kill the lamb and daub its blood on the doorposts of houses where people would see it. The flesh of the lamb was to be roasted and eaten with unleavened bread and bitter herbs. Care was to be taken that no bones were broken in the lamb, and any of the flesh that remained was to be completely burnt as an offering to the Lord.

The blood on the door witnessed to the Lord and the angel of death the faith and obedience exercised by those within, who would then eat the flesh of the lamb, which had died to preserve them from bondage and death. That all of the flesh would be eaten and all of the remainder be burnt symbolized the totality of the sacrifice of the lamb.

The unleavened bread represented the haste with which the children of Israel had to flee Egypt, since they did not have time to allow yeast to rise. The bitter herbs represented the bitter slavery imposed upon them. The Lord indicated one of the purposes of this festival when He said, "It shall come to pass, when your children shall say unto you, What mean ye by this service? that ye shall say, It is the sacrifice of the Lord's passover, who passed over the houses of the children of Israel in Egypt, when he smote the Egyptians, and delivered our houses" (Exodus 12:26–27).

From the fifteenth to the twenty-first day of the month, people were to observe the Feast of Unleavened Bread. Specifically, they were to abstain from eating leavened bread and remove all leaven from their homes. This reminded them of the first Passover when, because of haste, women did not have time to add leaven to their bread. They were to rest from their labors, remember the Lord who provided them with what they ate, and thus be reminded of the purity expected of the covenant people.

This festival, originally celebrated in the fall, became a spring celebration and thereby became enriched through time by its natural connections with the planting of crops and supplications to the Lord for abundance in crops and flocks. Because of the importance of this celebration, Jews flocked into Jerusalem from all over the world. By law, in the city each of the lambs eaten at the Passover meal had to be sacrificed in the temple. In addition, priests offered extra sacrifices at the temple during the Feast of Unleavened Bread.

Pentecost or Weeks

For seven weeks, forty-nine days after the Passover, people turned their energies to the harvest of the firstfruits of their fields. On the fiftieth day, they celebrated the Feast of Weeks, also called Pentecost, which is the Greek word for *fifty*. This was a joyous time, and people brought sacrifices of gratitude to the Lord from the firstfruits of their lands. As Passover commemorated the Exodus, so Pentecost, in Jewish tradition, came to represent the giving of the Law on Sinai because it was believed that the Law was given on the fiftieth day after Israel left Egypt. This festival was a time of thanksgiving, and it reminded people of their dependence on the Lord for the necessities of life. As at all the festivals, special offerings were made on Pentecost at the temple.

Day of Atonement

Israel celebrated two new years. Passover was celebrated on the fourteenth day of the first month, but a new year called *Ro'sh ha-Shanah* was also celebrated on the first day of the seventh month. The tenth day of the seventh month was the most holy of all days in ancient Israel—the Day of Atonement. The Lord stated the solemn purpose of this festival: "On that day shall the priest make an atonement for you, to cleanse you, that ye may be clean from all your sins before the Lord" (Leviticus 16:30).

The Lord gave specific directions for the celebration of this solemn day. People were to prepare themselves through fasting, prayer, and repentance. They were then to present themselves before the Lord, and the priests would offer a series of sacrifices for the purification of both the priests and all of Israel. After staying up all night for his own spiritual preparation, the high priest brought a bullock to the altar as a sin offering and a ram as a burnt offering for himself and his house as well as two male goats and a ram for "the children of Israel." He cast lots over the two goats, designating one as a sin offering to the Lord and the other as the "scapegoat," or the goat that would "escape" being slaughtered and that would be "for Azazel."

The term *Azazel* either represented a name of the evil one residing in the wilderness or was a name for the wilderness itself. The priest killed the bullock and the goat for the sin offerings and entered the Holy of Holies, stepping into the presence of the Lord. There he offered incense before the Lord and sprinkled the blood of the bullock and goat on the mercy seat, signifying the power of the Lord to cover over, or forgive, the sins of the high priest, his family, and all of the Israelites. The goat for Azazel was then brought forth, and upon its head the high priest confessed all the sins of Israel, symbolizing for the people that, through repentance and the blood of the Atonement, their sins could be removed. The high priest then offered the two rams as burnt offerings for his house and for the assembled congregation. Priests then took the scapegoat to the wilderness, where they released it so it would wander off, carrying everyone's sins away. It was a day of solemn cleansing.

Tabernacles

The Feast of Tabernacles was celebrated from the fourteenth to the twenty-first of the month of Chislev. This festival occurred in the fall and consisted of a joyous celebration of the harvest. It came to be associated with the forty years of wandering in the wilderness when the children of Israel lived in tents (booths or tabernacles) and were miraculously cared for by the Lord through water from the rock, the blessing of manna, and the gift of quail.

The children of Israel were commanded to live in temporary booths or tents for seven days to commemorate the wanderings in the wilderness (see Leviticus 23:42–43) and to take the boughs of "goodly trees, . . . palm trees, . . . thick trees, and willows" and rejoice (see Leviticus 23:40). Through time, the interpretation of these became citron (ethrog), myrtle, palm (lulav), and willow. It was a time of great joy and festivity.

The children of Israel were specifically commanded to read

the Law every seven years at the Feast of Tabernacles, symbolic of the renewal of their covenants with the Lord both as a nation and individually. Solomon's Temple was dedicated on this day as well as the rebuilt altar in the days of Zerubbabel.

Other Voices

Not all Jews felt the awe and anticipation of pilgrims who made their way to Jerusalem to worship in the temple at Jerusalem. The Essenes regarded the temple as polluted and the priesthood as illegitimate and therefore did not support or participate in the sanctuary (see chapter 15, "Essenes and Zealots"). As we have seen before, one of the aspects of their lives that separated them from other Jewish groups who worshiped at the temple was the calendar. They used a solar calendar of 364 days, whereas other Jews during the Hasmonean period used a luni-solar calendar that coordinates the lunar cycle with the solar year.

As noted previously, the Samaritans, who like the Essenes came to reject the temple at Jerusalem, established their focus on Mount Gerizim, where they built a temple that was later destroyed during the Hasmonean dynasty (see chapter 14, "The Samaritans"). Another group, led by the former high priest Onias III and his son, fled to Egypt during the period of Antiochus IV's persecution and founded a temple at Leontopolis. That temple was similar to the temple in Jerusalem and was a place of sacrifice. Although those who built this temple did not reject the temple at Jerusalem, the fact that they were willing to build a second temple indicates that they differed from most other Jewish groups who believed that Jerusalem was the only legitimate place to build a temple. Apparently, their justification for building the temple came from a passage found in the book of Isaiah (see Isaiah 19:18–22). It was eventually closed by the Romans in A.D. 70.

CONCLUSION

Feasts and festivals accentuated the daily rhythms of life for most Jews of the period just as the temple provided them a physical focus for their world. Since the establishment of the monarchy under King Saul, nearly a millennium before, the temple and its feasts and festivals had been the center of their life. While the synagogue became an established institution by the second century B.C., or even earlier, the nearness of the temple in such a small state meant that most worshipers could come to the holy sanctuary regularly, especially at the times of annual festivals. Luke notes such a tradition within Jesus' family (see Luke 2:41–42). Even for those in the Diaspora, the ideal was to make a yearly pilgrimage to participate in one of the major festivals at the temple and to regularly donate to its maintenance, tying Jews together in a special and unique way.

FOR FURTHER READING

Shaye J. D. Cohen, *From the Maccabees to the Mishnah* (Philadelphia: Westminster Press, 1987), 60–103.

David Noel Freedman et al., eds., *Anchor Bible Dictionary* (New York: Doubleday, 1992), s.v. "Temple, Jerusalem."

Richard Neitzel Holzapfel and David Rolph Seely, *My Father's House: Temple Worship and Symbolism in the New Testament* (Salt Lake City: Bookcraft, 1994), 55–79.

Jacob Milgrom, *Leviticus 1–16*, The Anchor Bible 3A (New York: Doubleday, 1991).

CHAPTER 18

JEWISH LAW

Ezra rolled his thoughts through his mind. He was to meet—again—this morning with clan and city leaders. During the past few months, his efforts to bring fellow Jews in Jerusalem to a state of heart wherein they would take the law of Moses seriously had met with only limited success. Why could people not accept the Law with all of their hearts? Why did they not remember the bitter lessons of Nebuchadnezzar's capture of the city 150 years ago? Why did they not share his passion for God's words to them? Why had their leaders, especially the priests, not kept the promises they had made with solemn oaths to follow the Law? This morning he would try to convince people that true safety and prosperity lay in obeying God's words. He had decided to ask people on the spot to separate themselves from their foreign spouses. That way, he had reasoned, they would have to make an irreversible decision that, he hoped, would finally mean something to them, even if the decision was terribly difficult. Turning toward the temple while standing in his room, he prayed. Then he removed the phylacteries from his right arm and forehead and took off his prayer shawl. With a brisk, determined stride, he went to the door and stepped out into the pouring rain.

At the heart of every enduring society stands law. No civilization can continue long without it. For Israelites, both before and after the exile, the law of Moses was the central focus of their lives, whether they lived by its precepts or not. Prophets and teachers and commoners measured their society and their own performance against its precepts. We think, for example, of the reforms of King Josiah (640–609 B.C.). In accord with Mosaic law, he banished idolatrous priests and demolished the sanctuaries and altars that citizens and others had erected around his kingdom to foreign deities (see 2 Kings 23:3–20). After the exile, the prophet Malachi inveighed against priests who, contrary to the Law, had been offering "polluted bread" and "lame and sick" animals on the altar of the temple (Malachi 1:7–8). Both examples illustrate that people might stand condemned before the Law when it was properly understood and applied. They also demonstrate that laxness, as illumined by the bright light of the law, was common. It was this aspect of people's personalities that challenged Ezra when he came to Jerusalem. He was passionate about the Law; many in the society were not. His genius was to hit upon a way to impress indelibly onto people's hearts the sobering, eternal fact that obedience to the Law meant everything.

The Interpretation of the Law

From the time of Cyrus' edict freeing the Jews to return to Jerusalem (538 B.C.) to the fall of the city to the Roman Titus (A.D. 70), interpreting the written law became the most pervasive religious and intellectual activity in Judaism. To be sure, the temple held the center of gravity in people's lives. But the priestly and Levitical managers of the temple represented only one of the twelve tribes, that of Levi. And while priests were generally held in admiration and were influential to a point, most people came to the temple for only one or more of the annual festivals. They did not go to the temple daily or even weekly, and therefore their contact with priests, and even the temple, was infrequent. What is important to see, however, in any review of the Mosaic law, is the fact that this law governed all that went on within the temple enclosure. Moreover, the Law is what mandated that all males go to the temple three times a year for the festivals (Passover, Tabernacles, and

Pentecost). The fact that women did not live under this requirement, because they bore the main responsibility for the nurture of children, is also a matter of law and its interpretation.

In general, the Mosaic law rests on those portions of the Bible known as the Decalogue (Exodus 20:2–17), the Covenant Code (Exodus 20:22–23:33), the Holiness Code (Leviticus 17–26), and the Deuteronomic laws, all found in the first five books of Moses or in what Jews call the Torah, a term meaning "teaching." However, most scholars agree that the Law preserved in the Torah does not include all the legal facets that governed life among ancient Jews. Some are alluded to in the Bible, others have not been preserved, and still others developed outside the Bible through the growth of custom and tradition. Finally, in the Bible is a subset of laws not found in the Torah. These laws came to ancient Israel through the prophets. In all these cases, Jews held that the laws in their multiple forms came from God and that He was, therefore, the ultimate authority behind them.

Some Jews, at least, understood that the Law required interpretation and application. Following the loss of the monarchy after the destruction of Jerusalem by Nebuchadnezzar, the authority to interpret the Law was invested in the priests (see Deuteronomy 33:8–10), as was the case with Ezra when he returned to Jerusalem at the head of a group of exiles in 428 B.C. Whatever functions the king held previously were either transferred or dropped, and the office of high priest became correspondingly much more important. In the case of Ezra, he came with the full power of Artaxerxes I, the Persian king (465–424 B.C.), to impose the Law on the community there (see Ezra 7–8).

The triple combination of the Law, temple, and priests became the central focus of Judaism during this early period. The primary role of the priests, as guardians of the temple and interpreters of the Law, was assured because, in the Jewish temple state, there was no higher authority than the priests. Of course, the highest political authority resided in the king of Persia; nevertheless, the temple and the priests remained the central unifying symbol and authority of Judaism in Jerusalem and its environs. Moreover, during this early period, it seems impossible to separate the interpretation and enforcement of the Law from the daily regulations that shaped people's lives in general. Hence, the Law and the priests were indispensable.

However, alternative voices claimed authority to interpret the Law. For example, the Samaritans ultimately rejected the Jerusalem temple and priesthood and therefore the priests' right to interpret the Law (see chapter 14, "The Samaritans"). Later, the Essenes also discredited the temple and the priests in Jerusalem and offered alternative interpretations of the Law (see chapter 9, "The Dead Sea Scrolls," and chapter 15, "Essenes and Zealots"). In addition, the cadre of scribes that grew up, either because of priests' disinterest in the Law or because the scribes disagreed with priests' interpretations, became a formidable force for understanding the Law chiefly in the Pharisaic way. Ultimately, the only viable segment of Judaism to survive the revolts against Rome in A.D. 66–70 and again in A.D. 132–135 were the rabbis, the spiritual descendants of the Pharisees. It was they who thereafter held the power to interpret the Law and enact needed legislation. Hence, with the destruction of the temple in A.D. 70, the priests disappeared as guardians and interpreters of the Law.

The Hasmonean Period

As discussed previously, the Zadokite family of the Oniads lost their moral authority as defenders and interpreters of the Law as a result of increased Hellenization and, in particular, the last of the Oniad high priests, Jason, who displaced his brother by bribing the Seleucid king. Hellenization and abuses of power among the priests, of course, eventually led to the Maccabean revolt (see chapter 4, "The Maccabean War"). In the early days of the war, a religious crisis arose over interpretations of the Law. The Maccabees were willing to defend their religion by force of arms, whereas other devout Jews believed that such action would violate the Law. Among those who agreed that military defense was not a violation of the Law were people who seriously questioned the Maccabees' decision to fight on the Sabbath. For some unknown reason, by the beginning of the intertestamental period, military action had become equated with work. However, the Torah does not explicitly prohibit fighting on the Sabbath, and earlier biblical stories about warfare do not seem to include any helpful information on the subject.

Because of this lack, as we have seen, Mattathias, the aged non-Zadokite priest who spurred the war forward, interpreted the Law in a way that allowed him and his fellow soldiers to defend themselves on the Sabbath. What is not clear is whether he believed that it was harmful to wage an offensive campaign on that holy day. In any event, the decisive Maccabean victories during the initial period of the revolt led them and their admirers to believe that God approved their actions and thereby their interpretation of the Law.

Another issue dealt with how Jews should relate to their neighbors—that is, should they tolerate gentiles in their midst or should they force them out of the land if they were unwilling to convert? Of course, this issue became more acute as the Maccabeans' continued victories greatly expanded the territory under their control, including gentile areas.

As we know, a growing number of people who had initially supported the Maccabees began to reject their leadership and therewith their understanding of the Law. One group, the Sadducees, believed that it was their duty to preserve and interpret the Law and therefore sought control of the temple where the Law intertwined visibly with its activities. To safeguard their interpretations of the Law, they made the Torah supreme. And while they did not reject the authority of the prophets and the writings, the other two sections of the threefold developing canon, they nevertheless believed that these latter sections were not authoritative. Additionally, they rejected the Pharisees' oral tradition (also known as the oral law), indicating that any interpretation or application that could not be explicitly supported in the written law was null and void. The Pharisees, of course, rejected the Sadducees' appeal to only written law.

THE ESSENES

It seems certain that some of the priests who went to Qumran were either descendants of or had affinity with those who had originally supported the Maccabean revolt. Their support seems to have rested on at least two bases: first, they could not abide the horrific anti-Jewish persecutions of Antiochus IV and, second, the appointment of the non-Zadokite high priest Menelaus was highly offensive to them.

Their attachment to the Zadokites' legitimate claim upon the office of the high priest, whether they were of the Zadokite lineage or not, led to their breach with the new Hasmonean rulers in Jerusalem. This apparently began to develop when the Hasmonean Jonathan came to the high priestly office with the help of Seleucid foreigners in 152 B.C. The breach continued to widen. Most scholars agree that the "wicked priest" mentioned in the Dead Sea Scrolls is most likely a reference to Jonathan's brother and successor Simon, who, according to the Habakkuk commentary, was accused of usurping authority through violence and wickedness and of persecuting their leader, the Teacher of Righteousness.

This Teacher of Righteousness was a priest (also called the "Righteous Teacher") who possessed the recognized authority to interpret the Law for Essenes. At Qumran, new members were required to take an oath to observe and obey everything that the Teacher of Righteousness had revealed—that is, to hold to the correct interpretation of the Law. Following his death, new members promised to follow the Zadokite priests because the leadership of the community fell to these priests. And they, of course, had embraced the views of the Teacher of Righteousness on the Law.

As we have seen, there were a number of differences between the Essenes and the priests at Jerusalem. Essene literature is filled with both biblical and nonbiblical legal interpretations. The *Temple Scroll* (11QTemple) opens one of the clearest windows into the legal thinking of the community gathered near the shores of the Dead Sea.

As we have pointed out, the *Temple Scroll* is an exciting document because it turns the biblical laws about building a temple from third-person accounts to a first-person account, thus claiming the words to be the very words of God. In this light, the author evidently felt inspired to make such dramatic changes and was therefore not merely correcting or harmonizing biblical texts. From all appearances, he believed that he was revealing the words of God Himself. In other parts of the *Temple Scroll*, we find not only interpretations and revisions of the Law but also new laws known from no other source. As a result, the *Temple Scroll* is sometimes identified as "the Additional Torah." For example, New Year's Day was the day for consecrating Aaron and his sons (Exodus 40:1, 12–15). This ceremony was a once-and-for-all experience. But the *Temple Scroll* requires that all priests be consecrated, mandating that a ceremony be held every year for such purposes. In this way, the Essenes went beyond what priests were doing, or not doing, in Jerusalem. Moreover, the *Temple Scroll* introduces new festivals (see chapter 17, "Feasts and Festivals") and reveals that Essenes followed a solar calendar, which meant that Essenes celebrated their festivals on different days from those celebrated by the priesthood in Jerusalem. Such variances arose from differences in interpreting law.

Non-Priest Interpreters

To this point, our discussion has focused on debates inside and outside the priestly community about the authority to interpret scripture. An important text from the Apocrypha (see chapter 10, "Apocrypha and Pseudepigrapha"), Ecclesiasticus (Ben Sira), reveals additional fractures within the Jewish community around 180 B.C. Many scholars have assumed that scribes who copied the Law were also priests. However, Ben Sira indicates that scribes not only copied the Law but also studied and interpreted it. In effect, he sets them off from the priests. Additionally, Ben Sira seems not to have been a priest, yet he studied the Law. His actions, therefore, suggest that the interpretation of the Law is not an exclusive privilege of the priests (Ecclesiasticus 38:24–39:11).

Conclusion

Interpreting the Law was the central focus of Judaism during the intertestamental period. Originally, at least from the time of Ezra, priests possessed, taught, and interpreted the Law. Within a short time, however, others took up the pleasant task of studying and trying to understand the Law. Thereafter, questions began to arise over who was authorized to interpret the Law and how the Law should be applied in the daily lives of the devout. This growing crisis of authority helps explain the multiplication of divisions within Judaism. As time went on, different interpretations of the Law were articulated. Certainly, many Jews must have been conscious of the differences. Matthew, like the other Gospel writers, preserved the people's reaction to Jesus' teaching, which was unlike that of the scribes (see Matthew 7:28–29). Divisions manifested over the fundamental question of who was authorized to interpret the Law highlight the most important religious reality of the day: Mount Sinai continued to cast its long shadow over the religious landscape of the period.

For Further Reading

David Noel Freedman et al., eds., *The Anchor Bible Dictionary* (Garden City, New York: Doubleday, 1992), s.v. "Law."

Lester L. Grabbe, *Judaism from Cyrus to Hadrian*, 2 vols. (Minneapolis: Fortress Press, 1992).

Helmut Koester, *History, Culture, and Religion of the Hellenistic Age*, 2 vols. (Philadelphia: Fortress Press, 1982).

Jacob Milgrom, "New Temple Festivals in the Temple Scroll," in Truman G. Madsen, ed., *The Temple in Antiquity* (Provo, Utah: Religious Studies Center, 1984), 124–33.

Yigael Yadin, *The Temple Scroll: The Hidden Law of the Dead Sea Sect* (New York: Random House, 1985).

CHAPTER 19

THE WORLD OF JESUS

Matthew stared vacantly at the small but bright lamp on his table. He had purchased the table from a man who had bought it from Joseph the carpenter of Nazareth, father of his beloved Master, Jesus. It seemed fitting that he begin to write the astonishing story of Jesus on this table. At this moment, however, he was trying to think how to begin his story about the Savior, who had unexpectedly come into his life by simply passing by his customs office just west of the town of Capernaum and inviting him to come with Him. To be sure, Mark, Peter's traveling companion for a number of years, had already written a brief account of Jesus' life and final suffering and resurrection, including much from Peter's preaching. But Matthew knew about other dimensions of Jesus' experiences, and he wanted to write them down for the benefit of other believers, particularly his fellow Jews. Then, in a flash, he knew where he should begin. He would begin with Jesus' royal ancestry, tying Him to King David and those who ruled after him. He would help readers see that Jesus was the true king of His people, the Messiah of Israel.

Herod the Great ruled Judea and adjacent territories as a client king of the Roman Empire. The political, economic, and religious center of the Jewish world was Jerusalem. However, it was a large and spacious site within the city that was the very heart of Judaism. Known as the "Mountain of the House [of God]," the enormous raised platform, with its huge retaining walls to bear the weight of the fill and the structures built above, was nearly 172,000 square yards, making it the largest building

Divisions after Herod the Great

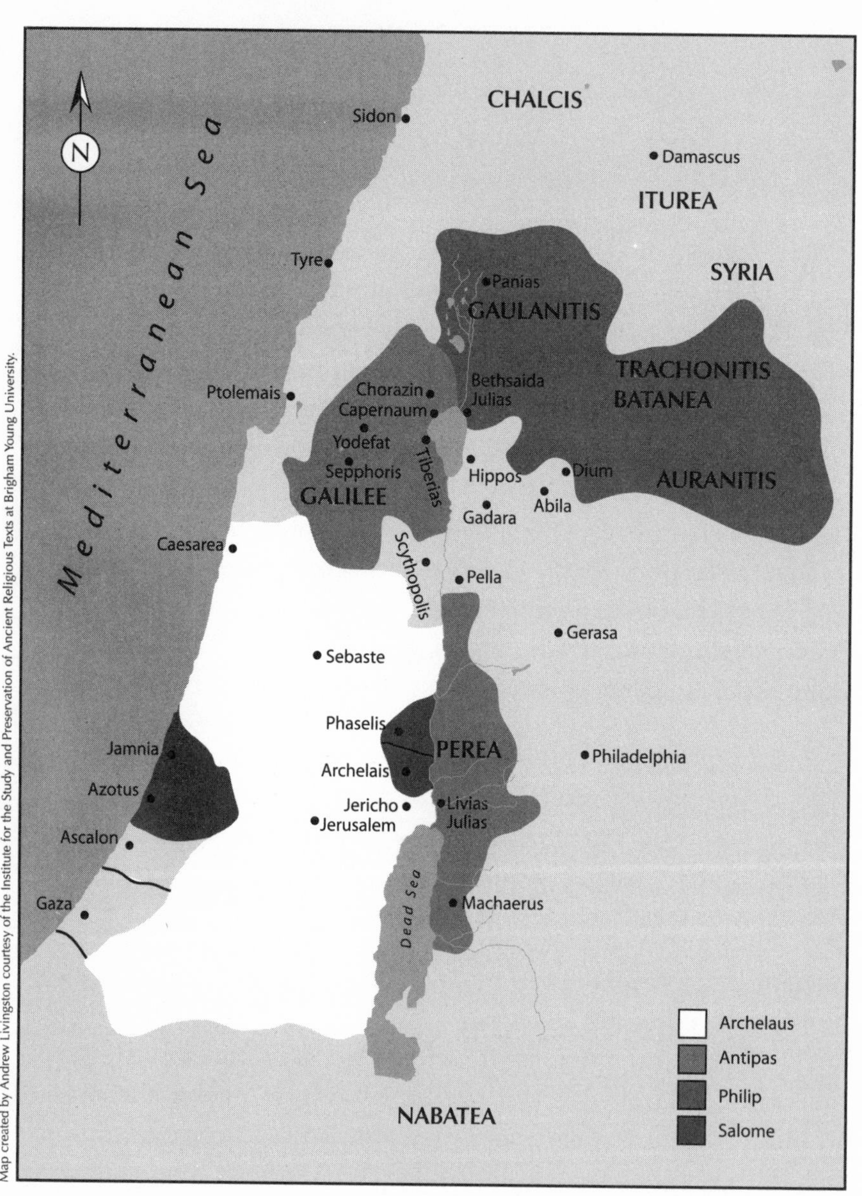

Map created by Andrew Livingston courtesy of the Institute for the Study and Preservation of Ancient Religious Texts at Brigham Young University.

platform in the ancient world. On this spacious, raised site was the jewel of Jerusalem—the holy temple. Radiant on the Holy Mount, it stood isolated from the city by a large courtyard. Its brilliant, white marble stones and gold-covered façade reflected the sunlight directly into a person's eyes and created a sense of celestial awe and wonder among visitors.

Matthew's story of Jesus' birth begins far north of Jerusalem, in Galilee, in the small village of Nazareth: "Now the birth of Jesus Christ was on this wise: When as his mother Mary was espoused to Joseph, before they came together, she was found with child" (Matthew 1:18).

Ancient Galilee

For centuries, the inhabitants of Galilee had suffered under one international power after another. Beginning with the initial deportation of Galileans and others by the Assyrians in 732 B.C., followed soon by the second in 722, much of the population of the northern Israelite tribes was forcibly relocated to distant places within the Assyrian empire. Other peoples took their places (see 2 Kings 15:29; 17:6, 24).

The general consensus is that a substantial Israelite population, though poor, remained in the northern valleys and mountains of Galilee as well as in the central highlands of Samaria. In succession, these people found themselves living under the rulership of the Assyrians, the Babylonians, the Persians, the Ptolemies of Egypt, and the Seleucids of Syria. In 164 B.C., when the forces of Judas Maccabee finally lifted the yoke of the Seleucids off of Jerusalem and rededicated the temple for the citizens in the south, the people of Galilee remained under Seleucid control. But their days under these Syrian overlords were numbered.

In 104 B.C., the high priest and King Aristobulus sent forces north to Galilee from Jerusalem and subdued the inhabitants, including those of Israelite stock and the non-Israelite Itureans.

The Hasmoneans enforced Jewish practices in the region, including circumcision and payment of tithes and offerings, making Galilee Jewish as it was before. So that government matters would remain on a proper footing, the Hasmoneans sent officials from the south to take up residence in Galilee and to manage Hasmonean political and economic interests.

Such people probably returned regularly to their family homesteads in and around Jerusalem at times of national celebration and when they "retired" from public service, but a substantial number of them undoubtedly sank roots in Galilee and raised their families there. This brings us to Mary and Joseph. One possible reason why the families of southerners, such as those of Mary and Joseph, were living in northern towns like Nazareth is that their forebears were among those who moved northward almost a century earlier either as Hasmonean functionaries or as people who saw an opportunity for a different kind of life after Galilee had come under Hasmonean control.

Another possible reason is that the forebears of Mary and Joseph, with genealogical ties to the royal family of David, would see Galilee as a place to escape potential retribution by the Hasmoneans, who would view Davidic family members as competitors for the throne of the Judean kingdom.

These families, whose roots reached back to Judea, would have come into possession of properties in the north while still retaining connections to the south, including property. It is this sort of situation that we seem to meet in the story of the journey of Mary and Joseph to take care of tax matters in Bethlehem, where both of them were to register to pay taxes (see Luke 2:1–5). Family origins in Bethlehem for Mary would also help explain her descent from the tribe of Judah and the line of David because Bethlehem lay within the old tribal area assigned to Judah and was David's hometown. As seems plain, ancestors of Mary and Joseph had moved north to Nazareth.

NAZARETH

Nazareth, where Joseph and Mary lived, is not mentioned in the Old Testament. Like Bethlehem, Bethsaida, Nain, and Sychar, it did not deserve to be called a city. Nazareth was, along with these other villages and towns, insignificant during Jesus' lifetime. Only later when Christianity became the dominant religion of the empire did it take on significance and become a place of pilgrimage and now, some twenty centuries later, a place of tourism.

Unlike Jerusalem, Nazareth was unwalled and small, with boxlike houses huddled close together on the side of a small hill, some distance from the main road. A simple one-story synagogue probably stood at the highest point in the village. Most of its two to four hundred inhabitants were farmers, but a few worked as craftsmen, like Joseph.

Joseph and others like him may have found work in Sepphoris, the most important city in Galilee, which lay just over the hill, three miles northwest of Nazareth. The town was the administrative center in Galilee and, presumably, the demand for skilled craftsmen during Joseph's youth would have been high. Then in 4 B.C., while Joseph and Mary were in Egypt (see Matthew 2:14–15), Sepphoris revolted against Roman rule upon the death of Herod the Great.

In response, the military forces of Varus, the Roman governor of Syria, sacked Sepphoris, burning it to the ground and enslaving its inhabitants. When Herod Antipas, son of Herod the Great, inherited Sepphoris and the surrounding territory in the same year, he immediately initiated a major rebuilding program of both the town and its walls.

Thus, after Joseph returned from Egypt (see Matthew 2:19–23), it may well have been more attractive for him to resettle in Nazareth, where life was quiet and he could find work at a good wage in nearby Sepphoris, than to make a living in

Jerusalem. Besides, as we have already observed, Joseph's family ties to King David may have held potential trouble for him in Jerusalem.

HERODIAN JUDEA

Luke's report of the annunciation by the angel Gabriel to Mary of the birth of her firstborn son, her journey to the home of Elisabeth her cousin, and her trip back to Nazareth again (see Luke 1:26–56) are followed by the story of the birth of John the Baptist (see Luke 1:57–80). These accounts link together two small centers in Herod's kingdom—Nazareth and Bethlehem. But events in those towns were played out on a larger world stage: "And it came to pass in those days, that there went out a decree from Caesar Augustus, that all the world should be taxed" (Luke 2:1). Augustus, who ruled the empire from 31 B.C. until his death in A.D. 14, had established the *Pax Romana*, which the empire enforced by military might. It was in this setting that Jesus was born.

Matthew, unlike Luke, moves more quickly to the birth of Jesus in his account, skipping Gabriel's annunciation, Mary's visit to Elisabeth, and the birth of John the Baptist (see Matthew 1). Matthew ties Jesus' birth and the fulfillment of messianic prophecies to the end of Herod's life: "Now when Jesus was born in Bethlehem of Judea in the days of Herod the king, behold, there came wise men from the east to Jerusalem, saying, Where is he that is born King of the Jews? for we have seen his star in the east, and are come to worship him. When Herod the king had heard these things, he was troubled, and all Jerusalem with him" (Matthew 2:1–3).

In light of this astonishing news, Herod told the wise men, "Go and search diligently for the young child; and when ye have found him, bring me word again, that I may come and worship him also. When they had heard the king, they departed; and, lo, the star, which they saw in the east, went before them, till it came and stood over where the young child was. When they saw the star, they rejoiced with exceeding great joy" (Matthew 2:8–10).

After presenting their gifts, the wise men departed for home without informing Herod. Joseph, warned by an angel, left Bethlehem and took Mary and the young child into Egypt (see Matthew 2:13–14). The story continues: "Then Herod, when he saw that he was mocked of the wise men, was exceeding wroth, and sent forth, and slew all the children that were in Bethlehem, and in all the coasts thereof, from two years old and under, according to the time which he had diligently enquired of the wise men" (Matthew 2:16). Herod would be known ever after as the murderer of children in Bethlehem.

Josephus records that, sometime between the events discussed in Matthew 2:1–18 and 2:19–23, it was widely announced that Herod was about to die (in his seventieth year, 4 B.C.). Upon hearing this news, Rabbi Judas (Judah ben Zippori) incited his students to tear down a Roman eagle that had been placed on the outside of what is know called Wilson's arch, the southwest entrance to the temple complex. Herod was incensed at their apparent ingratitude—he had built the temple and made every effort to balance the demands of Jewish tradition and Roman requirements. On March 12, the rabbi, along with the instigator, Matthias (Mattathias ben Margalit), and some of the students involved in the affair were executed. On the following night there was an eclipse of the moon, a symbol of the changes that were to befall Herod's kingdom. Shortly thereafter, Herod died at his winter palace in Jericho (see Josephus, *Jewish Antiquities* 17.4–5).

As we have seen, when Herod died in 4 B.C., his kingdom was divided among three sons: Archelaus became ethnarch of Judea; Herod Antipas served as tetrarch of Galilee and Perea; and Herod Philip became tetrarch of the northernmost regions, Trachonitis, Batanea, Panias, and Gaulanitis. Matthew informs us that, when Herod died, "an angel of the Lord appeareth in a dream to Joseph in Egypt, Saying, Arise, and take the young child and his mother, and go into the land of Israel: for they are dead which sought the young child's life. And he arose, and took the young child and his mother, and came into the land of Israel. But when he heard that Archelaus did reign in Judaea in the room of his father Herod, he was afraid to go thither: notwithstanding, being warned of God in a dream, he turned aside into the parts of Galilee: and he came and dwelt in a city called Nazareth" (Matthew 2:19–23).

JEWISH GALILEE

Luke provides only a brief statement about Jesus' life between the time that his family returned to Nazareth and his twelfth year: "And the child grew, and waxed strong in spirit, filled with wisdom: and the grace of God was upon him" (Luke 2:40). Matthew remains silent on Jesus' life from His birth to His appearance at the Jordan River to be baptized by John.

While Matthew and Luke offer little information about the years between the births of Jesus and John and the beginnings of their ministries, other sources speak about Galilee and Judea during the period between Herod's death in 4 B.C. and Pontius Pilate's arrival on the scene in A.D. 26. Viewed through the eyes of Josephus, it seems certain that Herod Antipas, who ruled Galilee following the death of his famous father, began to Romanize, urbanize, and commercialize the region, hoping to duplicate his father's economic and political goals in Judea and particularly in Jerusalem.

Archaeology is another source for understanding this era. Archaeological evidence suggests that, although the Galilee region showed extensive and expanded Hellenization, the character of Nazareth was Jewish through and through. However, this was a period of change and adaptation. Under the Hasmoneans and Herod, there were no royal palaces in Galilee.

Then Herod Antipas developed a royal presence in Galilee, creating a pronounced and fundamental social change.

As noted earlier, following his confirmation, Herod Antipas rebuilt Sepphoris as his first capital in 4 B.C. and later turned his attention to the western shore of the Sea of Galilee, where he built Tiberias as the capital and as a thoroughly Roman city, beginning construction in A.D. 19. Although changes escalated in the third decade of the first century, Galilee was still a different place from Judea. Apparently, there was no permanent presence of Roman soldiers in Galilee during Herod Antipas' rule. Therefore, there was at least a pretense that Jews in Galilee were ruled by one of their own. And although both Galilee and Judea had experienced more than three hundred years of Greek cultural imperialism, it was Judea who experienced direct Roman military imperialism.

Roman Judea

After his father's death in 4 B.C., Archelaus ruled in Judea, but only for about ten years, until A.D. 6. At that point the city became part of a Roman province under the direct control of the emperor. While few could have anticipated the ultimate impact of Pompey's capture of Jerusalem in 63 B.C., a continued Roman presence now seemed certain.

There were those of Jesus' generation who welcomed this new development, who willingly bowed to Roman hegemony. Their collaboration offended others, however. Some resented the fact that Jerusalem, the holy city, was occupied by Romans. Taxes apparently increased under the new arrangement, and Rome controlled both the high priest's office and his wearing of the sacred vestments. It was this new political reality that Jesus saw during his youth when he and his family made their trip to the temple at Passover time: "When he was twelve years old, they went up to Jerusalem after the custom of the feast" (Luke 2:42). His visit to the magnificent temple foreshadowed his ministry, which would offer people living under Roman domination the "kingdom of heaven." These people knew all about kingdoms and empires, rule and power, but they knew it in terms of heavy taxes, rents, tolls, mounting debt, malnutrition, sickness, disease, and emotional and physical captivity to forces beyond their control. Jesus offered something different from the other voices of resistance.

As during the Maccabean War, the Jewish response to occupation ran between the extremes of silent resignation and armed resistance. There were at least four separate and definable violent revolts against the Roman presence (4 B.C.; A.D. 66–70, A.D. 115–17; and A.D. 132–35). The ultimate results of these armed struggles included the consignment of the Judean ruling class to oblivion and the end of sacrificial worship in the temple. Many rich landowners were imprisoned, enslaved, or executed. Priests who surrendered when the temple was already on fire were put to death. Most of the Jews who escaped without physical punishment lost their land. Jews were required to pay the poll tax of two drachmas annually to Capitoline Jupiter, just as the tax had formerly been paid to the temple. This tax symbolized the deliberate destruction, not just of the Jewish nation, but of its religion and the society of Judea.

JOHN THE BAPTIST

Before these futile and tragic events, John the Baptist began his ministry, a ministry that prepared the way for the coming of the Anointed One: "In the fifteenth year of the reign of Tiberius Caesar, Pontius Pilate being governor of Judaea, and Herod [Antipas] being tetrarch of Galilee, and his brother [Herod] Philip tetrarch of Ituraea and of the region of Trachonitis, and Lysanias the tetrarch of Abilene, Annas and Caiaphas being the high priests, the word of God came unto John the son of Zacharias in the wilderness" (Luke 3:1–2).

Matthew also introduces John the Baptist into his story. From his record, John clearly plays an essential role in launching the Savior's ministry: "In those days came John the Baptist, preaching in the wilderness of Judaea, and saying, Repent ye: for the kingdom of heaven is at hand. . . . Then cometh Jesus from Galilee to Jordan unto John, to be baptized of him. But John forbad him, saying, I have need to be baptized of thee, and comest thou to me? And Jesus answering said unto him, Suffer it to be so now: for thus it becometh us to fulfil all righteousness. Then he suffered him. And Jesus, when he was baptized, went up straightway out of the water: and, lo, the heavens were opened unto him, and he saw the Spirit of God descending like a dove, and lighting upon him: and lo a voice from heaven, saying, This is my beloved Son, in whom I am well pleased" (Matthew 3:1–2, 13–17).

Following Jesus' fast in the wilderness (see Matthew 4:1–11), he began his mortal ministry: "From that time Jesus began to preach, and to say, Repent: for the kingdom of heaven is at hand" (Matthew 4:17). These events, which occurred in a tiny corner of the Roman Empire, were to have far-reaching effects.

Tiberius ruled the empire from A.D. 14 until his death in A.D. 37, spanning the whole of John's ministry. That Jesus' ministry began shortly after John began his own seems clear. Further, Tiberias was still on the throne when the culminating events of Jesus' mortal ministry came upon Him in Jerusalem: "And it came to pass, when Jesus had finished all these sayings, he said unto his disciples, Ye know that after two days is the feast of the passover, and the Son of man is betrayed to be crucified. Then assembled together the chief priests, and the scribes, and the elders of the people, unto the palace of the high priest, who was called Caiaphas, and consulted that they might take Jesus by subtilty, and kill him" (Matthew 26:1–4). Matthew continues the terrible and painful story of Jesus' experiences in Gethsemane, before the High Priest, before Pilate, and finally of his slow and painful death under the sagging weight of his bruised, stripped body on a Roman cross.

After the dramatic events of the following Sunday, that first Easter morning, Matthew changes scenes back to Galilee, punctuating the fact that the ministries of John and Jesus had taken place within a limited geographical region inhabited chiefly by fellow Jews but dominated by Rome. Matthew writes: "Then the eleven disciples went away into Galilee, into a mountain where Jesus had appointed them. And when they saw him, they worshipped him. . . . And Jesus came and spake unto them, saying, All power is given unto me in heaven and in earth. Go ye therefore, and teach all nations, baptizing them in the name of the Father, and of the Son, and of the Holy Ghost: Teaching them to observe all things whatsoever I have commanded you: and, lo, I am with you alway, even unto the end of the world" (Matthew 28:16–20).

Conclusion

The world of Jesus was made up of many dimensions and even contradictions, including a Roman Pilate and a collaborating high priest in Judea. In Galilee, Herod Antipas attempted to make the region like the Judea of his father, a Jewish world with a Greco-Roman veneer. But these elements are part of a continuing story from the past.

Much had happened to the Holy Land and its people during the nearly five centuries that separate the Old Testament period from the New Testament. It was far more than a mere chronological divide; it also represented a hefty cultural gap. The central difference between the peoples who lived at the end of the Old Testament period and those at the beginning of the New was the ever-shaping, ever-renewing passage of time.

Those nearly five centuries brimmed with far-reaching changes that included periods of crippling crisis, brilliant inventiveness, cautious adaptation, and painful transition. By all accounts, the major influence in that era was Hellenization. By definition, Hellenization sought to repackage the world as Greek. Making its relentless influence felt initially with the coming of Alexander the Great into the Near East in the late fourth century B.C., Hellenization affected people in profound ways and explains many of the differences in tone and texture between the Old and New Testaments.

For Jesus, John the Baptist symbolized the final transition from the Old Testament (covenant) and the beginning of the New Testament (covenant). The time of the Law and the Prophets had passed, and the time of the Messiah had arrived. John the Baptist, the last legal administrator of the Mosaic covenant, had one foot in each dispensation.

To say that the period from the birth of Jesus in Bethlehem until His death in Jerusalem is the most important epoch in world history is to say too little. No human's birth, life, and death have influenced world history as much as His and continue to do so today. For the faithful, of course, the story of Jesus' suffering and death does not close with His burial in a new tomb on a fateful Friday afternoon but with His resurrection on Sunday morning. The end, therefore, is not the end but the beginning.

For Further Reading

S. Kent Brown, *Mary and Elisabeth* (American Fork, Utah: Covenant, 2002).

F. F. Bruce, *New Testament History* (Garden City, New York: Anchor Books, 1972), 135–62.

John F. Hall, "The Roman Province of Judea: A Historical Overview," and William J. Hamblin, "The Roman Army in the First Century," in John F. Hall and John W. Welch, eds., *Masada and the World of the New Testament* (Provo: BYU Studies, 1997), 319–36, 337–49.

Stephen E. Robinson, "The Settling of the Gospels," in Kent P. Jackson and

Robert L. Millet, eds., *Studies in Scripture, Volume Five: The Gospels* (Salt Lake City: Deseret Book, 1986), 10–37.

E. Mary Smallwood, *The Jews under Roman Rule* (Leiden: E. J. Brill, 1976), 144–200.

Ben Witherington III, *New Testament History* (Grand Rapids, Michigan: Baker Academic, 2001), 61–131.

Chronology of Major Events

The following chronology, based on a similar chart found in John Bright's *A History of Israel* (1981), is to help readers visualize the passage of time and the important events that occurred therein. The inhabitants of the Old Testament kingdoms of Judah and Israel were often affected by events beyond their borders. It was the same for those who reinhabited these lands following the exile in Babylonia. No peoples live in isolation.

	EGYPT	JUDAH	ISRAEL	ASSYRIA
750	XXIII Dynasty ca. 759-715	(Jotham coregent ca.750)	(Amos and Hosea)	
		Jotham (Isaiah) 742-735	Zechariah 746-745	Tiglath-pileser III, 745-727
		(Micah)	Shallum 745	
		Ahaz 742-735	Menahem 745-738	
725	XXIV Dynasty ca.725-709		Pekahiah 738-737	
			Pekah 737-732	
	XXV (Ethiopian) Dynasty		Hoshea 732-724	Shalmaneser V 727-722
	Shabako ca.710-696	ca.716/15-663 Hezekiah 715-687/6	Fall of Samaria 722/1 ←	Sargon II 722-705
700		701 Sennacherib invades ←		Sennacherib 705-681
	Shebteko ca.696/5-685/4			
	(Tirhakah coregent ca.690/89)	688 Sennacherib invades?		
	Tirakah ca.685/4-664	Manasseh 687/6-642		Esarhaddon 681-669
675	← Invasions of Egypt; Sack of Thebes 663			Asshurbanapal 669-633?
	XXVI Dynasty 663-525			
	Psammetichus I 663-609			
650		Amon 642-640		
		Josiah 640-609		Asshur-etil-ilani 633-629?
		(Jeremiah)	Neo-Babylonian Empire	
625		(Zephaniah)	Nabopolassar 626-605	Sin-shar-iskun 629?-612
		(Nahum)		
		Jehoahaz 609	→	Fall of Nineveh 612
	Neco II 609-593	Jehoiakim 609-598	→	Asshur-uballit II 612-609
600		Jehoiachin 598/59	BABYLON	MEDIA
	Psammetichus II 593-588	(Habakkuk) (Ezekiel)	Nebuchadnezzar 605/4-562	Cyaxares 625-585
	Apries (Hophra) 588-569	Zedekiah 597-587		
		Fall of Jerusalem 587--Exile ←		Astyages 585-550
575		Deportations: 597, 587 and 582 ←		
	Amasis 569-525 ←	Nebuchadnezzar invades Egypt 568		
		Exile	Amel-marduk 562-560	
			Neriglissar 560-556	Cyrus overthrows Astyages 550

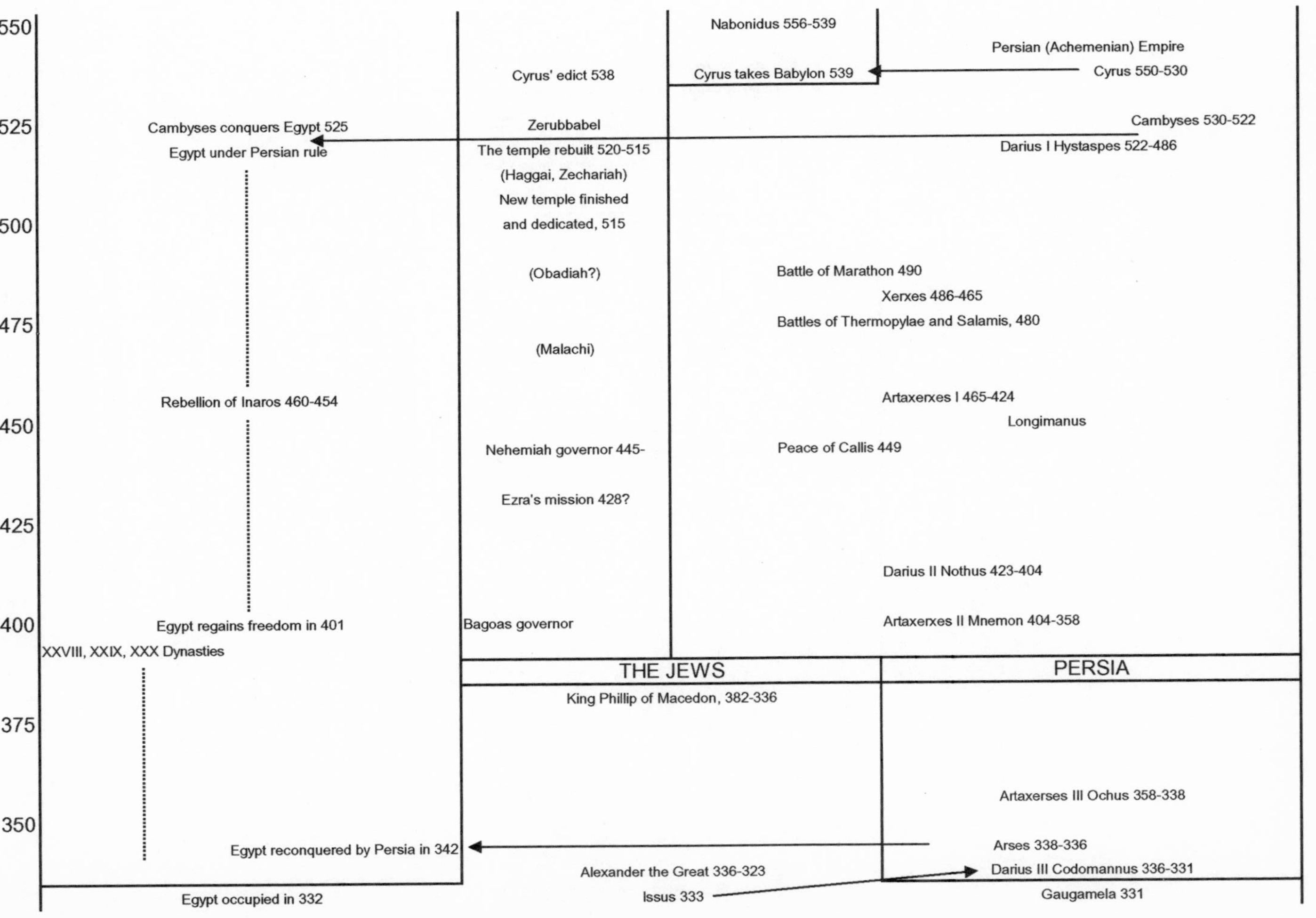

550
525
500
475
450
425
400
375
350
Nabonidus 556-539
Persian (Achemenian) Empire
Cyrus' edict 538
Cyrus takes Babylon 539
Cyrus 550-530
Cambyses conquers Egypt 525
Zerubbabel
Cambyses 530-522
Egypt under Persian rule
The temple rebuilt 520-515
Darius I Hystaspes 522-486
(Haggai, Zechariah)
New temple finished
and dedicated, 515
(Obadiah?)
Battle of Marathon 490
Xerxes 486-465
Battles of Thermopylae and Salamis, 480
(Malachi)
Rebellion of Inaros 460-454
Artaxerxes I 465-424
Longimanus
Nehemiah governor 445-
Peace of Callis 449
Ezra's mission 428?
Darius II Nothus 423-404
Egypt regains freedom in 401
Bagoas governor
Artaxerxes II Mnemon 404-358
XXVIII, XXIX, XXX Dynasties
THE JEWS
PERSIA
King Phillip of Macedon, 382-336
Artaxerses III Ochus 358-338
Egypt reconquered by Persia in 342
Arses 338-336
Alexander the Great 336-323
Darius III Codomannus 336-331
Egypt occupied in 332
Issus 333
Gaugamela 331

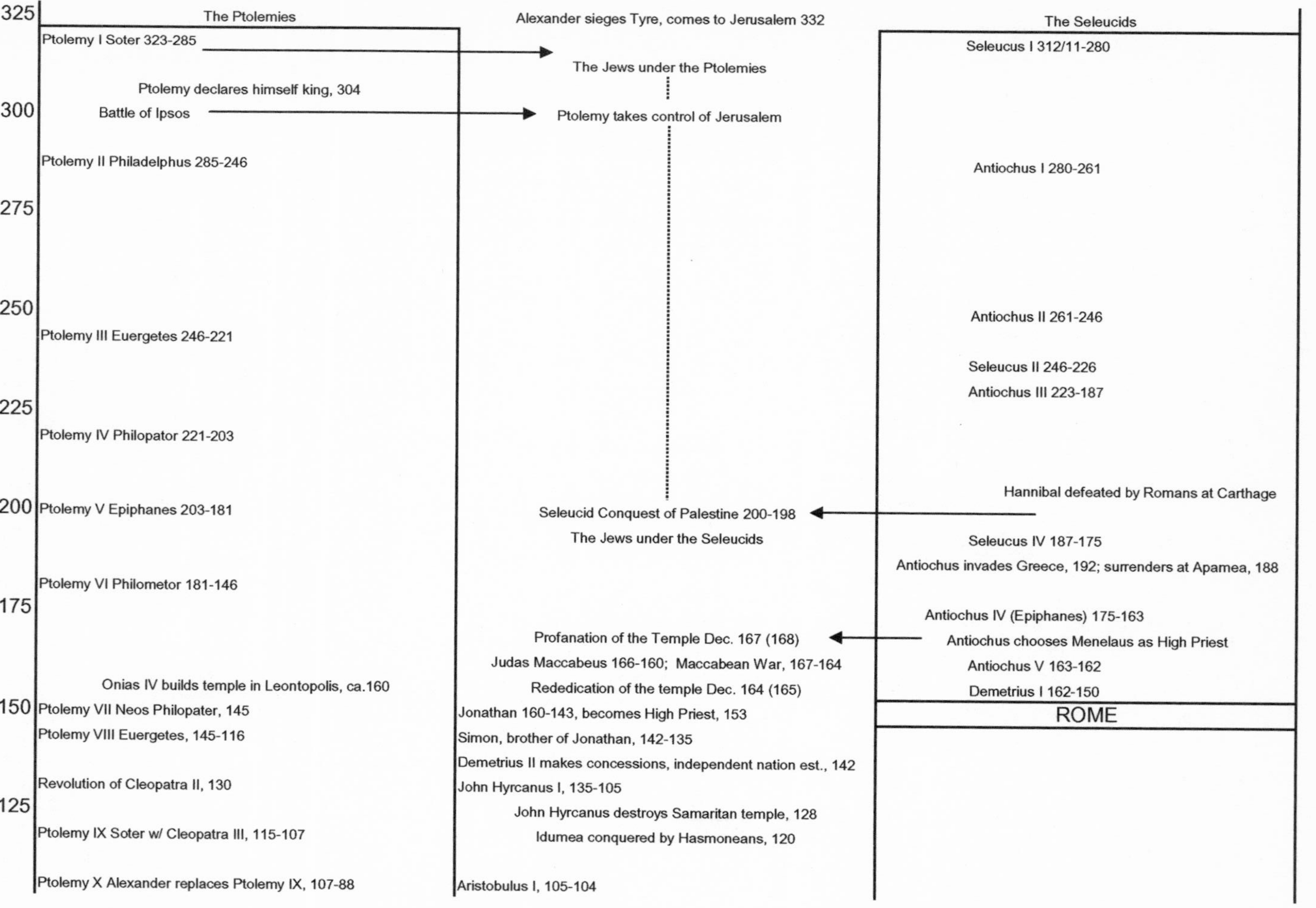
325
300
275
250
225
200
175
150
125
The Ptolemies
Ptolemy I Soter 323-285
Ptolemy declares himself king, 304
Battle of Ipsos
Ptolemy II Philadelphus 285-246
Ptolemy III Euergetes 246-221
Ptolemy IV Philopator 221-203
Ptolemy V Epiphanes 203-181
Ptolemy VI Philometor 181-146
Onias IV builds temple in Leontopolis, ca.160
Ptolemy VII Neos Philopater, 145
Ptolemy VIII Euergetes, 145-116
Revolution of Cleopatra II, 130
Ptolemy IX Soter w/ Cleopatra III, 115-107
Ptolemy X Alexander replaces Ptolemy IX, 107-88
Alexander sieges Tyre, comes to Jerusalem 332
The Jews under the Ptolemies
Ptolemy takes control of Jerusalem
Seleucid Conquest of Palestine 200-198
The Jews under the Seleucids
Profanation of the Temple Dec. 167 (168)
Judas Maccabeus 166-160; Maccabean War, 167-164
Rededication of the temple Dec. 164 (165)
Jonathan 160-143, becomes High Priest, 153
Simon, brother of Jonathan, 142-135
Demetrius II makes concessions, independent nation est., 142
John Hyrcanus I, 135-105
John Hyrcanus destroys Samaritan temple, 128
Idumea conquered by Hasmoneans, 120
Aristobulus I, 105-104
The Seleucids
Seleucus I 312/11-280
Antiochus I 280-261
Antiochus II 261-246
Seleucus II 246-226
Antiochus III 223-187
Hannibal defeated by Romans at Carthage
Seleucus IV 187-175
Antiochus invades Greece, 192; surrenders at Apamea, 188
Antiochus IV (Epiphanes) 175-163
Antiochus chooses Menelaus as High Priest
Antiochus V 163-162
Demetrius I 162-150
ROME

100		Alexander Jannaeus, 104-78	Caesar born, 100
	Ptolemy IX Soter returns, 88-80	Conquest of Gaza, 96	Mithridates VI massacres Roman citizens in Asia, 88-85
	Ptolemy XI Alexander, March 80-September 80	Culmination of Civil War, 88	
	Ptolemy XII Neos Dionysos, 80-57	Jannaeus' widow, Salome, reigns, 78-69	
75			
		Hyrcanus II, 69-63	Pompey defeats Mithridates and reorganizes the East, 66-63
	Berenike IV w/Cleopatra VI Tryphaena, 57-51	War with Romans, 66; Pompey conquers Jerusalem, 63	Augustus born, 63
	Joint rule of Ptolemy XII, Cleopatra VII and Ptolemy XIII, 51	Caesar Augustus, 63 B.C.- A.D. 14.; Hyrcanus ethnarch 63-40	First triumvirate of Pompey, Crassus and Caesar
50	Death of Ptolemy XII, 51	Death of Pompey, 48; Phillip made governor of Judea, 47	
	Death of Ptolemy XIII, 47	Julius Caesar assasinated, 44; Demise of Roman Republic, 31	Dictatorship of Caesar, 47-44 Caesar murdered, March 15
		Herod appt. governor over Coele-Syria,46; arrives in Rome,40	Octavian defeats Anthony at Actium, 31
	Death of Cleopatra VII, 30	Sosius captures Jerusalem for Herod, 37	Anthony and Cleopatra commit suicide, 30
25		Herod the Great's rule, 37-4 B.C.	Egypt annexed by Rome, 30
		Herod begins construction on the temple, 20/19	
		Death of Herod, 4	
0		Birth of Jesus Christ, Beginning of Christian Era	

INDEX